THE ALPHA PROJECT

RAIK LABJON

© 2011 Raik Labjon
Website: http://www.perfectdogs.de
ISBN: 9781499167061
Publisher: Raik Labjon
Second Edition, 2014
Translation: Globale-Kommunikation

Foreword

It's not uncommon for dog owners to find training their dogs overwhelming. Many are quick to lose enjoyment in their four-legged friends when they run into problems. New owners will also often expect their dogs to immediately differentiate between right and wrong and be able to anticipate what's required of them. The reality is unfortunately different, and training a dog can frequently become a laborious undertaking.

Dog training is nevertheless easier and more fun than you might think. You don't need to have exceptional talent or be a dog whisperer. If you want to understand your pet, you simply need to recognize him for what he is: A dog.

This book will help you to see the world from a dog's perspective. You'll learn how a dog thinks, how to correctly interpret his behavior, and how to deal with him in the right manner. Practical exercises play a secondary role in this training work. Knowledge of a dog's nature is far more critical to your success. You can only behave correctly toward your dog when you understand what's going on inside his head.

We humans aren't dogs, so we don't instinctively know how to behave correctly toward them. We first have to learn how to do this. Only when we're able to act in the right manner can we share a living space with this other species. You'll enjoy your dog more and also avoid problem behavior in the future. When you see the world through your dog's eyes, you'll be able to give him a happy and fulfilling life.

A dog lives in a world that's completely alien to us. He has his own way of communicating that's unfamiliar to us and his own set of rules and values. We want to spend a considerable portion of our lives with our dog, so we need to learn what his world looks likes – and we shouldn't expect him to learn to understand our world.

This book should provide you with an alternative perspective on mankind's oldest pet and similarly give you pause for thought. I'd like to make you question superficial knowledge and outdated training methods that you encounter in future. Drill right down into matters, and don't accept 'This is how it's always been'-style rules just because they've been written down somewhere.

Challenge this book's content and learn to question all that you come across.

There's a cause for each of your dog's behaviors. When you've answered the question as to why, you'll understand how problem behavior arises, how a dog learns, how you can change inappropriate behavior and how you can satisfy your dog's needs.

Training a dog is about more than learning commands. As with educating a child, command obedience has little in common with actual education work.

By 'training' we understand the guided practice of certain standards that are expected within a given setting. Training a dog requires holistic methods and follows different goals from the learning of commands.

The Alpha Project offers you a holistic training concept for both dog and human. You'll learn how to give your dog rules and routines from which he can take direction throughout his journey in life. Going forward, he should be able to find his way around a world that he considers entirely unnatural.

Everyone knows how important it is to provide a dog with security, to establish a trusting relationship with him, and to take over responsibility from him. This book will show you how and why to realize these goals.

This book doesn't claim to be a scientific tract. It's neither exhaustive nor scientifically accurate in every minute detail.

The first part of the book will teach you about a dog's nature. You'll find out how he's developed over time in contrast to humans, and also what influence the differences between our species have on training work. This knowledge forms the foundation for successful implementation of the book's practical part. Only when you understand your dog's nature and recognize him for what he is will you be able to treat him in an appropriate manner.

The book details the path of gentle, comprehensive dog training and helps you to help yourself in dealing with your dog's problem behaviors.

Daik Laljon

Content

1	Who are our dogs?	13
2	The most important time – Puppyhood	21
2.1	Puppy playgroups and dog re-socialization groups	23
2.2	How puppies learn through biting	29
3	Drive behavior	31
4	Territorial behavior	33
4.1	The family	40
5	Hierarchy	40
5.1	The employer	44
5.2	The boss	45
6	Social togetherness	47
6.1	The family pack	49
6.2	The pet human	50
7	Sensory perception in dogs	53
7.1	The control center	53
7.2	Seeing through a dog's eyes	54
7.3	How dogs hear even the smallest of pins drop	55
7.4	A superlative sense of smell	55
7.5	The sense of touch	58
7.6	Heat and cold	58
7.7	Selective perception	59
8	Emotions	62
8.1	The development of emotions	70
8.2	Building up a relationship	81
8.3	How do I establish trust?	92
8.4	Bonding through food	94
9	Taking responsibility	95
9.1	At home	97
9.2	Control in the outer territory	108
9.3	angers and unfamiliar territories	128

9.4	Recognizing the boundaries	128
9.5	Success through consistency	129
9.6	Attention – The importance of eye contact	131
10	**What dominance means**	**133**
11	**Tips for owning multiple dogs**	**136**
12	**Learning through conditioning**	**146**
12.1	Conditioning vs. training	146
12.2	It's not what you say, but rather how you say it	156
12.3	Using rewards for learning success	157
12.4	Why do we praise our dogs?	159
12.5	Food or toys as rewards?	160
12.6	How do I build up food drive?	161
12.7	Developing prey drive	164
12.8	Is acknowledgment a sufficient reward?	165
12.9	How do I reduce rewards?	166
12.10	How does a dog learn new commands?	167
12.11	Everyday life without commands	173
12.12	Acknowledgment using a clicker or 'Good boy'	174
12.13	Situational learning and generalization	175
12.14	Less is more	176
12.15	The 'No' command	177
12.16	How can I cancel commands?	178
12.17	For how long can I train?	179
13	**What your voice means to a dog**	**179**
14	**What a dog can and can't do**	**182**
14.1	Can a dog cry?	182
14.2	Can a dog have a guilty conscience?	182
14.3	Does a dog know love, faithfulness and allegiance?	183
14.4	Can dogs become friends?	183
14.5	Can a dog feel resentful or offended?	183
14.6	Does a dog have a sense of time?	184

14.7	Does a dog know what we can see?	185
14.8	Can a dog learn through observation?	185
14.9	Can a dog understand communicative indications?	185
14.10	Can dogs count?	186
14.11	Is it there or has it gone?	186
14.12	Noticed a detour?	186
14.13	You human, me dog!	187
14.14	Deductions, deductions	187
14.15	Can a dog learn rules?	187

15 Which dog is right for me? ... 189

15.1	Why do we need pedigree dogs?	190
15.2	A street dog	194
15.3	A dog from the pound	195
15.4	A puppy	196

16 What is problem behavior? ... 198

17 Explaining and handling problem behavior ... 200

17.1	Finding the cause	200
17.2	Help, my dog has too much spare energy!	203
17.3	Relieving stress and providing rest	204
17.4	Problem behavior at home	205
17.5	Stress on the leash	206
17.6	Unwanted hunting	207
17.7	Targeted aggression	210
17.8	When a dog bites	210
17.9	Begging	213
17.10	Garbage on the street	214
17.11	My dog isn't housebroken	215
17.12	Barking	216
17.13	Displacement behavior	221
17.14	Aggression	221
17.15	Dangers can grow	223

18 Managing fear ... 225

18.1	How do I recognize fear in my dog?	226
18.2	Relieving fear	227
18.3	Fear during walks	228
18.4	Habituation and systematic desensitization	229
18.5	Flooding	230
18.6	Fear of vacuum cleaners	231
18.7	Practical example: Habituation	231
18.8	Practical example: Flooding	232
18.9	Street noise	233
18.10	Separation anxiety	234
18.11	Shyness toward humans	235
18.12	Fear of other dogs	237
18.13	Uncommon stimuli	237
18.14	Touch and overcoming fear	238
18.15	Success in practice	238
18.16	Using your voice during fear therapy	239
19	**Mistakes in handling problem behavior**	**240**
19.1	Avoiding problem situations	240
19.2	Distraction and problem situations	240
19.3	Ignoring undesirable behavior	241
19.4	Castration and problem behavior	243
19.5	Punishing problem behavior	244
19.6	Training or coercion?	247
19.7	Training aids	248
20	**Contradictions in dog training**	**249**
21	**Behavior explained**	**250**
21.1	Enthusiasm for walks	250
21.2	My dog licks me	251
21.3	My dogs mounts me	252
21.4	My dog laughs	255
21.5	My dog is jealous	256
21.6	The wagging of the tail	257

21.7	Strangers and visitors	260
21.8	Canine greetings	261
21.9	My dog jumps up at people	264
21.10	Enthusiasm for other dogs	265
21.11	Making eye contact and baring teeth	269
21.12	Avoidance behavior and displacement actions	269
21.13	My dog suddenly stands still	272
21.14	Why does my dog paw at the ground after defecating?	273
21.15	Why do dogs roll around?	274
21.16	Why do dogs bury food?	274
21.17	Aggression while on the leash	274
21.18	My dog's tricking me	275
21.19	It's not a question of size!	275
21.20	Calming signals	276
21.21	My dog is inquisitive	278
21.22	False pregnancy	278
22	**What's meant by 'species appropriate'?**	**279**
23	**Keeping a dog occupied**	**285**
24	**Final remarks**	**307**

1 Who are our dogs?

If we want to understand and live alongside another creature, we need to know what this creature is, what its distinguishing features are, which values play a role in its existence, and how we can communicate with it.

Almost all problems in dog ownership arise because we don't recognize that our four-legged friends are dogs and not humans. It's not a dog's behavior that's at the root of our issues in living alongside him. The real problems are the training shortcomings that emerge due to misunderstandings between humans and dogs.

We can't understand that our dogs behave differently from what we expect from our fellow humans. It's not in our nature to think like a different species.

As dogs belong to a different species, they'll always behave differently from humans. Other rules and conformities apply to dogs than apply to us. A dog has different needs and values and a completely different purpose in life from our own. This is why it's important for us to get to know our dogs better.

If we want to understand a dog's nature, we need to question the degree to which his descent and domestication have influenced his behavior and character.

DNA analysis has unequivocally established that our dogs are descended from wolves. Analysis of mitochondrial DNA can only provide information about maternal lineage, however. Paternal lineage can't yet be traced. It's nonetheless likely that the original wolves only reproduced within their own species; cross-species genetic differences are normally so large that these pairings won't produce fertile offspring. Based on current knowledge, the mother of all dogs is the grey wolf. Since 1993, the domestic dog (canis lupus familiaris) has officially belonged to the wolf species (canis lupus), forming the 'familiaris' sub-species. The 'canis lupus familiaris' label translates to mean 'domesticated wolf'.

Even though we now know where our dogs are descended from, this information doesn't reveal much about their behavior. We don't yet have any way of mapping the behavior patterns that are associated with specific genes. What we do know about their lineage, however, tells us that our dogs are mammals that can be classified within the canine group. This group also includes jackals, coyotes and wolves.

A dog isn't a wolf, and not least because he behaves differently from his ancestor. Nevertheless, he still demonstrates typical canine territorial and social behavior. A good example of how dogs behave in the wild is shown in the Australian dingo. This is a domestic dog that became feral thousands of years ago and now lives independently of humans. Like our dogs, dingoes are descended from the gray wolf. Despite their prior domestication phase, dingoes now demonstrate behavior patterns that are comparable in purpose to those of their forefathers. Dingoes have a wide range of vocalization behavior, and they also mark their territories, scratch at the ground, are considered shy, and hunt when necessary in organized groups. Their social organization is comparable to that of wolves, even if not in all regards. Dingoes are inherently social creatures despite normally being seen alone; they form stable packs and live within fixed territories. A hierarchy is also established in dingo families as it is among wolves. Also like wolves, only the leading dingoes within a pack are permitted to reproduce.

You can see that our domestic dogs similarly behave like canines. We'd even label them as canines if we had to give them a biological classification without knowing anything about their ancestry. Why? Because of how they behave.

The parts of a domestic dog's territorial and social behavior that are relevant to dog training have a particularly clear link to his lupine heritage. They're also typical embodiments of canine behavior.

Ultimately, however, it was only speciation that meant that dogs could co-exist with humans. Wolves weren't able to co-exist in the same manner. Our dogs inherited lupine behavior patterns, but certain lupine characteristics had to change for dogs to live in symbiosis with humans. As in the past, it remains controversial whether humans domesticated wolves.

It's likely that wolves began to approach humanity when we became settled. Our settlements opened up new food sources for wolves, in turn making them less dependent on hunting success. Some animals were able to make use of this newly created environmental niche, increasingly seeking close proximity to human settlements and surviving from human garbage. The only wolves that could live in this manner were those that had both no fear of humans and a less pronounced instinct to flee. Other animals didn't possess these characteristics and so were less able to benefit from the newly created food sources. Human settlements grew over time, and at some point those wolves that lived from human garbage gave up hunting altogether.

The settlers tolerated tame and trusting wolves, but other wolves were chased away or killed if they posed a threat. The only animals that could reproduce in the new habitat were those with natures that had adjusted to life with humans. The wolf populations became increasingly separated over time until a new species eventually emerged. This new species is what we now call the dog.

The new species was distinguished by its trust for humans and its reduced tendency for both aggression and flight. The first dogs lived in loose association with humans, but later generations were selectively bred so as to develop certain attributes that were of use to us.

The theory that humans tamed wolves is very controversial. Why should a human want to domesticate a wolf? A human wouldn't benefit even if the wolf could be tamed. A wolf would never share his prey with a human, and he also wouldn't tend a flock of sheep for a human – even though such flocks didn't exist at that time.

A wolf's fear of humans is often raised as a problem when the taming issue is discussed. Nowadays, a wolf that's adopted by humans after he turns two weeks old is almost impossible to tame. This is one reason for assuming that domestication by humans would hardly have been achievable.

Nevertheless, I don't believe that wolves living 15,000 years ago had the same fear of humans as wolves today. There must logically have been some wolves with a less pronounced fear of humans, as otherwise no wolves would have been able to fill the new environmental niche that was created by humans. Some of these less fearful wolves probably lived entirely peacefully right among the settlers.

The tameness of some wolves subsequently initiated a process of natural selection among all the wolves that lived at that time. The wolves that didn't manage to approach humans because of their fear remained wolves as we know them today. But some wolves from this group still ventured to the edges of human settlements: Not to live there permanently, but rather to hunt humans' livestock. A new niche emerged when humans started to keep livestock around 8,000 years ago. Some wolves could now feed off the humans' animals.

Humans didn't tolerate this new feeding pattern, so we hunted wolves from this point on. They'd now become an enemy of humans. They were brought down wherever we saw them. They were ultimately represented as beasts and were hunted until they were completely eradicated in most parts of the world.

Our hostility meant that the only wolves that could reproduce were those with an extreme fear of humans. These wolves only managed to survive because they could never be seen or shot at. The fear of humans that wolves and many other animals exhibit today is the result of a selection process that was initiated by our hostility toward these animals. Fear toward humans isn't an intrinsic feature that wolves have always displayed.

The tameness that initially allowed wolves to live with humans was just one feature that developed through domestication. The biologist Dmitri Belyaev showed that the genes responsible for tame behavior in animals also produce a number of other features.

To prove his hypothesis, Belyaev procured 30 male and 100 female silver foxes from a fur farm in Estonia. He used these foxes for selective breeding. His selection criteria during the breeding process were very simple: The animals were bred if they were trusting and didn't demonstrate a tendency to flee from humans. When the cubs became sexually mature at between 7 and 8 months, the researchers separated them into different groups in accordance with their tameness.

In the early years, only 20% of the female animals and between 4 and 5% of the male animals were sufficiently trusting to be bred further.

Several years later, when the foxes had reached their sixth generation, Belyaev's team were able to introduce an additional grouping. The animals within this group were submissive and teachable, and they also sought out human contact. In short, they behaved like dogs. After another 4 generations, 18% of the animals were domesticated. After 35 generations, this figure rose to almost 80%.

Belyaev with his domesticated silver foxes.

But it wasn't just the foxes' natures that changed; other features changed as well. Some animals developed a mottled coat, floppy ears and curly tails while others' coats changed color, just like in our domestic dogs. Belyaev had proved that selection according to behavior also led to the development of other features. Although Belyaev only made his breeding selections according to one behavior, many other behavior patterns also changed in the foxes. They became sexually mature earlier, for example, and similarly became more playful, started to bark, and showed a lower tendency to aggression toward other silver foxes. All of these features equally separate the dog from the wolf today.

In another instance of domestication research, the zoologist Julius Kollmann discovered the phenomenon of juvenilization (neoteny). Neoteny is the retention of juvenile features, something that was also observed in Belyaev's silver foxes.

Among other matters, neoteny establishes the social compatibility of dogs with humans. This is what makes our dogs never fully grow up and so maintain the behavior patterns of young dogs even after they reach sexual maturity. Neoteny can be expressed very differently from dog to dog. As an example, the extensive range of vocalizations that our dogs maintain after sexual maturity is actually a behavior pattern of young wolves. Wolves only bark very rarely as adults, and even then in a rather monotonous voice.

In contrast, wolf hybrids can develop into full adults. As puppies and young animals, their behavior mostly leads to unproblematic co-existence with humans. When they reach sexual maturity at two or three years old, however, their lupine heritage breaks through in a frequently abrupt manner – often making wolf hybrids unsuitable for life within families. Humans become rivals for food to these wolves, so they'll often defend resources against them. Many wolf hybrids demonstrate absolutely no submissive tendency.

Despite a dog's speciation and moderated tendency to aggression, he remains a predator and selfish hunter that's primarily concerned with his own gain.

Most dog behavior patterns are aimed at bringing advantage or a direct benefit from an action. Like their forefathers, dog are predators. Predators are creatures that feed from other living beings while they're still alive.

There are also parallels between dogs and humans. We humans are by nature just as selfish as our dogs, for example. You can see selfish behavior in its original form by watching small children. Claims of ownership are asserted against others, and obtained items aren't readily given away. It's only through education that children learn to comply with rules, recognize boundaries, and respect the laws of social co-operation. We humans similarly strive for advantages with our actions. Just like our dogs, we strive to achieve our goals with the minimum possible effort.

Dogs live in packs and thereby form partnerships of convenience in which all individual members offer a benefit in the fight for survival. A pack increases the animals' chances of hunting success and therefore of obtaining food. The partnership offers increased security for each individual member, and it also increases the entire group's chance of survival.

Dogs demonstrate pronounced social behavior. Co-existence between dogs works according to completely different rules and routines from human co-existence, however, so it isn't comparable with human social behavior. Their structures, needs and values are fundamentally different from ours.

As with all predators, behavior patterns in dogs are determined by diverse motivations. The resulting actions are based in needs and can also be labeled as instincts. Instinctual behavior patterns first and foremost secure a dog's existence. If these instincts didn't exist, a dog wouldn't see a reason to look for prey, reproduce, or defend himself against attackers. There's a reason behind every dog behavior. If we want to understand a dog's various behavior patterns, we need to know the causes and motivations for his individual actions. If we then want to understand these causes, we need to know which of a dog's needs determine his actions. Only then can we integrate our dogs into our lives, avoid conflicts and satisfy their needs.

Who are our dogs?

Dogs were bred to fulfill certain tasks, so our dogs today have differing dispositions for developing particular skills. Differences in instinctual drives partly influence our dogs' natures.

The experiences that a dog accumulates over the course of his life nevertheless have a much greater significance for the development of his nature. No dog is born fond of children, loyal, or evil-minded, for example. There are also no fighting dogs, watchdogs, herding dogs or family dogs. The behavior patterns that a family dog demonstrates are too complex to be inherited. This makes it almost impossible to select a dog according to 'family dog' characteristics.

Border Collies target their prey.

Dogs that demonstrate such skills and characteristics learn these skills and characteristics during their lives. This means that only humans are responsible for what a dog learns and what kind of nature it develops. Even Retrievers, which are often seen as family dogs, can pose a danger to others if they're raised incorrectly. Yorkshire Terriers are also fighting dogs; in the last century they were trained to fight rats. A Border Collie similarly doesn't protect a flock of sheep out of instinct even though it's a 'herding dog'. No dog has a 'herding drive' or demonstrates innate hunting behavior. No wolf or dog will shepherd something that would normally be on its dinner menu. Herding behavior is really just hunting behavior, but with the difference that the final action, the killing of the prey, is suppressed. A herding dog first has to be trained to refrain from seizing his prey. He can't herd out of instinct.

Pointers follow the same example. A Pointer shows a hunter that he's found game. He pauses a certain distance away from the prey without making a sound, and then raises a foreleg to show that he's found something. No dog is born with this ability. It's hard work teaching him that he has to stay away from the prey and that he absolutely isn't allowed to grab it.

It's just like there are Dobermans – generally seen as watchdogs – that would sleep through any burglary, and there are Podencos that are too lazy to hunt. The character traits assigned to your dog aren't so important; far more important are the characteristics that you promote.

2   The most important time – Puppyhood

A dog learns most effectively during his puppyhood. His nature is determined by the experiences that he gains, or fails to gain, as a puppy. What he learns during this time shapes him for the rest of his life.

All a dog develops during his first few days of life are his sense of touch and his sensitivity to heat on his muzzle. This is how he finds his way to his mother's teats. His other senses develop during his first two weeks, the neonatal period. Puppies spend most of their first two weeks taking in food and sleeping.

Puppies aren't yet able to independently pass feces and urine during the neonatal period. They instead depend on their mothers to lick their anogenital regions. The licking acts as a trigger for defecation. They also aren't yet able to regulate their own body temperatures, so they maintain their temperatures through body contact with their mothers and littermates.

Their eyes and ears begin to open completely during their third week of life, the transitional period. Their neurological functions also show constant improvement, and the co-ordination of their muscles becomes significantly

The most important time – Puppyhood

better. Their first milk teeth break through their gums at this time, and they can also regulate their body temperatures and, for the first time, pass feces and urine by themselves. The puppies start to actively engage with their environment – alongside their mothers, their littermates and humans.

A puppy's socialization period begins in its 4th week of life and ends around its 16th week of life. This is the time in which a puppy develops the majority of its social behavior patterns. The vast majority of these behavior patterns have already been fully developed by the 8th week of life. The socialization period is the most important part of a dog's life. This is where he generates his bonds to individual other pack members and learns to interpret other dogs' communication signals. He also learns the rules and routines of the pack and the ordinary environmental stimuli that surround the pack and are part of normal, everyday life.

Whatever a puppy fails to learn during his development period can later foster insecure behavior or fear. This sensitivity makes sense from a biological perspective. During a puppy's development period, he learns all of the sounds, smells, pack members, behavior patterns etc. that are normal for the pack's everyday life. All stimuli that don't occur during this period also don't belong to the pack's everyday life. It's therefore likely that these things pose a threat. This makes it sensible for such unknown stimuli to cause uncertainty, caution or even fear in young dogs. Instinctive caution protects the dog from behaving carelessly toward unknown quantities that may endanger both that dog's life and the safety of the entire pack.

In consequence, if a puppy grows up around only a limited number of stimuli, he'll likely respond to everything that he doesn't already know with caution. This caution often later leads to fears or phobias. If a dog never learns what a streetcar is, for example, he'll probably demonstrate fear if he suddenly has to board one as an adult dog.

If you want a puppy to build up an intensive and trusting bond with you, it's important that this bond is shaped at the earliest possible stage during the puppy's socialization period. The earlier he has contact with you in this period, the strong his later bond to you will be. Regular visits even before the puppy's

8th week of life will help him to get used to you. He'll learn your smell and your voice early on, will associate you with his experiences from the start, and will recognize you as one of his social partners.

By making visits, you'll also make it easier for him to settle in during the first few days after you bring him home. Puppies often associate these first few days in a new home with considerable stress. They're separated from their mothers and siblings, all the smells are new, and nothing seems familiar. If your puppy already has a relationship with you, this will help him to quickly settle in with you and reorient himself.

2.1   Puppy playgroups and dog re-socialization groups

A puppy's socialization isn't normally complete by the time he moves in with you. This is the stage in his life when he should learn how to communicate with other dogs. Puppies already instinctively demonstrate the correct behavior patterns toward other dogs; they're born with the ability to use body language to express all of the signals that are important during their later lives. While they have this ability from birth, however, they still have to learn how to interpret other dogs' signals to them.

Puppies learn how to interpret other dogs' body language by playfully exploring the boundaries of their own behavior. They establish how to read other dogs' body-language gestures through contact with their siblings.

They learn less about this from adult dogs, as adult dogs respond to incorrect behavior from puppies with threats that they never subsequently carry out. An adult dog would never seriously endanger or injure a puppy as a result of his natural restraint against killing offspring from his own pack.

This natural killing restraint is also referred to as 'puppy license'. The license only extends to offspring within an adult dog's own group, however, and not to unfamiliar puppies.

In the wild, an unfamiliar puppy is just as much a rival as an unfamiliar dog; it consumes resources. An unfamiliar puppy would normally be killed if it stayed

The most important time – Puppyhood

in another pack's territory. It may be painful to consider such an event, but this behavior makes sense.

The biggest enemy in a dog's life is starvation. In consequence, a pack endeavors to protect its scarce resources. Animals that don't know one another are first and foremost rivals for food. It's not in a predator's nature to share food with others. Any animal would put his life on the line in a fight to protect this essential resource. Every predator sees a rival for food as constituting a survival-level emergency.

An unknown puppy would consume valuable resources at the expense of a pack's own offspring. In the wild, the survival rate for a pack's own offspring is around 50%. Packs can't even secure enough food for their own offspring, so they'll certainly never take on an unknown, unrelated puppy.

If your puppy meets an unfamiliar dog during a walk, there's no guarantee that this dog will allow your puppy to pass in peace simply because he's a puppy. The danger of the unfamiliar dog confronting your puppy in a hostile manner may seem small, but if a confrontation does occur, your puppy will be in a clearly inferior position. If a hostile confrontation escalates, the consequences for your puppy can't be foreseen. Your puppy may have already learned to show willingness to submit, but this doesn't mean that the other dog will automatically renounce his hostile intentions.

Puppies learn subordination through dealings with their siblings and parents. They quickly learn to assert themselves, submit, and interact with others. The parent animals instinctually strive to subordinate their offspring; the parents are normally the leading animals within the pack and will remain at this level. In this respect, the first lesson that puppies learn is to show subordination toward their parents. Toward their siblings, however, they quickly learn to assert themselves. Battles for rank already begin in the whelping box as siblings fight among one another for the best milk. At seven weeks old, puppies are able to use body language signals to gain advantages over their

The most important time – Puppyhood

siblings and to maintain these advantages on a permanent basis. Puppies can already form ranks among one another at this early stage[1].

When a puppy reaches eight weeks old, he's already basically able to interpret canine behavior whenever he sees it. He still doesn't generally know enough about signals from unfamiliar dogs with different appearances, however. Over the next few weeks, he should be given the opportunity to gain a more generalized perspective on what he's already learned.

A puppy playgroup allows puppies to be socialized with unfamiliar other puppies. However, it's not in a dog's nature to learn how to communicate with puppies from different packs through forced confrontation. If a puppy intrudes on an unfamiliar pack, he runs the risk of being killed. He'll therefore often instinctively avoid puppies from unfamiliar packs when he first meets them. He knows that this situation could present him with a significant threat.

Socialization with unfamiliar, unrelated other puppies in a puppy playgroup can't be a natural affair. It can therefore be assumed that such playgroups are held because we humans are all too happy to treat our dogs like little people who are glad to have playmates at a playground.

In actual fact, many observers consider the way in which puppies act when they're on the fringes of a puppy playgroup as rather questionable and alarming. They hear their dogs whine, howl, whimper, scream, growl and bark. Fun and games play no role, at least not for the puppies. New or fearful puppies are often bullied or forced into submission from the very first moment. A puppy will learn from this situation as well: He'll learn to defend himself. What he won't learn is how to interpret other dogs' body language signals.

Do you remember how you felt as a child when you were placed in a group of unfamiliar children for the first time, and no one asked you whether you wanted to be there? You looked for safety and support, something that you knew and trusted, your mother or father. A puppy feels exactly the same in an incorrectly run puppy playgroup. If the puppy's abandoned to his fate, he'll

---

[1] Cf. Ziemen, E. (1992): Der Hund, Munich 1992.

The most important time – Puppyhood

look for you, his caregiver. You'll then often hear: 'He has to make his own way'. No, he definitely doesn't. Quite the opposite, in fact.

Your dog should live alongside you, and not other dogs, for the rest of his life. This type of socialization makes sense if you're socializing wild dogs that don't have any connection to humans so that you can release them back into the wild later on. But this isn't the goal of puppy playgroups. Here, puppies should learn to correctly interpret other dogs' signals – not how best to assert themselves against other dogs.

To a certain extent it's natural for a puppy to assert his interests against others. But he also has to learn to step away from others when they show pain signals or gestures of appeasement or submission. If one of the puppies is permanently disadvantaged or afraid, he won't learn anything. Fear and stress inhibit the ability to learn. When in doubt, he'll learn that his submission signals aren't understood and that he therefore needs to develop new strategies to defend himself against others. The only option that usually remains open to him is to demonstrate aggression early on.

If your dog is overwhelmed in a confrontation, you're presented with an opportunity to show him the role that you'll play in his life. Your dog should eventually see you as the center of his universe, the God of all happiness, and as someone in whom he can place his trust for as long as he lives. Turn your dog's cry for help into something positive and assist him when he needs assistance. Stop the interaction whenever a game turns sour, whenever a puppy is permanently forced into submission, or whenever any flight or fear behavior is shown.

Wild dogs also don't force their puppies together or compel them to fight among one another. The puppies play with each other, and they therefore fundamentally enjoy their interactions with other dogs. A dog can only have fun if he searches out closeness with other dogs of his own accord and without coercion, and is also free to choose his own playmates. Even in the wild, if a puppy perceives a situation as overly threatening, he'll rather stop playing than be beaten up. If you force your dog to face escalation within a puppy playgroup, this isn't his decision. He's made to cope with the situation by himself and has to find his own ways of dealing with the unfamiliar dogs' attacks.

Watch your dog to see whether he enjoys the meeting with the other puppies – or whether he just runs at them because he feels threatened and attack is his strategy for coping with the danger. If in doubt, stay with him and offer him protection if he looks for it. In the future, he should live with you first and foremost, and not in a pack full of unfamiliar dogs.

The trust that your desperate puppy will develop in you during such situations will last for his lifetime. If you leave him alone with his problems and fears, he won't need you later on when there are conflicts to resolve. By this point, it'll be extremely difficult for you to influence the manner in which he resolves such future conflicts.

Don't forget that puppies and young dogs are also predators, and are so first and foremost rivals for resources. It's not in a predator's nature to make friends with other predators, and especially not with unfamiliar others.

What's true for puppy playgroups also extends to dog re-socialization groups that are made up of so-called 'problem dogs'.

These dogs mostly demonstrate aggression during their everyday lives. Then, as if by magic, they should be re-socialized in re-socialization groups. You'll often hear the following in such a situation: 'The dogs need to work it out among themselves.' No, they absolutely don't. You're responsible for your dog's safety, and you want him to trust in you. He should learn that you're able to provide him with safety. If you can't do this, he'll have to learn to defend himself.

A re-socialization group won't teach him to give up his self-defense strategies. In most instances, exactly the opposite will occur if you can't offer him an alternative. Your dog already doesn't trust you, and he'll trust you even less after visiting a re-socialization group. Undesired behavior can become strengthened in a group like this and ultimately grow into a danger for other humans and dogs.

The most important time – Puppyhood

If you want to bring your dog together with other dogs, stay with him and offer him protection if he seeks it. Control the situation. Lead him individually up to other dogs or keep the groups small. Only two dogs can interact with one another at a time in any case. Give him the option of playing with the same dogs on a more regular basis. He needs time to test and refine the behavior that he learns, and this will work best if he often has contact with the same animals, like in a real pack. When your dog has learned that his behavior produces the same effect in other dogs, he'll generalize what he's learned and then in future be able to correctly interpret all signals, even if they come from completely unfamiliar dogs. Your dog will gain this experience within just a few weeks.

This study from 1969 shows how important it is for dogs to have contact with other dogs during the development period.[2] Two groups were formed from various Chihuahua litters. One group's puppies were adopted by cats, while the puppies from the other group were raised by their own mothers. After 16 weeks, the puppies from both groups were brought together and the behavior of the two groups was compared. It was established that the puppies that lived among cats for their first 16 weeks had developed timidity toward their siblings of the same age that were raised by dogs. They tucked in their tails and remained close together. They didn't know how to interact with the other puppies; they considered them as strangers.

The study uncovered two interesting results: Dogs have no self-perception; and they can still quickly learn how to interact with other dogs even after their 16th week alive. The two groups were brought together permanently after the first meeting. In just two weeks, the puppies that were raised by cats had learned how to interact with their siblings from the other group. After this point, they played and behaved in a completely normal fashion.

Fox's study showed that even once the development period has passed, dogs can still learn how to interact with other dogs and are also very quick to pick up on how to deal with one another.

---

[2] Fox, Michael W.: *Behavioral effects of rearing dogs with cats during the critical period of socialization*, Behavior Vol. 35, 1969.

2.2 How puppies learn through biting

Puppies and young dogs have underdeveloped bite inhibitions that teach them how well they've understood other dogs' signals. When a puppy uses his sharp teeth without restraint, the resulting bite quickly causes pain and teaches another puppy that his behavior was incorrect. A puppy also learns when he's bitten too hard himself from other puppies' reactions; a game will end or the bitten puppy will turn away. The puppies learn that biting too hard can lead to

Puppies learn while playing.

The most important time – Puppyhood

negative consequences. They then learn how to control their biting strengths and instead apply them in correct accordance with the circumstances. A grown dog's bite inhibition serves to protect his pack from injury-causing fights and so maintain the group's hunting capability.

To a certain extent, it also ensures the health of the individual social partner. But this natural bite inhibition doesn't extend to animals that don't belong to the pack. When it comes to defending territory against unfamiliar dogs, bites are made without restraint and without regard to any subordination gestures that the opponent makes. Your dog will also gain a bite inhibition through his dealings with you. If your puppy bites too hard during play, you should stop whatever you're doing immediately.

This allows your puppy to gain a natural learning experience, and also denies him the opportunity to learn to bite for his own gain. Alternatively, your can let out a short and intense scream that briefly frightens your dog and causes him to take back his behavior. He'll then notice that his behavior has caused something that he hadn't intended. When the previous situation occurs again, he'll change what he did so as not to disrupt the game once more.

3 Drive behavior

The term 'drive' is predominantly applied to a behavioral cause that has a biological root. Such behavioral causes generally serve the preservation of life, species and self. A drive arises from a physical state of stress (need) and provokes behavior that leads to that drive's satisfaction (need satisfaction).

Although the existence of unknown, internal behavioral causes – such as instincts – is debated, there are a number of endogenous (internal) and exogenous (external) factors that trigger drives and so provide motivation for goal-directed behavior.

An example of an endogenous factor is hunger, with hunger triggering the food drive. An example of an exogenous factor is a threat, as a threat may trigger protective behavior.

Even when we talk about drive, all we're basically talking about is the cause or motivation for a behavior. You can also call a drive an instinct, motive, urge or compulsion.
You can see motivation-based actions or drive behaviors in our dogs. If you want to explain a dog's behavior, it's essential to know what motivates him into certain actions. A stimulus is always required to trigger a drive-based behavior. If your dog sees a running hare, for instance, this stimulus can trigger his hunting drive. If a dog feels hunger, this feeling can induce him to go on a search for food.
A dog always needs a motivation for doing something. Doing nothing, for example, satisfies a dog's need for rest. Every behavior is backed by a motivation or stimulus that encourages or provokes a certain action. Your dog is goal-oriented in this regard, just like us humans. Most of his goals have direct or indirect significance for his existence. As examples, a dog's prey, flight, protection and food drives are all primary drives that directly ensure his survival. In contrast, a dog's aggression drive is of rather secondary significance; it supports the behavior associated with his primary drives. Aggression is important for hunting, self-defense and the defense of territory and prey, so like the primary drives, it's always for the most part about ensuring survival.

Drive behavior

When a stimulus activates a drive in a dog, it triggers a behavior that should quench the dog's desire for that drive's satisfaction. Such a behavior is called an 'appetitive behavior'. An appetitive behavior can either be learned or occur due to instinct.

If your dog feels hungry and starts to look for food, this is undirected appetitive behavior. The behavior is caused by the hunger, and the dog will continue to act in this manner until the drive has been satisfied.

If your dog sees a moving object, this can be sufficient stimulus to trigger an appetitive behavior within him and motivate him to give chase. This is called a goal-directed appetitive behavior. Initially, the desire to grasp the prey or the object develops inside your dog. If he can successfully act out his drive, he'll be left with an expectation for drive satisfaction in similar future situations. He'll become aggressive so as to seize the prey; aggression is useful to him in hunting. Until he bags the prey, he'll continue to demonstrate further behavior patterns that all have a single goal: Drive satisfaction. He'll eventually experience satisfaction when the prey is grasped. However, if he can't successfully act out his drive in the first instance and so has no prospect of obtaining satisfaction, his appetitive behavior will also adjust.

4 Territorial behavior

A territory denotes a spatial area that's surrounded by boundaries and over which a claim to power or sovereignty is exerted.

A dog's territory is one of its most important resources. It's divided into the inner territory where the pack lives, sleeps, plays and maintains relationships, and the outer territory where the pack finds its food.

Like most of a dog's behavior patterns, he inherits his territorial behavior from his forefather, the wolf. A wolf's territory is where the wolf finds his food, security and social partners. The size of a wolf pack's territory varies according to the size of the pack and the food supply, but is on average some 200 km². Wolves expand their territory in winter and during periods with low amounts of prey. Territories of 1,500 km² and more are then not uncommon.

The manner in which territory is possessed was also passed on to dogs from wolves. Scents are left in urine or feces for this purpose. Marking behavior serves to claim a resource. The markings act as 'boundary stones' for the territory, as it were, and are spread across the entire territory on paths and intersections. Their locations are a clear indication to other dogs as to who holds sway in that territory. Urine markings fulfill additional functions within the pack. Wolves use group urine markings, for instance, to demonstrate their togetherness and their communal claim on their territory.

Responsibility for controlling and marking the territory lies solely with the alpha wolves, the leaders of the wolf pack. These are also the only animals in the pack that raise their leg while they urinate.

Wolves will generally only move within their own territorial boundaries and will respect other packs' territorial boundaries and property. If multiple packs share a territory, these groups will mostly be related to one another. When wolves leave their territory, they will usually move outside of other territorial boundaries. They'll only cross another pack's territorial boundaries in very rare cases when food is scarce. The intruders then know that this behavior will inevitably lead to a confrontation with that territory's dominant pack. Such

Territorial behavior

altercations end with either a timely escape by the intruders or a fight to the death.

If your dog demonstrates controlling and marking behavior, you can assume that he's claimed the territory that he controls and marks. A number of problems can arise from this situation.

If your dog claims a territory, he may also defend it against threats. He'll want to control his territory.

He'll constantly run ahead so as to recognize dangers in a timely manner and satisfy his enormous need for information. You therefore can't expect such a dog to walk well on a leash. He's also likely to become aggressive toward other dogs that refuse to accept a subordinate role in his territory or pose a threat to his resources. This behavior toward other dogs will occur regardless of gender and will primarily depend on what your dog claims to own.

The longer your dog's territorial behavior is consolidated, the stronger his ownership claim will become and the more aggressively he may defend his territory against dangers. Only he knows what he considers as a danger or a threat. It'll often be things that he's unfamiliar with, whether roller-skaters, children playing, disabled people, cyclists or mothers with strollers. In most cases, however, it's unfamiliar dogs that will pose the greatest threats.

A dog will also consider us humans to be other predators and rivals if we don't live within that dog's social group. However, they're mostly quick to learn that humans don't generally pose a threat.

A dog watches us even while he's a puppy. He looks closely at how we behave and how we move. Using his observations, he quickly learns when we're in a peaceful mood and how we behave when we're in this state. He memorizes our movement pattern, for instance, and connects this with our mood. While he's a puppy, he may still bark and perceive a threat when he sees an unfamiliar human during time outside. As an adult dog, however, he'll note the human's behavior and realize that no threat is posed; he's already memorized and recalled the human's movement pattern. If he sees a human whose movement pattern differs from what he knows, he'll primarily see this as meaning danger.

It's mostly disabled, drunk, elderly or fearful adults or children that deviate from the standard movement pattern and so are perceived as threats. A dog will similarly perceive a threat if a person's external appearance is unusual. The older a dog becomes, the more movement patterns he'll have memorized and the more tolerant of his surroundings he'll usually be.

Take the time to observe your dog's territorial behavior. His marking behavior will often change, for instance, when he enters an unfamiliar area. In older human-dog relationships that have predominantly been lived in the same single territory, you'll see that the dog marks very often and barely lifts his nose from the ground when he enters somewhere new. The shorter the time between markings, the greater the dog's claim to that area. This claim determines how energetically and aggressively the dog will defend his property and bark at rivals.

When a dog lives together with us humans in a social group, he considers this social group as his pack. In biological terms this is a symbiotic relationship, but the dog isn't aware of this fact. He'll live in the social group – where he resides permanently alongside other social partners – in accordance with the rules that he knows, which are the rules of a pack.

It's now normal for many packs to live together in an area that would usually be claimed by a single pack. This is especially the case in urban areas. A pack's average territory size corresponds roughly to a city such as Stuttgart or Hannover. In the wild, this area would be for a single pack. Now, however, thousands of packs have to share the same territory.

Dogs that don't live together in the same family will always regard one another as belonging to different packs, and therefore as rivals. In the wild, dogs from different packs that meet in one another's territories will see each other as mortal enemies. But dogs don't just regard other dogs as belonging to different packs if they don't live together. Other species such as humans and cats are also seen as rivals. If cats belong to your social group, you'll be able to see that your dog behaves differently to your cats than to unfamiliar cats that you meet during walks. Some dogs see unfamiliar cats as prey, while other dogs see them as rivals.

Territorial behavior

If a friend visits you, your dog will first see this friend as an intruder, as a rival from a different pack. If your dog were a wolf, he'd kill your friend immediately. It's only thanks to our dogs' weakened aggressive tendencies that we're able to receive visitors. Nevertheless, many dogs still show aggression toward intruders – and often from when the danger is first announced with the ringing of the doorbell.

Every dog that lives within the same territory but comes from a different pack will claim the territory for himself, showing his ownership claim through his marking behavior. If two dogs meet and claim the same territory but come from different packs, conflict is normally inevitable.

Each morning, territory markings will show your dog that many unfamiliar other dogs are also claiming his territory for themselves. He'll then know that many rivals are on the move in his territory.

The stronger one of these rival animals' area claims, the stronger that animal will defend his own claim against rivals. You can generally say that the more equal two area claims are, the higher the risk of an escalation if these two dogs meet. If one dog only has a low ownership claim to a certain part of a territory, he'll quickly bow down to another dog with a strongly pronounced counter-claim.

Such a situation is hardly imaginable in nature. Territories normally border one another and are not shared with unfamiliar other dogs.

Imagine this situation from your own perspective: Dozens of people walk through your apartment each day and tamper with your property. You'd be outraged by their audacity, right? This is exactly how your dog feels each morning when he goes to a lamppost and discovers that someone has once again illegally claimed his property as their own.

Now you want to talk to the people who are hanging around in your apartment. But when you go up to them, all they do is abuse and insult you. Your dog has to put up with this every day. Unfamiliar dogs want to bark him out of his own territory or complain about his presence at the tops of their voices. It's outrageous, isn't it?

Territorial behavior

If dogs from different packs meet on neutral ground or signal that they're not laying claim to each other's resources, their readiness for aggression is considerably reduced. This is also important from a biological perspective, as pack formation would otherwise be impossible.

If you want to derive guidance from this knowledge, you can only come to the conclusion that as a dog owner, you shouldn't leave territory to your dog, but should instead claim it for yourself (see Page 95, "Taking responsibility"). Our dogs then won't have to become aggressive, as they won't have an ownership claim over anything. They won't defend something that doesn't belong to them. Even rivalry and competition will come to an end. If nothing belongs to the dogs, there's nothing that's worth their while to compete over.

Territorial behavior isn't limited to the area outside of an apartment, however. Most problems arise because a dog claims an apartment, the inner territory, for himself. If he takes possession of the apartment or parts of the apartment, he may also defend his territory and whatever lies within it. He'll then decide against whom or what to address his defensive aggression. In the case of doubt, he'll even defend his property against you; as we already know, a dog considers us as nothing more than other predators, and therefore rivals.

Over time, your dog may come to consider visitors, strangers and even family members as threats to his resources against whom he'll defend his property. This process can develop over several years until all of a sudden it's: 'But he's never done this before!'

You might think that this permanent control is an inherited lupine behavior and is therefore completely normal. But if you watch a wolf pack, you can see that the animals mostly wander through their territory with their heads held high. The tasks of controlling and marking the territory are reserved for the leading wolves.

Territorial behavior

The leading animals within the pack are generally the alpha male and the alpha bitch. They lead the pack together. The female controls and marks the territory as well, even often lifting her leg like the male when she leaves markings. Lifting the leg is done to leave markings either high up or at a higher point than an existing marking, allowing the scents to be carried further by the wind and so detected by other wolves early on. In contrast, animals that are further down in the pack structure don't lift their leg when urinating and also don't leave markings. If your male dog doesn't lift his leg when he urinates, this doesn't mean that he still needs to learn how to do this or that he's 'effeminate'. All it means is that your dog has probably found his position within your home pack and isn't asserting any independent ownership claims over the territory. Congratulations.

A dog marks his territory.

Territorial behavior

If you have a plot of land or a garden in which your dog can move freely, he probably already barks at unfamiliar people or dogs from the fence, or will do so at some point in the future. This behavior is a sign that he considers the land to be his property and now feels responsible for defending the area from rivals. You've unwittingly ceded the property to him, along with a great number of associated responsibilities.

You might think that the fence would deter intruders and so prevent your dog from having to become concerned. A fence is sufficient protection for the land; your dog can't cross it, so unfamiliar dogs also won't be able to threaten his territory. But don't assume that your dog is capable of logical thought. As far as he's concerned, fences don't exist as boundary markers. His territory boundaries are set by urine markings. We humans can't image what our dogs consider as their territories and where the borders lie. Fences, doors, windowpanes and barriers only hinder a dog from checking and defending his territory. These obstacles cause a dog considerable stress. He can react hysterically, bark and become aggressive, for example, if a fence stops him from checking his territory. If you let him through to the other side of the fence, he'll stop barking, carry out his duties and check intruders' intentions. If he sees a relevant threat, he'll bark to warn the pack of the danger. He'll only become aggressive and accept all of the consequences associated with defending his territory if he has no other option for warding off the threat.

A privacy screen can remedy this situation, but better still is claiming the territory for yourself (see Page 95, "Taking responsibility"). Your dog won't want to monitor territory that he doesn't own.

4.1 The family

Like wolves, dogs in the wild live within a social structure. A pack is first and foremost both a family and a partnership of convenience. The community offers each individual animal an increased chance of survival.

Wolf packs have very diverse social structures. Wolves can live alone, in pairs or in groups of up to 36 animals, although this last configuration tends to be the exception. A pack normally has between six and eight animals, all of which are related.

Both wolves and dogs are social creatures. They co-operate with the aim of ensuring the community's survival and they have a clear family life. Pack members don't just work together when hunting large prey. Adolescent and already sexually mature young animals help to rear puppies, providing the bitches with food while they care for their offspring and so can't hunt for themselves. Later on, other pack members watch the puppies while the parents go out to secure food. Rearing offspring is treated as teamwork.

5 Hierarchy

Wolves and dogs live in hierarchies. It's through a hierarchy, or a ranking system, that rights and duties are regulated within a group and laid down for a long period of time. Internal disputes are then kept to a minimum and violent confrontations between group members are avoided.

Some people dispute the existence of hierarchies or ranking systems among dogs. This may be because the terms have been greatly misunderstood in the past.

A hierarchy has nothing to do with the human concept of military organization, and neither wolves nor humans are responsible for its invention. This social structure existed long before humans gave it a name, and almost all creatures that live in groups develop ranking systems. Even we humans live in hierarchies. A ranking system permanently regulates resource access among social partners. It has a clear biological value and serves the survival of the species. A group has an evident evolutionary advantage if its hierarchy gives it the ability to safeguard its members from injuries and so prevent wider group decimation.

Stray dogs also have ranking systems, even when they don't live in packs. Anyone that permanently uses resources alongside others will eventually form a ranking order. If this weren't the case, members of a group would be forced to compete afresh for food and water on a daily basis. Competition costs energy, which unfortunately exists in nature only in very limited amounts.

Animals' relationships among one another are called rankings. An animal's comparative rank determines his freedom. 'Freedom' in this context shouldn't be confused with the human understanding of freedom, as it more accurately describes a group member's scope for making decisions. This description can be used to make statements about an individual group member's rank position. In this case: The greater a pack member's scope for making decisions, the higher that member's rank within the pack.

The leading animals have the greatest scope for making decisions, and they also control the resources. They therefore have the highest rank within the group and bear the most responsibility. The pack's lowest-ranking animals can make almost no decisions. They lie where no one else wants to lie and eat what the other pack members leave over.

Only a pack's highest-ranking males and females will normally mate. In larger packs, other animals may also reproduce if resources permit. Aggression and threatening and combative behavior increase within a pack during food shortages and the mating season. Even mating partners will become rivals for food when food supplies are scarce.

A wolf pack is usually a family unit, with the parent animals taking on the leading roles. Unrelated animals from other packs may be present as well, but they'll normally occupy low positions within the ranking systems.

Leading animals aren't always the strongest and largest animals. Like with us humans, such control is much more about leadership ability, intelligence and experience. Only very few animals possess what's required to lead a pack. The

Hierarchy

leading animals' decisions contribute directly to the pack's preservation and welfare. Not all animals are up to the job and aspire to the position. Most would rather bow to a leading animal's decisions than take on this enormous responsibility themselves.

Conflicts about rankings are usually resolved in a peaceful manner. Serious ranking challenges aren't a daily occurrence within a pack. If confrontations do occur, bitches often interact with one another far more aggressively than their male counterparts, even biting other animals without warning. Male ranking fights are mostly preceded by display behavior and threatening gestures. A serious confrontation will only follow if an animal's rank remains challenged in spite of these actions.

Ranking isn't enforced through aggressive behavior. Lower-ranking animals instinctively show submissiveness toward higher-ranking animals. Their submissiveness signals ensure social harmony and are therefore important to the preservation of the pack's hunting ability. These signals aren't learned, but are instead shown directly from birth. If a dog submits, he'll instinctively convey the appropriate signals to his counterpart.

Wolves and dogs communicate through certain postures. A threatening wolf doesn't just growl and bare his teeth, for example. He also stiffens his shoulders, raises his tail and puffs himself up so as to appear larger and more threatening. A threatened wolf will conversely distort his mouth into a defensive grin, cower, pull in his tail and crouch down to the ground so as to appear smaller.

Despite a fixed ranking order, serious confrontations always occur within a pack during the mating season as the young animals challenge the old. This is because even the best leading animals can't satisfy one of their pack members' needs: The need for reproduction. When males become sexually mature, their mating urge compels them to fight for the leading animal's privilege; only the leading animal is entitled to reproduce.

Sexually mature males will normally leave their packs so as to establish their own families, although some will remain and become integrated within the existing hierarchies.

No wolf will challenge a leading animal for as long as that leader is able to satisfy his pack's needs on a constant basis. At some point, however, even the strongest wolf will grow weak. When this occurs, the changeover of power will usually follow in a completely peaceful manner.

Another animal will take over a leading animal's role when he becomes too old or weak to continue. No single animal will decide on his replacement; the pack will decide as a group. A pack member will only become the leading animal following recognition from the entire rest of his pack. It's to every pack member's advantage to submit to the leading animal, because he's best able to make the important decisions.

Leading animals usually demonstrate particular leadership qualities even during their adolescence. They bring more to the community than other animals, help where they can, and thereby gain considerable acceptance among all pack members. If the parent animals are no longer able to fill their leadership positions, the pack will automatically realign itself around such younger animals and their decisions. The old leading animals will often remain in the pack, submitting to the new leading animals and frequently adopting 'beta wolf' positions. The young leading animals will continue to benefit from their elders' experiences while now possessing the final decision-making authority.

What does this knowledge mean for dog training?

If you want to take on the leading role in your relationship with your dog, you have to show him that you're better able to do the things that are important in his life. Only then will he hand over responsibility to you and be able to trust in you when it comes to securing his most basic needs. You can't force this recognition from your dog; you have to earn it.

5.1 The employer

A pack functions in accordance with simple rules. The leading animals control the resources (e.g. food, prey, territory) and decide which animals can claim how much of these resources. They determine the freedoms that are due to each pack member and can seize any resource for themselves. They equally bear responsibility for social harmony within the community and the overall safety of the pack.

Leading animals don't necessarily eat first, although they can always do so. They also decide who can lie where and may claim any resting place as their own. Every animal within a pack will take it upon himself to carry out all tasks in accordance with his abilities. He'll intervene where his abilities are required and so compensate for the group's shortcomings.

Tasks aren't distributed in a pack in the same way as in human society. If you're supposed to take on a task in your company, you'll normally receive an order from your boss. If no one tells you what to do, you won't do anything.

A dog, on the other hand, will take on all tasks that he considers important as soon as he becomes an adult. This will inevitably cause him to poke his nose into areas of responsibility that don't concern him. Whoever holds an area of responsibility benefits from the associated privileges and won't just give up these privileges. The animals therefore defend their respective areas of responsibility and won't just allow a young dog to challenge their freedom.

If a young dog is refused a task, he isn't permitted to take on this task. Conversely, any task that he is allowed to complete or that he can claim from another pack member does fall within his prospective range of duties.

A dog that lives in a human family won't normally be prevented from carrying out his tasks. We ban him from certain things that aren't tolerable from a human perspective, but we don't take away his tasks. In this respect, our dogs take on all tasks that exist within their worlds.
They also use our behavior to discern which tasks we're able to complete and which tasks we can't handle.

Our dogs perceive us as mostly behaving in a completely anti-social manner. We stay out of confrontations. We show no sign of wanting or being able to defend our territory. We don't monitor or claim a territory, and we also don't hunt for prey. We don't even follow tracks.

From a dog's perspective, we're not able to protect our pack, our territory or ourselves. We don't claim ownership of a territory, so how should we obtain food? In consequence, our dogs have no choice but to take on these tasks themselves. Because they believe that we're not able to protect ourselves, they also take on this task when we're out and about together.

5.2 The boss

The leading animal is the boss of the family business; the employer that bears all of the responsibility.

No leading animal will leave responsibility for his pack to a lower-ranking pack member, as doing so would equate to handing over his ownership claim. The animal that owns a pack can claim all prey within that pack. But the leadership position doesn't just come with advantages. The animal that claims the privileges associated with this rank must also take on an associated amount of responsibility. Additional rights always involve additional duties.

Leading animals have the greatest scope for making decisions, but this position means that they're similarly responsible for the pack's security and internal social stability. They also make decisions during hunting, place themselves in the most dangerous situations when fighting with prey, and kill the pack's prey with the final bite.

If we want to co-exist with our dogs without giving undesirable behaviors the chance to arise, we need to learn how to control all resources and take on a leading animal's position of responsibility. Only then will our dogs see sense in submitting to us.

Our dogs can't understand that we've found other, more effective ways of securing our existence. They don't consider a supermarket to be an alternative source of food. As such, they can't just ignore resources that are essential to

Hierarchy

their survival. Our dogs will claim ownership over all survival-critical resources that we don't claim for ourselves. If we don't complete tasks to secure these resources, they'll instinctively take on these security tasks as well.

Imagine that you're on the Titanic. You can see the iceberg approaching as the ship moves unstoppably toward it. When you look around, you see that no one's manning the ship's helm – so you instinctively take up the position yourself.

This is exactly what happens with our dogs. If we can't take on the tasks that they consider important, they have to take on these tasks themselves. In a dog's world, these tasks are essential for survival. If we unknowingly abandon our territory to our dog, we simultaneously present him with a great number of obligations. He'll want to monitor, guard and defend his resources. Many dogs are completely overwhelmed by such demands, becoming stressed and developing problem behaviors as a result. Only a tiny fraction of animals have what it takes to become real leading animals.

It's decided in the whelping box which animals will later have what it takes to lead a pack. Puppies struggle unrestrainedly and crawl to one of their mother's free teats as soon as they're born. This is where the fight for food resources begins. The more successfully a puppy asserts itself during the struggle in the whelping box for the best milk, the more likely it is that this puppy will later have what it takes to become a leading animal. Even during his first day on earth he's collecting learning experiences that will help in the struggle for resources. The greater a dog's assertiveness, the greater his chances of survival. It's a simple survival principle.

A similarly predetermined fate is also revealed at this early stage for omega animals, the lowest-ranking members within a pack. The puppies with the least assertiveness will remain at the bottom of the ranking order in later life. Dogs today shouldn't fall into either extreme, and alpha and omega animals are often very difficult for breeders to sell. This is why breeders influence puppies' behaviors as soon as they're born. They'll watch closely for puppies that are disadvantaged and ensure that these puppies are always the first to receive milk. The puppies are mixed around well so that no puppy goes short.

We're then left with a problem, however: Our dogs no longer learn how to be alpha animals. They're subsequently often overwhelmed by the tasks that we unknowingly give to them within our families.

6 Social togetherness

Many parallels emerge when you compare a family company with a pack of wolves or dogs. Like in a pack, every employee within a family company has a role. A family company also has hierarchy levels and management structures that operate in spite of family relationships, once again like in a pack. Work life and family life in a family company are both closely connected and strongly separated. The family pulls together when it comes to earning their means of existence, and members also drive each other forward and require every individual to perform so that company goals are reached.

The children in a family company learn from their elders and don't normally have any responsibilities of their own. They learn the rules that apply in the family through observation and education. Unrelated employees generally have very little say and take a back seat with many decisions. If the parents become too old or infirm to run the company, another family member will take over the management. The young, new managing director will often still profit from his predecessors' experiences and continue to respect these family members even though they no longer stand at the company's helm.

The larger the company and the stronger its competition, the greater the pressure on that company to perform. If it becomes more difficult to secure an existence from the company's ever-decreasing profits, everyone starts to look after themselves. They all try to seize the largest piece of the cake before the others do the same. In extremely difficult times, employees even begrudge the dirt from underneath their colleagues' fingernails. Everyone develops their own strategies for obtaining the greatest benefits for themselves.

If new employees join the company, existing employees will often fear that their positions are under threat. In particularly hard times when profits completely fail to materialize, quarrels and disputes will even arise among the

Social togetherness

parents, the company's bosses. The atmosphere within the company sinks to a low, and questions are frequently asked as to whether it's the right time to bring in new company management.

Competition means rivalry. Employees may not like each another, but they respect one another so long as everyone remains in their own area.

The employees rest and relax during breaks, when work is over, and in their time off. They may even meet up and have fun together. But when their leisure time ends, other things take priority once more. The job calls!
The parents run the company and set the business strategy. Their decisions ultimately determine how much each employee earns at the end of every month. If disagreements occur or employees are bullied, it's normally down to the parents to resolve these conflicts. If ambiguities emerge about responsibilities or authorities and the employees can't work out these issues between themselves, the parents will also step in to provide resolution and restore harmony among colleagues.

Family companies train apprentices, as well. These are usually the family's own children or grandchildren, nieces or nephews. They don't yet have to generate profit for the company or take on any responsibilities. They'll later decide whether they want to leave the company, become part of the team, or if they're able to lead the business.

This situation gives you a rough impression of what happens in a pack and what values apply within a dog's world. There are various responsibilities in a pack. Some dogs are responsible for hunting while others follow tracks or protect the pack's offspring. In bad times, everyone acts for themselves in the fight for food. Food and security play the same roles in a dog's life as money does in our lives; a dog will do anything possible to secure these survival-critical resources.

Unrelated animals from other packs are generally seen as rivals and threats.

If pack members leave or rejoin the pack, there's always uncertainty about how this affects the rest of the pack. It creates insecurity about the future allocation of tasks, the claims to resources and the division of rights and duties within the group. If ranking orders change, freedoms always change as well – directly affecting the survival security of those concerned.

Dogs rely on their leading animals' decisions. They follow their leading animals because these animals are in the best position to secure resources and make the correct decisions for the survival and social harmony of the community. A dog will submit to his leading animals because he trusts them. He allows the leading animals to control the resources, and in return he receives a secure existence. This is just like in a company, where employees leave the important decisions to their bosses and in return receive their salaries on time each month. The bosses in a pack are responsible for all important decisions, and they strive for social peace and harmony within the group.

The leadership will change if the current leading animals are no longer able to secure the pack's needs or if another animal is better suited to the job. This handover will usually take place peacefully. The new leading animals will mostly have qualified for these positions of responsibility long in advance. They'll normally enjoy a high reputation and will have shown the relevant leadership skills from an early stage.

Only when a dog has met all of his obligations and finished for the day will he play with other dogs or demonstrate behaviors that he enjoys.

Puppies are the apprentices within a pack. They don't take on any responsibilities, don't have to concern themselves with obtaining food, and are protected by the adult dogs. They learn social behavior from one another and pick up rules and routines by watching the adults.

6.1 The family pack

Your dog knows that you're not a dog. As you're neither related to him nor a member of the same species, he also won't recognize your family as a pack in the sense of a family unit. To him, you're just a non-canine social partner who's involved with his life. Since he's the only dog in your family, he'll instinctively take on the tasks that secure survival in his world. He'll behave like a loner, necessarily taking on the tasks of a leading animal whether he wants to do so or not. There's no one else there, after all. It's common for our dogs to subsequently become overwhelmed by the tasks that they've taken on. They don't possess the necessary leadership skills, and they've never really learned how to bear responsibility. They'd much rather take direction from someone that they trust.

A dog can only think in terms of the social structure of a pack, so he'll only submit to you if he's learned that you can control resources, make the correct decisions and satisfy his needs. If your dog makes every decision by himself and dominates all resources that are important to him, there's no reason for him to submit to you.

6.2 The pet human

Join us on a trip to Planet Hasso and experience the everyday life of a pet human. Use this small role-play to gain an insight into how your dog might perceive our world.

Imagine that you wake up one morning and find yourself on Planet Buddy. Huge, powerful predators, the Buddys, control all of the resources here. They control all of the food, the water, the territory and the raw materials on the planet. You live as a human pet to the Buddys, completely separately from all other humans. The Buddys are concerned about species-appropriate human ownership, so you live in a two-room apartment with a shower, your own toilet and a television. You can't understand the Buddy language, and the Buddys also can't understand what you say. In everyday life, you try to meet the Buddys' requirements. You don't want to annoy or provoke them under any circumstances; you want food from them, after all. You've learned to judge their moods based on their body language. You can sometimes infer from their gestures that they require you to show a certain behavior. If you show this behavior, you receive a tasty reward. They sometimes address you with sounds, however, and you can't interpret what these sounds mean.

You can leave your apartment three times each day to go outside. Your Buddy mistress takes you on a leash, and sometimes you're given a candy bar at irregular intervals. You meet other people during your times outside; they're also kept as human pets, but you often don't know them. The Buddys think that they're doing you a favor by letting you have frequent contact with these strangers, so whenever possible, they look out for other Buddys who are walking with their human pets. Unfortunately, you've never met another human and got along well with him or her. So far you've only met dangerous criminals and crooks with whom you've wanted absolutely no interaction. When you encounter these people, you have to run for your life or fight for your candy bars. Your Buddy mistress interprets the scraps that occur as playing, so she always heads specifically toward the criminals in the hope that you'll be able to play some more. You often leave this 'playing' with burst lips and black eyes, but your Buddy mistress thinks that this is normal for humans. It's just what happens when humans play.

After a while, you learn self-defense because your Buddy mistress won't protect you from the criminals. Now you often end up fighting with other people even when you're still on the leash. But your Buddy mistress doesn't want you to become aggressive while you're on the leash. She yells violently every time and pulls on the leash whenever you try to defend yourself. You naturally don't want to get into trouble every time there are problems with other humans. You learn to suppress your tension, and now instead of arguing, you launch straight into an attack whenever you meet a criminal.

When you're back in the Buddys' home, the doorbell rings. The Buddys have a visitor. Since you don't know whether what's about to happen will affect you, you run to the door and watch closely for what occurs. You know the visitors and already have a sinking feeling in your stomach. What do they have planned for you this time? You become nervous, shake your head and scream; you've already anticipated what's about to happen. The Buddys interpret your behavior as joy, so they pick you up and cuddle you like there were no tomorrow. The visitors pat you all day long, playing with your ears and rubbing your stomach. The Buddys have read somewhere that you like this.

The sun goes down and the Buddy house starts to smell like dinner. Today there's tasty meat. You'd never normally be given any of this meat, but you've learned that if you stand at the table and make a decent amount of noise, there's always someone who'll throw you a scrap. This is why you stand at the dining table each evening and cry your heart out – before you return to your apartment and the whole game begins once more the next day.

Social togetherness

One day, your Buddy mistress reads in the newspaper that humans are supposed to walk 20 km on a daily basis. They're hunters, after all, and spent millions of years on their home planet hunting prey over very long distances. Your Buddy mistress wants to treat you in accordance with your species, so you now have to walk 20 km each day before breakfast.

As some point, she goes to a human shelter to find you a friend so that you'll have someone to play with during the days. You're unfortunately not allowed to go with her to look for your new partner.
The new human moves in with you on the very same evening, sprawling out over your couch and eating your candy bars. You can't bear this new person right from the start, and you end up fighting. Your Buddy mistress thinks that you're playing and is sure that she's done you a favor by getting this new playmate.

This is how you spend your life, shaped by misunderstandings day in and day out. What a dog's life! How great your life could be if only someone took an interest in your real needs.

7 Sensory perception in dogs

A dog needs a predator's senses to complete his tasks. It's only dogs' and wolves' excellent, habitat-adapted sensory perception that allows them to survive in the wild.

Imagine that your dog pulls completely unexpectedly on the leash, barks at the top of his voice, becomes nervous or is abruptly very attentive and easily scared. He suddenly behaves in an entirely incomprehensible manner during what seems to be a totally everyday situation. When your dog behaves in way that you see as having no apparent justification, there's usually a cause that humans don't perceive, or at least not to the same extent. The differences between what humans and dogs perceive are greater than many dog lovers think.

7.1 The control center

A dog's brain is divided into different parts. The medulla oblongata controls all of his vital functions such as his breathing and his heartbeat. The cerebellum controls his spatial orientation and motor function. The midbrain processes his emotions and impulses. The midbrain is also the site of his limbic system, which determines how he perceives his world. The amygdala and the hippocampus, both of which are found in the temporal lobe, are parts of the limbic system.

The sensory organs deliver neutral stimuli to the brain. The amygdala provides these stimuli with emotional meanings and plays an important role in your dog's emotional assessment of stimuli and recognition of situations.

This information is then matched with saved memories in the hippocampus before being forwarded to the cerebrum. The cerebrum is where conscious thought occurs. Sensory perceptions are processed and potential actions are formed in the associative cortex; prior experiences play a significant role at this stage. Conscious decisions are then eventually reached.

The limbic system is the control center for the emotions. Emotions serve to maintain contact between the brain and the body. They're controlled via biological processes. As an example, the hormone oxytocin is released when your dog is touched in a way that he finds pleasant. The oxytocin results in the breaking down of the stress hormone cortisol, thereby creating a soothing effect.

Neurochemical research connects oxytocin with mental states such as love, trust and calmness. Numerous studies have confirmed oxytocin's significance for feelings and actions, although it should be noted that complex mental states such as love don't correspond to any single biological process.

7.2 Seeing through a dog's eyes

A dog's eye is similar in structure to a human's eye. The lens is larger, however, and therefore less flexible. This means that dogs require longer than humans to focus their eyes. They also have more than twice as many rods on their retinas as humans. The tapetum cellulosum lucidum in a dog's eye, a reflective cell layer on the back of the retina, allows dogs to see much better than us at dusk and during the night. This cell layer reflects light that's already passed through the retina back through it again, thereby increasing the total amount of light that's collected.

Unlike humans, dogs have only two cone types in their eyes instead of three. This means that the world is considerably less colorful for a dog than it is for a human. Dogs see reddish and greenish shades less well than blues and yellows, and their vision is also less rich in contrast and only about half as sharp as human vision.

A dog's sense of sight is specially adapted to match a hunter's needs. This includes a wider field of vision than humans. In contrast to a human's eyes, a dog's eyes are more on the side of his head. This means that he can see things that approach from the side at a much earlier point. He can also detect movements far better than he can detect stationary objects. The disadvantage of this eye position is much poorer spatial vision; a dog's eyes overlap considerably less in their individual fields of vision. Depending on skull shape, a dog's overall field of vision is between 180 and 270 degrees.

A dog has much a higher flicker rate than a human. The flicker rate is the number of images per second that are necessary for perception of a moving image instead of many individual images. Humans have a flicker rate of between 50 and 60 Hz, after which we see a series of images as a moving image. In contrast, a dog has a flicker rate of 80 Hz. He sees television programs as slide shows; he can only see a moving image at 80 Hz. This characteristic means that a dog can react far faster than a human to optical stimuli.

7.3 How dogs hear even the smallest of pins drop

Humans and dogs share the same inner ear structure. Both species have their sound receptors located in the cochlea, the most important bone in the inner ear. In contrast to humans, dogs additionally have receptors that respond to extremely high-frequency sounds. They also have far more sound receptors than humans overall; a dog can localize sounds up to 10 times more precisely than a human. Dogs can hear sounds up to 40,000 Hz, while humans can only hear sounds up to 20,000 Hz. They can similarly hear sounds from up to four times further away than humans. Disobedience is therefore not an indication that your dog is hard of hearing. Most dogs continue to hear better than humans even into old age. Dogs can similarly locate sound sources better than us. A dog can precisely identify a currently active sound source from within a circle of 64 sound sources. A human can only complete the same precise identification with a maximum of 16 sound sources.

7.4 A superlative sense of smell

A dog's most important sense organ is its nose. If you show your dog an object, he won't look at it as a human would, but will first sniff at it instead.

A dog has an average of around 220 million olfactory cells. In contrast, a human has only around 5 million of these cells. Dogs are a million times better than humans at detecting and distinguishing between even the subtlest of scent traces. Dogs can't just perceive a wider variety of smells: They're also able to accurately detect a scent trace's path and direction. Such incredible performance is possible because a dog's brain stores smells in spatial terms and analyzes them in chronological order.
The Jacobson's organ (vomeronasal organ) allows dogs to taste smells. In total, roughly one tenth of a dog's brain is exclusively dedicated to the processing of

scent information. Many people even believe that dogs can smell our emotions, although this isn't entirely correct. We start to sweat when we're stimulated, and this action causes scent molecules to be released from the surface of our skin. It's these scents that a dog can perceive. He then connects our emotional state and our body language with this smell, and in future can recognize our state of mind from our smell alone.

The Chinese already knew some 3,000 years ago that dogs can use their extremely sensitive noses to smell illnesses in humans. A Polish-American research team has since been able to teach five dogs in just 16 days the difference in smell between cancer patients and healthy volunteers.[3] Scientists from the Pine Street Foundation in Marin County, California, specialized in the detection of lung cancer. Breath samples were taken from test subjects and saved in plastic bags. 83 of the 169 test subjects were completely healthy, while biopsies had recently diagnosed 55 of the subjects with lung cancer and 31 of the subjects with breast cancer. The breath samples were presented to the dogs. Subjects with lung cancer were recognized in 99% of cases, and subjects with breast cancer were recognized in 88% of cases. The dogs even outperformed the accuracy of mammograms in detecting breast cancer.

Dogs equally communicate with their own scents to a large extent. They produce pheromones that are conveyed though the air after being given off by various glands, e.g. the glands at the end of the rectum that add scents to the feces. Anal glands add secretions to the feces as well. There are also the perianal glands at the anus and the violet gland at the base of the tail. A dog's urine contains pheromones that deliver information about social rank position or a bitch's reproduction readiness. Marking behavior is similarly encouraged by the smell of other dogs' urine markings.

The nose at work
Like dogs, wolves have astounding cognitive abilities. They have a much better cartographic memory than humans. A wolf's sense of smell allows him to precisely memorize his routes and territorial boundaries, and also where

---

[3]McCulloch M., Jezierski T., Broffman M., Hubbard A., Turner K., Janecki T., Pine Street Foundation: *Diagnostic Accuracy of Canine Scent Detection in Early and Late Stage Lung and Breast Cancers*, Integrative Cancer Therapies, Jan. 2006.

within his territory there's potential prey and where dangers, enemies and competitors lurk. A wolf knows how his prey moves within his territory, when young animals are expected, and when's the best time for hunting. Wolves also always find their ways back, even over the most difficult terrain; they follow their own scents that they leave on the way out. They take their bearings from their own urine, feces and the scents that the sweat glands in their paws leave along their routes.

Dogs spend most of their time collecting information about their territories. A dog relies almost exclusively on his olfactory abilities for this task, i.e. his sense of smell. Our four-legged friends gather information with their noses that we'd gather with our eyes. These hunters use their extremely sensitive senses of smell to collect information about the health of prey animals. A dog can pick up smells at a distance of over 10 km if the wind and scent concentrations are correct. He can determine whether the prey animals that live in his territory are healthy by examining the saliva, feces and other bodily fluids that these animals leave behind. He can also smell when his prey animals are wounded or if their wounds are healing poorly or are infected. As he patrols his territory, he'll use his nose to monitor the animals' healing or recovery processes. He can similarly determine their condition from the smell of their feces and urine. He uses all of these indications to select prey animals for hunting. Sick, old or injured animals are at the top of his wish list. A wolf has excellent sensory performance, but his hunting results will be usually quite poor: On average, only between 5 and 8 of his every 100 hunting attempts will end in success.

Most dogs have already forgotten how to hunt, so they'd probably have an even worse rate of success than their forefathers.

The controlling behavior exhibited by our dogs is a legacy from the territorial behavior exhibited by wolves. It serves to satisfy their need for information. The stronger a dog's urge for control, the stronger his need for information. Dogs collect information for the same reasons as their ancestors, but they can often find this process to be hard work. They use the information that they collect to work out actions and problem solving strategies – despite neither still being needed for co-existence with humans.

7.5 The sense of touch

Dogs also explore their surroundings through their sense of touch. This includes physical contact, cold, heat and pain. When we stroke a dog, he feels our touches via receptors that sit underneath his skin. Whether he regards our touches as positive or negative depends on the experiences that he's already connected with this feeling.

A dog's paws contain nerves that tell him what surface he's walking on. This becomes clear when you watch a dog on an icy surface. His paws transmit the feeling to his brain, and he then begins to walk in an uncertain manner because the surface is slippery.

The hairs on a dog's muzzle (vibrissae) provide another important sense of touch. These hairs transmit information about his surroundings to his brain. They're thick, strong and deeply embedded in the skin. As soon as an object approaches, his forward-facing whiskers feel it first and pass this information on to his brain. The dog will then stop because of the information that he's received about the obstacle. This explains why even blind dogs slow down and stop instead of colliding into obstacles. To gain a feel for an object, a dog's whiskers first brush over it and so determine its physical characteristics and surface.

7.6 Heat and cold

Dogs can only sense heat with their noses, as it's only in their noses that they have heat receptors. These receptors are important for helping puppies to find their mothers after they've been born. A dog's body is otherwise only equipped with cold receptors. He's therefore unable to sense heat; if one of his body parts becomes too warm, it's his pain receptors that respond. A dog feels the effect of extreme heat in the same way that humans feel pain.

A dog's body temperature is between 37.5 and 38.5°C (up to 39.5°C in puppies). Dogs mainly regulate their body temperatures through panting instead of through their skin. Water evaporates through the mucous membranes in the mouth, pharynx, trachea and lungs and is also exhaled in the breath. This evaporation removes heat energy from the body and thereby regulates the body's temperature. Regular water intake is therefore especially important for dogs in summer. A cooling bath and water that's absorbed via drinking will also regulate a dog's body temperature.

It's a misconception that longhaired dogs fare better in summer if they're sheared. Dogs don't have any sweat glands on their skin; their only sweat glands are on the soles of their feet. Unlike humans, this means that they can't benefit from the cooling effect of evaporation on sweat-covered skin. A dog's coat has a biologically in-built thermal effect that keeps his body temperature low during warm periods as well as warm during cold periods. That we think that a dog with short hair will fare better is down to our human empathy (see Page 62, "Empathy"). We humans take off our thick coats after the winter has ended, so the same should also be good for our dogs – or so we believe.

7.7 Selective perception

A dog's world is determined by environmental stimuli, with the stimuli that he experiences having a significant influence on his behavior. In order to process environmental stimuli, he needs to differentiate between important and unimportant sensory perceptions. Selective perception assists him in this task.

Selective perception allows only certain environmental stimuli to be detected. Other stimuli are blocked out. This perception is based on one of the brain's basic mechanisms: Pattern recognition. The brain is constantly searching for patterns so that it can better incorporate new information alongside existing information. As such, selective perception is the search for specific patterns that are of relevance to a dog. Sensory stimuli are filtered for relevant patterns prior to processing by the dog's brain. Only information that's important for the dog is passed on for further processing. This filtering prevents sensory overload and is necessary if the dog's brain is to cope with the wealth of information that's conveyed from his sensory organs. Information about the dog's position is perceived more prominently, while other information is suppressed.

We humans react very strongly when we hear our names. We even hear our names clearly when they're mentioned in conversations that we only hear in passing. We react in this manner because when we've heard our names in the past, what's been said has normally affected us in a direct sense. Our dogs also react to vocalizations if they learn that these vocalizations affect them.

If we humans were suddenly given a dog's meticulous sense of smell, our first few days with this new sense would be extremely demanding. Selective perception only develops with experience. We already filter out unimportant stimuli that we encounter while we continue to process other stimuli further. This phenomenon is evident in people who live next to train lines. When we visit such people, we find the sound of trains to be extremely disturbing. In contrast, the inhabitants have learned over time to completely block out this background noise. The sound becomes normal and no longer disturbs them.

Selective perception soon causes most dogs to stop attaching importance to human speech. This is because dogs don't understand human vocalizations, and

Selective perception makes deep sleep possible – without missing dangers.

most human vocalizations also provoke no response in them. The same applies when we speak in whole sentences: A dog will soon block out a normal human voice and stop responding to human vocalizations. He'll only pay attention when our voices significantly differ from their everyday tones. This means that a dog has to be yelled at in all different pitches if he's to show any reaction to our voices. As a dog has excellent hearing, however, the secret to an obedient dog doesn't lie with volume. Instead, use your voice very specifically and limit the total vocalizations that you direct toward him. He'll then pay considerably more attention to sound commands and vocalizations in the future.

Sounds or other sensory perceptions that are unfamiliar to your dog or that could indicate danger may provoke unwanted behavior patterns, insecurity or anxiety. Only when you've positively conditioned your dog to a new stimulus (see Page 229, "Habituation and systematic desensitization") will he associate this stimulus with a desired action and a positive experience and also deal with this stimulus in a more confident manner.

If your dog demonstrates unwanted behavior when he's faced with new stimuli, avoid punishment or any form of compulsive behavioral correction. He's behaving in accordance with his species and won't understand your punishment. Your dog is behaving correctly if he barks loudly on hearing a sound that's unfamiliar to him or that he considers dangerous. He's warning you to be vigilant, as an unfamiliar sound may indicate danger.

8 Emotions

It's important to know whether a dog can experience feelings and, if so, which feelings. This knowledge allows us to give our dogs comfortable and fulfilling lives. It's only when we know what makes our dogs happy, when they feel joy, and what their needs are that we can treat them properly and build up a positive relationship with them.

Empathy
We humans possess a very special gift: We can feel for others. We call this ability 'empathy'. When we empathize with others, mirror neurons are activated within our brains. A mirror neuron is a nerve cell that triggers the same stimuli in our brains when we see an event as would otherwise be triggered if we experienced that event for ourselves. Mirror neurons are also activated when we merely imagine situations. The process draws on our wealth of experiences and our own feelings. The way in which mirror neurons work was discovered by the Italian neurophysiologist Giacomo Rizzolatti and his colleagues in monkeys in 1995. The neurons form the neurobiological basis for our intuitive knowledge and our understanding of what others feel. They tell us what other people feel and allow us to share in these other people's joy or pain.

Empathy enables us to share in sorrow, happiness or euphoria even if we only hear about these emotions from a distance. This is why we're so glad to sit in front of the television and switch from one emotional experience to another. Although we don't experience the situations that we see on the television for ourselves, we can still empathize with the protagonists' emotions. Football fans often come close to heart attacks during penalty shoot-outs or suffer agony if their team loses a home game against their archrivals. They feel humiliation, shame, frustration or anger despite not being on the field themselves. Fans of action movies vividly share in the heroes' thrills even though they're sitting in armchairs and watching the movies with bags of popcorn. But it's not just unbearable tension that captivates us: We're equally fascinated by love-pains, sorrow and misery. We feel all of these emotions alongside the performers.

Empathy determines our entire everyday lives. We watch our fellow humans so that we can assess their moods. We often only see a situation from afar, but we still know how the people involved feel. This is a good thing, as it allows us to react to other people's moods in an appropriate manner. People with a particular capacity for empathy usually have very good social integrity. On the other hand, people who are less competent in this regard come across as rather cold-hearted and emotionally dulled. They often respond to other people's emotional states in completely inappropriate ways, and this frequently leads to their ostracization. People who suffer from autism, for instance, have a neural disorder that prevents them from empathizing with other people's feelings. They experience the feelings themselves, but they can't feel them when they see them in others.

Empathy plays an incredibly important role in dog training. We don't just feel what we observe in other humans: We also think that we can feel what our dog feels.

Empathy isn't the result of conscious thought. Instead, we look at something and are subconsciously able to share in the emotions of what we've seen. This even applies if the objects that we look at aren't capable of feeling emotions. If we see a statue, for example, we might recognize joy within it because it's smiling. If we look at a car, we can tell whether it seems evil or friendly. Your subconscious makes a decision long before you consciously know what the subject feels. We can react to someone else's emotional states within 200 milliseconds if necessary, but conscious actions only follow after between 1.5 and 7 seconds. This means that we evaluate situations subconsciously.

We also see when our dogs are happy, angry, ashamed or jealous. We even think that we know when they want to annoy us or when they're offended or being stubborn. We transfer what we see in our dogs into our own emotional worlds.

But a dog isn't human, so he'll experience situations and feel emotions differently from a human.

Emotions

Findings from evolutionary emotion research show that the closer two creatures are related in evolutionary terms, the greater the conformity in how these two creatures will subjectively perceive emotions. Creatures with weaker evolutionary relationships tend to perceive emotions in more divergent manners. In consequence, members of the same species have a relatively high degree of conformity in their emotional repertoires. The closer an animal is related to humans in evolutionary terms, the more similar this animal's emotions are likely to be to human emotions.

If you now look at how closely humans and dogs are related in evolutionary terms, it quickly becomes clear that nothing connects us. Hominids split off around 90 million years ago, so humans have gone through completely different evolutionary processes from dogs for the length of this period. Humans probably have a completely different emotional repertoire and will subjectively experience situations entirely differently from dogs. It's even difficult for us to say how another human experiences emotions such as love or grief. Do you remember how you felt when you fell in love for the very first time? People normally experience this feeling in an extremely different manner once many years have passed.

This difference isn't just caused by the limbic system's messenger substances that are responsible for how we feel emotions. It also involves our acquired knowledge such as our worldview, religion, beliefs, values, desires and dreams. All of these factors differ tremendously between humans and dogs.

The example of grief illustrates the real magnitude of the differences that exist between how humans and dogs perceive emotions.

The history of grief began around 2 million years ago. This was then the ancestors of modern man, Homo erectus, began to leave piles of stones over those who passed away. To this day, no other creature on Earth is known to do this. But why did Homo erectus do it? It's assumed that they wanted to protect the corpses from scavenging animals. But why should a dead body be protected? It's likely that our ancestors were now grappling with death for the first time and believed that something would happen to people's bodies after they died.

A 1.8 million year-old grave was found in the northern Spanish city of Atapuerca. It contained an interesting find: A hand axe that was made from a material that wasn't available in that area at that time and that had demonstrably never been used. This made the hand axe a burial object. Whoever left the tool in the grave must have thought something of it. It was probably at this point that our ancestors began to believe in a life after death. The burial object was likely supposed to be of use to the deceased in his next life.

These processes indicate an increase in Homo erectus' mental capacity that other animals, including dogs, have not developed in the same form.

Humans subsequently found faith and attributed everything inexplicable to a higher power. We now call this power 'God'. The most diverse religions developed across the world, all with their own idea of what happens after we die. Some believe in reincarnation, while others believe in Heaven and Hell. The diversity of religions is matched by the diversity of subjective feelings of grief. If someone knows that a deceased person will be reborn or enter paradise, they'll feel grief differently from someone who sees death as a final farewell.

It's therefore very difficult to describe how an individual human will subjectively feel grief. A dog is also certain to feel this emotion in a completely different manner from you or me. He's gone through entirely different evolutionary selection processes from humans, and this ultimately means that his less-developed brain will interpret emotional states in a different way from our highly developed brains.

Even we humans can only understand death after a certain age. Pre-schoolers still can't grasp the finality of death, with life and death being interchangeable in their minds based on their previous experiences. They believe death to be limited in time and so reversible at any point. In a child's emotional world, death means darkness, separation or sleep. Many children also believe that you can be dead to a greater or lesser extent, and this notion finds expression in how they think that the dead are asleep and will wake up again, or that they continue to live on underground.

Emotions

Only when children are old enough to start school can they understand the difference between 'alive' and 'dead' and also the finality of death. This is when their brain development reaches a new stage of intellectual maturity. The new maturity allows them to grasp the meaning of death in stronger emotional terms and experience these emotions in a more intense manner. They now devote far more thought, and especially worry, to the death of their loved ones or pets.

An older child will also be increasingly able to contain himself, control his feelings and postpone the satisfaction of his needs. He'll similarly be able to concentrate better and learn in a goal-oriented manner. The growing maturity of the frontal lobe facilitates logical thought, judgment making, numeracy and social behavior.

It's during puberty that young people speculate about a life after death. They experience intensive periods of grief during this time, and these periods raise their awareness of the finality and irreversibility of death. Their grief is associated with powerful emotional mood swings, and they express their feelings in very diverse ways, from rage and aggression to withdrawal and the suppression of feelings. This concrete, close-up experience of death if often accompanied by physical symptoms such as headaches, stomach pains and sleep problems.

Even though most mammals have brains with similar structures, their subjective interpretations of emotions are extremely different and depend strongly on individual mental capacities. An emotion can't just be demonstrated through chemical messengers: It also has to be individually interpreted. An emotion is not the result of the limbic system alone, but rather interaction between many parts of the brain.

What's going on in our dogs' heads when we think that they're grieving?

If a family member dies, the whole family will usually grieve and so behave differently from how they would on normal days. A dog will be very aware of these behavioral changes, but he'll be unsure as to why you're behaving in this different manner. He bases his entire day around you. Suddenly all of the daily routines and familiar habits change, and anticipated routines cease to occur. Perhaps even his caregiver is no longer there – the person who previously determined his entire daily routine. Your unsettled behavior causes him to question his position and his prior security within the family.

Who can he now take direction from? Who will take over responsibility for his security? Who can he trust in future?

Your dog will show his insecurity and will also behave in an unusual manner. He'll whine, wander around aimlessly, paw at you or show you other reassurance signals until he's learned to find his bearings within this new situation. His insecurity will soon disappear if the old routines reappear of if he learns a new daily routine. From a human perspective, it might be said that the dog is grieving as well. But he's not human.

When two wolves live together in a long-term partnership and one of the wolves dies, the other wolf will sometimes die just a short while after.
This phenomenon can also be seen in other animals, e.g. in birds. It's especially well known that parrots suffer enormously when they lose their partners.
Humans don't experience these extreme emotional reactions that in some cases lead to death. I therefore believe that it's inappropriate to talk about 'grief' when we refer to dogs. We humans can't empathize with the strength of emotion that an animal experiences in this situation. Their feelings are probably fundamentally different from the human emotion of grief.
As such, we should avoid the anthropomorphization of other creatures' emotions and instead recognize that a dog can experience feelings that we'll most likely never understand.

If we want to understand emotions, we need to have experienced these emotions for ourselves or be able to imagine them. Even if you've never been hit by a car, your experiences are sufficient to imagine how being in this situation would feel. In contrast, you can't imagine certain other things because you don't have sufficient experiences. I have no idea how heartburn feels, so I can't empathize with someone who complains of this condition.

As you can see, it's difficult for us humans to always understand other humans' emotions in the correct manner. It's even more difficult, if not impossible, to use our human empathy to correctly understand our dogs' emotions. But this doesn't stop us from making decisions that concern our dogs from a purely human perspective. Empathy works on a subconscious level, so we don't have any choice but to treat our dogs like humans.

But why is it so important for us to be able to assess our dogs' moods?

Every dog owner has his dog's best interests at heart. He only wants the best for his four-legged friend, who should have a good life and want for nothing. If we see that our dogs are joyful, we naturally want to maintain this state and do everything that we can for them to experience this moment of happiness more often and for as long as possible. But what if our dogs aren't really joyful and we're misinterpreting what we see? Then we end up encouraging an emotional state that's less pleasant for our dogs than we suppose.

If you don't know what's going on in your dog's head, you can't behave in the manner that he expects.

Empathy doesn't allow us to think about these questions; we're convinced that we know how things appear to our dogs. Our subconscious minds already make decisions before we're able to apply conscious thought. But if you take the trouble to seriously question your dog's emotional repertoire, you'll be able to build up a much stronger relationship with him than you can even imagine at present.

There are some advantages in dogs having a different emotional repertoire. A dog can't bear grudges, for instance. He equally can't understand when we bear grudges against him.

A dog similarly can't yearn for or miss something. He can't compare current situations with prior situations that were more advantageous for him, and he also can't miss these prior, more advantageous situations. Such an ability would cause frustration and be accompanied by his striving to recreate these prior, more advantageous situations. A dog can't consciously reminisce in this manner.

If a dog is exposed to a familiar stimulus (e.g. a smell, sound or sight), he'll often seem to be able to reminisce. This doesn't reflect reality. The stimulus just triggers the emotion that he previously experienced when the stimulus occurred and that he therefore associated with the stimulus. If he'd never been re-exposed to the stimulus, he'd never have thought back to the associated situation or miss that situation.

We humans have been able to improve our skills through our abilities to remember past situations and establish why past and present situations differ. When we use ten tools, for example, we can later remember which tool worked best and why this was the case. We can think back and thereby improve our strategies for solving problems. If a dog finds a solution to a problem, he won't later try to optimize this approach or find a better solution by attempting different approaches. Dogs just aren't humans.

In consequence, if you adopt a dog from an animal shelter, he won't be eternally grateful to you or show daily appreciation for how much better his life is now than it was while he was back in the shelter.

A dog lives in the present and evaluates his mental state in accordance with the currently prevailing situation. There are some dogs that feel comfortable in an animal shelter. There are similarly dogs that run away from their owners because they don't feel comfortable living alongside them.

Empathy is important for our dogs as well, as they also have mirror neurons and so can empathize with others. Just like we constantly humanize our dogs, they constantly see us in their own terms.

Like humans, dogs can only reflect on emotions that they know. It's therefore incorrect to think that a dog can sense our tempers and moods. He can connect our moods with smells, so if he smells our sweat when we're uncertain or afraid, he'll associate this smell with our state of mind. But he can't smell our mood per se; he can just connect a stimulus (a smell) with a situation (a mood).

Behavior patterns that he can't interpret will usually unnerve him. He'll equally interpret gestures that he thinks he recognizes in accordance with his own experiences. If you lie on your back in a meadow to take a short break, for instance, your dog will come over to you in confusion and probably lick your face or show other reassurance signals. In a dog's world, presenting the stomach area is a sign of submission. Your dog doesn't know why you're behaving like this, so he'll react in an insecure manner.

Our dogs interpret many of our well-meant gestures in ways that are totally different from our intentions. Dogs assess situations from their own perspectives, and these perspectives are those of predators and not humans. We're then all the more surprised by how our dogs react. When we want to lovingly embrace them, for example, they growl at us. A dog simply isn't a human. In a dog's world, predators only embrace when they want to go for each other's throats. You wouldn't put up with an action like that, either!

8.1 The development of emotions

When considering the development of emotions, the question arises as to emotions' biological function. Emotions enable the selection of need-oriented, situation-appropriate behavior patterns, and they also regulate these behavior patterns' intensities and durations.

Emotions developed because they offered a survival benefit (selective advantage) to someone or their relatives.

Our evolutionary development allows us to experience many emotions that exist in almost no other living creatures.
Vital to the development of our present emotions was our learning to control essential resources during the course of our evolution. This enabled us to develop unique needs. Our needs form the basis of our emotional world: A creature with no need for recognition, for instance, won't be able to feel shame, honor or pride.

But how could our needs develop?

The process was initiated by climatic changes in present-day Ethiopia that forced our ancestors to find new resources. The shifting of India to the Eurasian continental plate formed the Himalayas, in turn causing enormous climate changes. The tropical climate that had so far provided our habitat with paradisiacal conditions slowly became very dry. The resulting decrease in vegetation brought about a crucial process of selection among our forefathers. We once ate only fruits, but now only those people who were able to find new food sources could survive. We subsequently discovered meat as a food source and so developed into hunters.

Some of our ancestors were able to walk upright due to an abnormality in their hips. This method of movement allowed us to hunt in a very efficient and energy-conserving manner. Although we weren't predators, over millions of years we became the most successful hunters that the world has over seen. We were ultimately able to source more food than we needed for our survival. It was only with this excess of food and the resulting excess of energy that our brains could develop further. Meat was an excellent brain food, and it triggered the first push in the rapid growth of our intellectual faculties. Our brains are real gluttons for energy: They're nine times larger than would be expected for a mammal of our size, and their metabolic rate is more than 20 times higher than that found in our skeletal muscles. In total, they need around 20% of all the energy that we absorb from our food, along with 15% of our oxygen and 40% of our blood sugar. The ratios are even more extreme in embryos and small children: Their brain growth takes up between 60 and 70% of their total available energy.

Our qualities as intelligent hunters were what allowed our brains to grow. Our cerebral cortex was disproportionally affected by this enormous growth. The cerebral cortex is responsible for thinking, planning, memory and speech.

Our intelligence also enabled us to ensure the safety of our communities. We could assess dangers, think ahead and plan for the future. At some point, we no longer faced either dangers or natural enemies. It was only from this point

Emotions

onward that we could afford, from an evolutionary perspective, to develop interpersonal feelings.

There's no clear evidence to show exactly when our present emotional world developed. It can be supposed, however, that emotions had obtained a special place in our forefathers' lives and were continuing to develop by the time humans discovered fire. We began to cook our food with fire around a million years ago. From this point forward, if not before, some humans collected food instead of simply eating what they found. This food was brought to fireplaces where people often ate together. When the food had been cooked over the fire, it then had to be redistributed. Everyone had previously eaten what they had found themselves, and without paying particular attention to those around them. Critical issues now had to be resolved: How should the food be distributed? Who would get how much?

Humans began to engage with their fellow humans and question their frames of mind, health, needs and feelings. This allowed them to consider what the weak, ill, old and needy required for survival when it came to redistributing food.

Statistical analyses of human mitochondrial DNA have shown that we possess very low genetic diversity, and perhaps even the lowest genetic diversity of any mammal. This leads to the assumption that there could have been a genetic bottleneck in human evolution around 70,000 to 80,000 years ago. There were only about 1,000 to 10,000 individual Homo sapiens alive after this bottleneck, and it's from these few individuals that the world's entire present population is descended.

The events of the bottleneck that so decimated the human population also presented a further selection process. Ultimately, the only humans who could survive were those who could feel human emotions and so increase their tribe's chances of survival.

But what does this have to do with a dog's emotions? A great deal. Dogs never underwent this development. They probably also never experienced the events that affected the selection process in humans, of if they did, they experienced them in an entirely different way. In addition, a dog's ancestors most likely spent this development period in Asia, whereas humans only populated Africa. Our two species' varying living areas alone had an unavoidable, differentiating effect on the influential factors that shaped us both.

A dog still today doesn't share his food with anyone apart from his offspring. He may leave something behind when he's full or tolerate others eating at the same time, but only if resources permit. He similarly doesn't grill his meat over fire like a human. His brain also hasn't grown, and has even decreased in size as he's developed. He never needed to develop feelings during the course of his evolution, whereas for us humans, doing so may once have secured our survival.

It was more important for early humans to be recognized by their communities and stand out from the crowd than it was to be at the very front of the line when food was distributed. Being recognized by everyone was now an advantage that was essential for survival. Recognition couldn't be forced, and only those people who had stood up for the community earned recognition from the other community members. Individuals therefore had to be able to identify other people's needs. This is how human emotions such as honor, loyalty and pride developed, as well as the need for individualism and appreciation of one's own person.

There was an evolutionary advantage if emotions such as compassion, shame, jealousy, grief, pride or love existed within a community structure. Over the course of millennia, those tribes that were able to feel these emotions prevailed over other tribes that had not developed such feelings. These emotions presented an advantage in the fight for the species' continued existence.

As evolution progressed, new needs developed that went beyond what was necessary for existence and provided less of a selective advantage in the fight for survival. These new needs instead gave us an advantage in our dealings with other social partners. Some emotions also remained from earlier times, however, and these emotions can threaten our existence today. As examples, only we humans know feelings of hate or revenge.

Emotions

Our present emotional world is inextricably linked to our needs and is unparalleled in its current form. It's therefore important to know which needs we've developed during the course of our evolution and how these needs differ from those of our dogs. If we're to understand the differences between human and canine needs, we need to know how these needs arise in the first instance.

In 1943, the psychologist Abraham Maslow published the model of a 'hierarchy of needs' in pyramid form.
Human needs form the levels of the model's pyramid, and levels of need are built on top of one another. According to Maslow, humans first strive to satisfy the needs in the pyramid's bottom level before the needs in the next level can take shape. A need from a higher level can in principle never develop for as long as a need from a lower level remains unfulfilled.

Maslow's model of a 'hierarchy of needs'

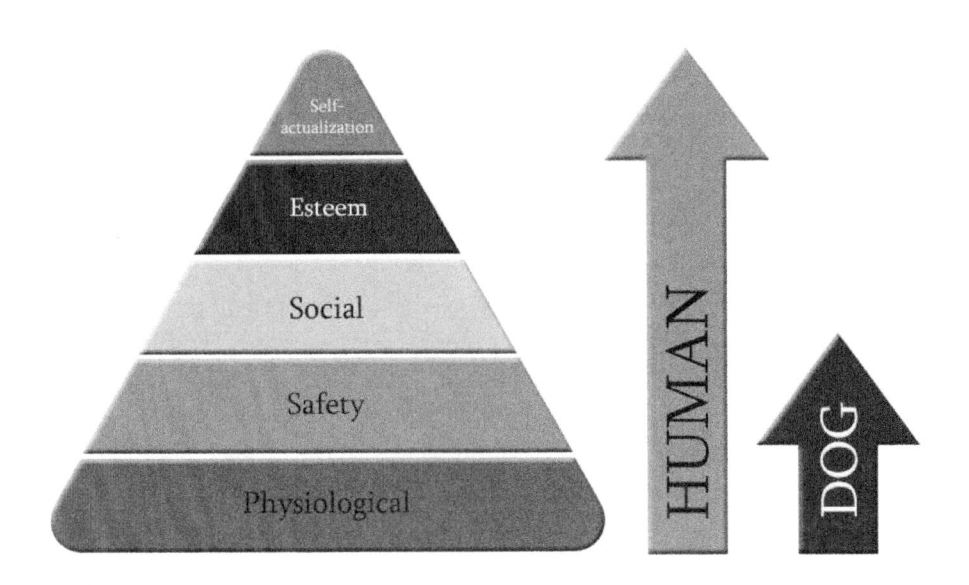

Emotions

Maslow's hierarchy of human needs:

1.) **Physiological:** Metabolism, Regeneration, Reproduction;

2.) **Safety:** Law and order, Protection from dangers;

3.) **Social:** Family, Friends, Partnership, Love, Intimacy, Communication;

4.) **Esteem:** Increased appreciation due to status, Respect, Recognition (awards, praise), Prosperity, Influence, Private and professional successes, Mental and physical strength;

5.) **Self-actualization:** Individuality; Talent development; Perfection; Enlightenment; Self-improvement.

Humans could only develop their present diversity of social needs once they could secure their physiological and safety needs on a permanent basis.

If our ancestors had our current emotions while they still had natural enemies and competed with others for food, these emotions would have endangered their existence and rendered the continuation of the species impossible. Our ancestors couldn't afford to have feelings of compassion, pride, consideration, shame or guilt during their fight for survival.

The same applies to our dogs today. Human emotions would be comparable to a death sentence in terms of a dog's survival. In the wild, it's survival of the fittest. Whoever foregoes food out of concern for others is in danger of starving themselves.

A dog lives in the present. He can't think ahead or make plans like a human, and he therefore doesn't know if and when he'll find food again. If a dog or a wolf allows a prey animal to escape out of pity, this behavior doesn't just endanger his own life, but also that of his community. If a group member dies, the other pack members won't feel grief in a human sense. A group member's death can even be an advantage for individual animals in the fight for survival: The available resources now have to be shared among fewer competitors.

Emotions

If a mother wolf could feel pity, she wouldn't be able to kill ill or weak cubs as soon as they were born. This concept might be painful for us, but it makes complete sense from a biological perspective. Ill or weak offspring consume food resources at the expense of the stronger cubs. As you already know, a wolf cub's chances of survival in the wild are about 50%. If the mother wolf is to increase the chances of survival for the litter's strongest members, she can't allow weak or ill cubs to live out of pity. Human emotions would hamper this natural selection process, which in turn would endanger the continuation of the species.

Wolves, like dogs, similarly can't afford to feel emotions such as sympathy, antipathy or love when it comes to choosing a mate. In the wild, the animals that mate decide on the continuation of the species. Only those animals that assert themselves against others are allowed to mate. This natural strategy ensures that only a species' most successful animals are able to pass on their genes to the species' offspring. Human emotions such as antipathy would hamper this type of selection or even render it impossible.

As such, before we impose human emotions on our dogs, we first need to question whether these emotions exist in dogs in the same form. The greatest danger in anthropomorphizing our dogs is allowing wishful thinking or our own subjective feelings to give them human emotions that they don't know and can't reciprocate. We subsequently interpret their behavior patterns entirely incorrectly and treat them in a different way from if we judged their actions in a correct and objective manner that was based on their natures. Our dogs respond in turn with undesirable behavior. And so begins a vicious cycle in which the ultimate victim is always the dog.

Use your intelligence to understand your dog.
Don't expect your dog to understand your world.

Humans and dogs have developed entirely separately from one another for the last 90 million years. It'd therefore be presumptuous for us to want to know how these completely different creatures experience feelings. We'll never be able to empathize with how a dog experiences his feelings; all we can do is guess.

Dogs certainly have feelings on a social level and can build up relationships with one another. But it's rather unlikely that these feelings can be compared with what we call 'friendship'. How feelings of friendship are subjectively perceived already differs from human to human, so it can't be assumed that a completely different type of creature will experience any feeling in exactly the same way as us. His feelings may be more comparable to the human experience of euphoria. We'll never know for sure. There are certainly also animals with feelings that are completely unknown to us and with which we can't empathize.

If a member of a dog pack dies, the feeling that a remaining dog experiences in response will fundamentally differ from the subjective perception of human grief. A dog's relationship with its pack leader similarly can't be compared with employee-supervisor feelings in a workplace. We'll also probably never know whether two dogs can feel affection for one another in a manner that approaches human feelings of love.

Only a dog can know how a dog experiences feelings. A pain, for example, may sting, burn, throb or tickle. How he perceives this feeling will remain his secret. We'll never even be able to assess whether he experiences a feeling as positive or negative. We should therefore avoid projecting our emotions onto a dog, and we also shouldn't expect him to be able to understand or reciprocate human feelings. It's otherwise impossible to treat a dog in accordance with his nature.

If Maslow's needs pyramid model were to be applied to a dog, its levels would have to be reduced to physiological needs, safety needs and, in part, social needs. A dog doesn't have any need for self-actualization. He also doesn't have any need for esteem, as he doesn't have any self-awareness; he doesn't know that he exists.

He doesn't care about the color of his fur. He doesn't need to have the most expensive leash or visit the trendiest dog hairdresser so as to gain recognition from others. A dog's happiness is similarly less dependent on Christmas gifts or a bouquet of flowers. In contrast, these things are important for us humans. We need recognition and praise from our social surroundings and we require colored hair, eccentric clothing, tattoos, expensive cars or personalized trips to stand out from the masses and develop our own identities. We take recognition and appreciation as meaning security for our social status. Appreciation contributes directly to our happiness because we've developed a need for it over the course of our evolution. Our dog doesn't know or need any such thing. None of his pack members come up to his sleeping place after he's finished work and pat him on the back for his excellent performance. A dog can't feel pride because he's never developed a need for it. He won't understand such behavior and so won't be able to reciprocate the feeling. It has no influence on his happiness. He's more likely to react with uncertainty if anything, as he won't know what's just taken place.

The needs that a dog develops on the social level aren't comparable with human social needs. The primary reasons for predators coming together in a pack are hunting and rearing offspring. A pack is therefore comparable with a partnership of convenience. Other needs only appear on the social level when the more important needs have been satisfied and the animals are aware of this satisfaction.

In consequence, a dog won't establish friendly relationships with other dogs if there isn't enough food. He also won't want to play if he's busy monitoring or guarding his territory, hunting prey, or can see a threat to his safety. New needs will only arise when his physiological needs have been secured on a long-term basis.

Needs play an important role in motivational psychology. Only when you recognize other people's needs can you positively interact with them or motivate them to carry out actions via the prospect of need satisfaction.

We gladly and often show behavior that results in a positive experience, but we avoid behavior patterns that lead to unpleasant consequences. Our dogs behave in exactly the same way. If we want to motivate them into showing certain behaviors, we need to know what gives them pleasure. If we want to motivate them to do something, they have to be given the prospect of having one of their needs satisfied. A dog doesn't do anything for you: He does what he does to satisfy his needs.

If our dogs are going to happily subordinate themselves to us, it's important that we know their needs and can also satisfy them.

If you want to give your dog rules from which he can take direction on a permanent basis, these rules have to make sense from his perspective and also contribute to the fulfillment of his needs.

If you expect your dog to walk on a leash, for instance, you should be able to ensure his safety. He needs safety, so before you can expect him to remain beside you during critical situations, you need to be in a position to satisfy this need for him.

If you require him to guard your property, you should realize that he'll then decide who can and can't enter the property.

Your dog will take direction from you in future because only you will satisfy all of his needs. You'll become the team leader in your relationship with him. You'll learn to control resources, provide him with security and build up a trusting and intense bond with him. He'll subsequently place more trust in you and learn to hand over responsibility to you. He'll also only take on tasks that you consciously assign to him. This will help both of you to avoid stress and uncertainty going forward.

You'll be in a position to change already-established problem behaviors and prevent the development of new problem behaviors. You'll take away a large portion of your dog's obligations and so give him the freedom needed to have more fun in his life.

Almost all of the problems that we experience with our dogs in everyday life result from natural behavior patterns that they demonstrate to protect their resources. It's therefore important for them to learn that we're responsible for all resources. Only then will a dog submit to us and stop showing problem behaviors.

Most dog owners see their dogs as loyal partners, friends and companions. But a dog will never be able to fill these roles. You can't build up a friendly relationship with your dog.

A friendly relationship between two social partners can only be formed on the same hierarchy level. Neither partner then owes the other anything or is dependent on him. All relationships in a dog's life will see one partner take the lead and bear the responsibility. If you don't do this, your dog will instinctively take on the leadership role himself. If he does so, he'll have greater freedom for making decisions than you. In the worst-case scenario, he'll decide who can claim which resources. You should therefore decide who will take over the leadership role in your relationship: Will it be you or your dog? Don't look at your dog as a friend, but rather as a ward for which you bear responsibility.

If you're going to be recognized as a leader by your dog, you need to learn how to develop a leading personality. You have more experience and authority than him when it comes to dealing with the problems of civilized everyday life. This is exactly what you need to impart to him. Act in a calm and determined manner, don't demonstrate any uncertainty or fear, and always be sure of your actions. You'll automatically be self-confident when you deal with him if you know what you have to do and understand why you're doing these things.

8.2 Building up a relationship

It's less important for you to learn exactly what to do in every moment than it is for you to understand what's going on in your dog's head. If you know what he's feeling at a given point, you'll automatically respond in the correct manner. Only then will you be more confident and determined in your dealings with your dog and stop doubting in you own decisions. You'll also be predictable for your dog and a help to him in everyday life. He'll look to be close to you, and a bond will be established between the two of you that's unlike anything else in the world.

Your dog can't trust you if you're unsure of yourself. If you behave indecisively or show a lack on consistency, he'll see you as unpredictable and will continue to live in accordance with his own rules because you can't provide him with reliable direction.

Your bond with your dog is what connects you together. If you want to strengthen this connection, you need to know how relationships arise and how you can influence them.

A relationship between two social partners arises through interaction. The more often these interactions occur, the more intense the relationship will be. We establish more intense relationships with people with whom we have frequent contact than with other people whom we only meet on a sporadic basis. A relationship can take on a positive or negative form depending on the type of interactions that occur. A relationship that lives from punishment, pain or coercion is more likely to be perceived negatively, and the two social partners will probably separate. In contrast, if both partners in a relationship are able to recognize and satisfy the other partner's needs, a strong bond will develop that's marked in a very positive manner. Both partners will enjoy the closeness of the other partner, and the desire to maintain the relationship will grow.

Emotions

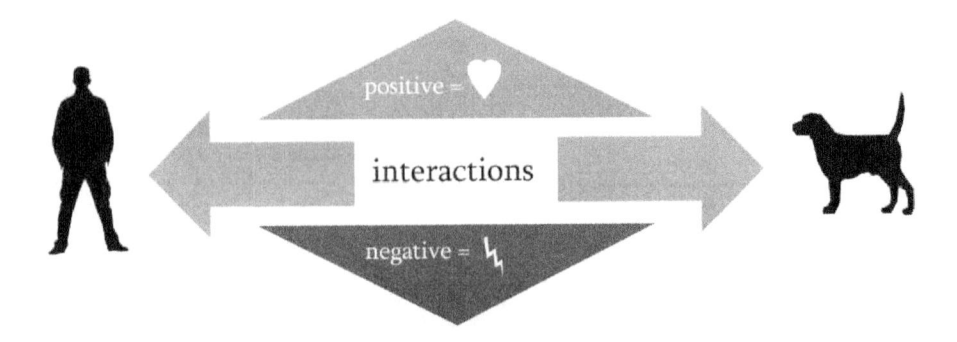

As a result of dogs' evolutionary development, they're only able to meet one another's needs to a very limited extent. In the wild, undesirable behavior is corrected through punishment, i.e. through negative interaction. Desirable behavior is also not rewarded, as a dog doesn't possess the necessary resources for this form of positive interaction.

Examples of positive interaction between dogs include lying next to each other, playing, grooming and licking. A dog can equally provide another dog with security to a limited extent by protecting him from danger, and thereby satisfying one of his survival-critical needs.

We humans are able to build up unique relationships with our dogs. We can do this because we're able to interact with them in a way that won't ever be possible for other dogs. We're at the top of the food chain, so as well as controlling all of the resources that are important for our own survival, we also those resources that are important for their survival. We don't have to worry about food, at least not in industrialized nations. We decide how often, how much and what we want to eat, and we can similarly satisfy our dogs' needs for food at any time. This isn't possible for other dogs.

We don't have to punish our dogs for undesirable behavior or cause them pain. We can praise them for desirable behavior instead. This is something else that other dogs can't ever manage. It's also why food plays such an enormously important role in building up relationships with our dogs.

Humans can even awaken and satisfy needs in a dog that the dog wasn't previously aware existed.

A dog has no need for human touches or strokes in the wild. Dogs don't stroke one another and they also don't need such strokes. Unlike humans, they haven't developed a need for this form of touch. Our need arises within us as infants in the womb, and it's a legacy of our primate existence that we stroke everything that's dear to us with our hands and use caresses to show our affection to one another. An unborn child in the womb already perceives these touches and connects its first impressions and emotions with these strokes. Dogs develop in an entirely different fashion and aren't familiar with being stroked by other predators. They only learn the meaning of our touches over the course of their lives.

When a dog learns that our touches mean something positive, namely that we have amicable intentions toward him, he'll quickly acquire a liking for our strokes. Dogs don't have this need in the wild, so it's only though our positive interaction that this need can arise within them.

We can also recognize and evaluate dangers that another dog doesn't know to assess and will never learn to assess. This provides us with another opportunity for positive interaction.

Our ability to think logically and with foresight allows us to evaluate dangers and assess risks like no other creature on this Earth. We can let our dogs benefit from this privilege by showing them that we're able to recognize dangers and offer protection against them. No dog can provide this kind of security. Even the most powerful leading wolf can't offer protection from the dangers of our civilized world, whether traffic, elevators, subways, construction sites or shopping malls. All wolves, regardless of how strong, are helpless against dangers of this sort.

We can therefore meet more of our dogs' needs than other dogs. We can also strengthen our relationships with them by means of predominantly positive interaction. Such relationships will have a much higher value for our dogs than any relationships with other dogs.

Most dog owners unfortunately don't take advantage of the opportunity to build up positive relationships of this type. If a dog barks while on the leash,

Emotions

controls his territory, yaps at every visitor, constantly runs behind his humans at home, pulls on the leash or monitors or marks his turf, these are all signs that the human-dog relationship still has considerable development potential. If the dog's everyday life is also regulated through commands, vocalizations, punishment or coercion, it's no wonder that he runs away from his humans when he's on the leash or even escapes over the garden fence.

We humans can use the unique position in nature that evolution has afforded us to foster relationships that could never exist among dogs. We just have to make sure that this occurs.

I'd like to use an experience that I had with two dogs to show you how our four-legged friends assess relationships with humans. The two dogs concerned chose one another and so constitute my personal reference-point for a canine relationship.

Olanda, a mongrel bitch from an animal shelter, was born into a foster family in Germany and left for her new home at eight-weeks old. She came back to the foster family a year later while her human parents went abroad for a few days. The foster family had a new litter of puppies when she returned.

She went home with her owners when they came back from their vacation. They noticed that something was wrong with her on the same day that they picked her up. She was extremely downcast, wouldn't eat, whined incessantly, and lay down in her place frustrated and without motivation. Her parents called the foster family to find out why she was so depressed. They then found out that while she was with the foster family, she'd adopted a puppy from the new litter just after the puppy had first opened its eyes. Without further ado, Olanda's parents drove back to the foster family and adopted the little puppy. Olanda was soon happy once more, and meaning seemed to have been restored to her life. The puppy, called Molly, had subsequently grown up and the two dogs remained inseparable.

I had the good fortune to host both of the dogs for three weeks, and it was beautiful to see the precious nature of their relationship.

I spent the first few days working one-on-one with each dog, building up individual relationships that were defined by positive interaction. After a week, we chanced upon an astounding observation.

My wife and I were both sitting on chairs about three meters to the left and right of where the dogs were lying. We were absorbed in our work, so neither of us was paying attention to the dogs. After a few minutes, Olanda came up to me and lay down under my chair. A short while later, Molly ran over to my wife and lay at her feet. That evening, when I was sitting alone on the couch, Molly came over and crawled onto my lap. We saw the same behavior outside: After a while, each dog independently decided to leave the partner that they'd known for more than a year and instead be close to us. We don't talk with our dogs or use commands to make them demonstrate certain behaviors, so they were evidently making these decisions by themselves. They opted to be close to us instead of close to their partner. They chose closeness to us of their own accord, and after just a week!

As this example shows, it's not about the number of relationships, but rather about their quality. Everyone's felt this. When you walk through the city, you only interact with the smallest fraction of the people you meet. You could interact with more of them, but you don't do so: You don't care about most of them. You're only attracted to and enjoy the company of those people with whom you have a positive relationship. The same applies for dogs. Not every social contact is of a high quality and enriches your dog's life. In general, dogs can only meet one another's needs to a limited extent. A relationship with a social partner who can satisfy more of these needs is considerably more valuable. You can therefore assume that a dog attaches only minor importance to relationships with dogs that are unfamiliar or don't live within the same household. These dogs are first and foremost rivals.

You can become the social partner in your dog's life who satisfies more of his needs than anyone else and is so of more value to him than any other dog.

We humans like to think that it's somewhat strange to build up a more positive relationship with a creature of another species than to another human being. I wouldn't leave my wife to snuggle up to an unfamiliar predator, for instance.

But this is exactly what dogs do every evening across thousands of living rooms. It's incredible, right?

It's completely normal that we can't imagine this, as no other species controls our vital resources. In consequence, only a human can satisfy another human's needs. But you can become the key partner for your dog: You just have to make this happen.

In one study, it was proven that dogs value closeness to humans more positively than closeness to other dogs.[4] The study looked at eight adult mongrels, assessing how they reacted to changes in their surroundings and what role their respective social partners played in these situations. The group of dogs was made up of littermate pairs that lived together in kennels after turning eight-weeks old. They lived constantly in their pairs and were also accustomed to normal dealings with humans. If one pair member was subsequently placed in an unfamiliar kennel, his stress level increased by more than 50%. The increase was detected by measuring the dog's cortisol level. The measurements increased to the same extent when a pair entered unfamiliar surroundings together. In contrast, when the dogs' human caregiver remained with them, their cortisol levels only increased to a negligible extent. The dogs considered closeness to humans to be significantly more reassuring than closeness to another related dog.

If you want to influence your relationship with your dog, you need to know about positive and negative influencing factors.

What are positive interactions?

You can interact in a positive manner whenever you satisfy one of your dog's needs. In contrast, he'll perceive your actions in a negative manner if you deny him need satisfaction or work against one of his needs.

---

[4] D. Tuber, S. Sanders, M. Hennessy, J. Miller: *Behavioral and glucocorticoid responses of adult domestic dogs (Canis familiaris) to companionship and social separation*, Journal of Comparative Psychology, Vol 110 (1), Mar. 1996.

Food

If you give your dog food and he takes it from you, you can be sure that you've just interacted in a positive manner. It's therefore important that you become part of how your dog experiences food. No interaction will take place if you just fill his bowl in the kitchen and then walk away. The dog will satisfy his need himself without establishing a positive link to you, and you'll have just thrown away a whole bowlful of interaction opportunities. It's better to satisfy your dog's need for food by using it throughout the entire day.

If you feed your dog out of your hand, he'll associate your smell and your presence with food. This means that you can interact with him in various ways across the most diverse of situations, and you'll always be at the center of these interactions. Give him food over the whole course of the day instead of merely in two moments in the mornings and evenings. Let happiness rain down time and time again. You can do something that no other dog can manage. Take every opportunity to show your dog all the good that you can do for him.

Meeting expectations

If you arouse an expectation in your dog, you can positively interact with him by meeting this expectation. If you place food in your hand and allow him to sniff it, for instance, his need for food may increase. If you now satisfy this need, you'll have interacted in a positive manner.

If you call your dog after you've successfully conditioned a recall (see Page 146, "Learning through conditioning"), he'll return to you with the expectation of receiving a reward. If you then provide him with a reward, you'll meet his expectation and so positively interact with him.

You can also interact positively by rewarding demanding behavior such as begging, although there are problems associated with giving rewards in these situations (see Page 213, "Begging").

Rest

Another need that every dog has is the need for rest. Use your dog's rest periods and become the center of this need satisfaction on a more regular basis.

Emotions

Rest together with your dog, as doing so will help you to develop a trusting relationship and a bond. Lying against one another is a sign of togetherness among dogs, so your dog should have the option of lying next to you if he wants to be close to you. You can safely share the couch or your bed with him if he likes doing this and you permit it.

Security

Give your dog security if he needs it. This is one of your dog's physiological needs, and you need to satisfy it if he's to later hand over responsibility to you. Throughout this book you'll learn when and how to provide your dog with protection in a manner that he understands.

Touch

Touch can also satisfy a dog's need, but we should be aware that it isn't normal for a dog to be touched. The sense of touch has a different meaning for us humans than it does for dogs, and the same applies to received touches. Humans descend from fruit-eaters who used their hands to work, just like many types of primate still do today. A primate's hands pick fruit from trees, pull their bodies along branches or produce primitive tools. They're also used to maintain relationships with other social partners, both for grooming and exchanging hostilities.

We humans use touches to show our connections to other humans. We perhaps use touches in this manner more than any other creature that's alive today. We also want to express our connections to our dogs via touch. Dogs, in contrast, have no need for touch.

A dog has never used his paws to interact with other social partners. Paws primarily act as feet and are used almost exclusively for movement. His sense of touch also provides him with information about the nature of what he's walking on. Paw-contact among dogs doesn't have the same meaning as hand-contact among humans. Unlike a chimpanzee, for example, a dog can't use his paws to grab, climb or groom.

A dog doesn't know what touches mean, while we consider touches to be expressions of our attachment to other humans. We think in this way because it's how we've thought throughout our evolutionary development. We use touches to show affection for one another and strengthen our relationships with one another. We can similarly determine our partners' emotional states via touches. Children who grow up with minimal exposure to human touch often have very poor or even non-existent attachment to their parents. When these children reach adulthood, they display a fear of touch and frequently have impaired social lives.

Dogs show their affection for other social partners in completely different ways, e.g. by lying next to one another and licking. Mutual grooming is another important method for signaling affection.

When we touch our dog, he first has to learn what our behavior means. If he doesn't establish this meaning, he'll react in a rather shy, indifferent, uncertain or fearful manner. Touching a dog in an already-stressful situation can even increase his stress and uncertainty (see Page 238, "Touch and overcoming fear").

Your dog interprets your behavior from his own perspective: He sees a huge predator reaching out at him with its paw. No animal would be excited at this prospect in the wild, but our dogs normally tolerate our handling as a result of their reduced flight tendencies. When your dog tolerates your touches, he also learns what effect these touches have on you.

We're normally relaxed when we touch our dogs or stroke their fur. This teaches them that we're in a friendly mood when we touch them. They'll then seek out this situation again in the future, as it provides them with a clearly recognizable sign of our state of mind. If you're stressed or in a bad mood when you touch your dog, he'll become stressed during future touches or may avoid subsequent touches altogether. Your dog will only relax and be able to enjoy your touches once he's learned that they have a positive meaning for him.

What are negative interactions?

Punishments, restrictions and sanctions
Dogs perceive punishments, restrictions and sanctions in a negative manner. These actions always work against a dog's needs. Negative interaction leads to frustration and can also encourage stress and avoidance behavior.

In addition to obvious negative interactions such as physical violence and coercion, there are also interactions that only appear negative on closer inspection.

Commands
I believe that work with commands constitutes a form of interaction that's more negative than positive. A command arouses an expectation of a reward within a dog. The dog then shows us the behavior that we expect so as meet the requirements for this reward. It's therefore his expectation of a reward that makes him so eager to work with us. If the reward is no longer given, the dog has a negative experience. We aren't meeting his expectation, and this leads him to become frustrated. If he isn't rewarded for an extended period, he'll at some point stop seeing sense in showing the behavior that we've encouraged.

We act against our dog's needs when we give commands that aren't rewarded. If he's supposed to walk by our side and we give him the 'heel' command, for instance, he may do what we demand. But what's going on in his head at this point?

Your dog probably isn't by your side when you give this command. If he were, you wouldn't have needed to give the command at all. He's not by your side because he has a need to do whatever else he's doing in that present moment. You're now requiring him to stop what he wants to do and walk alongside you instead. If he'd wanted to walk alongside you, he would have done so in the first instance. You're therefore preventing him from satisfying one of his needs and also demanding him to act against his will. Even if your dog does come back to you when you call him, you can't assume that he's doing this for your sake. It may be advantageous for him to follow your request even though he knows that there won't be a reward: Doing so will allow him to avoid a sanction.

You should similarly question why it's necessary to command your dog to come over to you when you're on the couch in the evenings. If he isn't looking for closeness to you by himself, you need to work on your relationship with him. Respect his need if he feels more comfortable somewhere else in that moment. If your dog wants to be next to you of his own accord, you won't need to call him. Present him with an offer to let him know when he's allowed to lie on the couch. If he doesn't take up your offer, he's content in his current position. You can present him with the offer by working with discriminatory stimuli (see Page 149, "Discriminatory stimuli").

Touch
Not every dog perceives touch in a positive manner. How he reacts is dependent on what he associates with touch. If we try to use stroking to reassure a fearful dog that's never previously been touched by a human, he'll connect our stroking with his current emotional state. If we then stroke him again whenever he's afraid in future, he won't come to perceive our touches in a positive manner. When we reach out to touch him while he's resting and unafraid, he may evade our approaches.

Even if your dog generally enjoys being stroked, he'll differentiate between touches and strokes that he receives when he's resting and those that he receives when he's outside and occupied with other matters. If he's following a trail or is busy monitoring his territory, for example, he may consider your strokes as an inconvenience. Later on, when there's nothing more important to do, he'll enjoy being stroked once more.

8.3 How do I establish trust?

A positive relationship is the foundation for strong mutual trust between you and your dog. But what is trust?
Trust is the conviction to assess a situation and foresee its consequences.
You should separate your bond and your trust in your relationship with your dog. They're simultaneously independent and interdependent. You can't build up a bond if your dog doesn't trust you. On the other hand, you always need to consider the specific situations in which you expect your dog's trust.

As an example, I have a strong bond with my wife, but I wouldn't place my trust in her during an altercation with another man. Then again, I would trust that she could independently assert herself against children.

A bond is first and foremost a positive relationship to another social partner. When it comes to trust, however, each partner may make a different evaluation based on the situation at hand.

If you want your dog to trust you, your actions don't just have to make sense to him or provide him with clues as to what's going to happen next. Instead, you have to be predictable for him. You need to always behave in the same way when you deal with him: Think and act in accordance with routines and make him feel as if you know exactly what you're doing in every situation.

Trust toward humans
If your dog is to trust in you as a human, he first needs to know that you don't pose him any threat. He should associate you with peaceful situations. It's only when he's completely relaxed with you that he'll feel safe and associate closeness to you with an inner sense of security. Give him the opportunity to relax both at home and outside. Avoid speech, commands, tug or prey games, and contact with unfamiliar dogs. Avoid situations in which your dog becomes aggressive, fearful or stressed.

Create moments of calm and ensure that your dog has the rest periods that he requires. Take the time to rest together with him more frequently, and do the same outside of your home as well. Body contact is extremely important here.

Resting together strengthens your bond and promotes your sense of togetherness.

Trust on an everyday basis
You should also use your everyday life with your dog to show him that you're able to handle any situation.

You may have to pick your dog up, for instance, providing that you're physically able to do so. If you hold him securely, he'll learn that he's safe in your arms and so won't mind being picked up. If he's tense and stiff, however, you should again show him that he's safe when you lift him. Always carry your dog with the same hold if possible, and always approach him in the same way. He'll then know what you plan to do and will make the process easier for you in future. He'll recognize from your body language that you're offering him help and will be glad to take you up on your offer.

When you provide your dog with assistance, you should also ensure that what you're doing is actually helping him. Dog owners' intentions are often good, but the end results aren't always ideal for their dogs.

If you do carry your dog, move quietly and take your time when placing him down. This is when he'll feel most uncertain. Place him down in slow motion to begin with so he can learn that you're always in control of the situation. He has to really feel how the ground approaches. If you repeat this exercise regularly, he'll know in future that he's safe in your arms.

Act in a quiet and confident manner if you help him down from a wall, over a barrier, or to get in and out of your car. Avoid talking to him constantly in a soothing voice; you want to help him, not hypnotize him. Only quiet has a genuinely calming effect. You should really avoid talking to your dog in stressful situations in general. Dogs don't calm one another with vocalizations, but rather with confident actions. A confident, calm demeanor will give your dog more direction than speech.

Your dog similarly expects confident guidance when you roam with him across rough terrain, pass through crowds of people, or make your way around

Emotions

marketplaces. You're responsible for your dog, so you should keep dangers away from him and provide him with assistance in difficult situations.

Your dog shouldn't ever find himself in danger while you're nearby. Closeness to you equates to safety for him. Only when he knows this will he entrust you with responsibility for his security. If you leave him alone with his problems or act in an unconfident manner, he'll ultimately prefer to make his own decisions as to what's best. In cases of doubt, he'll also choose to defend himself against threats.

8.4 Bonding through food

Food provides one of the most important interaction opportunities for building up a positive relationship with your dog. There's no question that a dog has a need for food, so you can guarantee the establishment of a strong bond by dealing with food in the correct manner.

It doesn't matter whether you're at home or out on a walk: Feed your dog out of your hand whenever possible. You should offer him the food from close up to your body, as this will teach him to associate you with positive feelings. If he accepts your offer, he'll want to take the food. If he doesn't accept, the food won't have any rewarding effect. When he comes close to you and takes the food, he'll associate your smell with the food experience and so often seek out closeness to you in future.

Your dog should always attach great importance to food. If he has it in abundance, there won't be any reason for him to do anything for it. If your dog is full, he won't consider food as a reward.

If your dog doesn't value food, you lose the opportunity of using it for positive interaction. You should therefore control this resource. Put food down in a deliberate manner that strengthens both your own position and the value of food as a reward.

Your dog won't be given any treats or extra portions. He'll get his everyday food, provided it can be fed by hand.

The only difference that a dog will often perceive between treats and his everyday food is smell. If given the choice, he'll favor food that smells more intense or rich. There's barely a difference for him in terms of taste. Dogs have only around one-fifth as many taste buds as humans, so their ability to taste is much worse than ours. This makes it quite acceptable to use their everyday food as a reward.

In the future, you should decide when, how much and even whether to give your dog food. He'll then learn that you're the only one in charge of this resource, and he'll therefore take direction from you more readily. Your dog should only receive food from you. He'll then be dependent on you to satisfy his need and so will seek out closeness to you more often.

9 Taking responsibility

Starvation is the greatest enemy in a dog's life, so dogs value food above all else. A dog finds the food that secures his survival in his territory. If he's to safeguard this food for himself and his pack, he needs to claim the largest possible territory and, in the case of emergency, also defend this territory from rivals.
Most dogs spend all day monitoring their territories so as to know what's happening within them.
Monitoring a territory is stressful for a dog. He can never let his guard down, and it's up to him to react if anything occurs that could threaten either him or the territory. He has to constantly make decisions and work out problem-solving strategies from the information that he collects.

Taking responsibility

A research team led by the biologist Laurence Gesquiere conducted a study into the stress burdens suffered by leading animals. The study[5] examined fecal samples from 125 adult male baboons over a period of nine years, measuring the concentrations of the stress hormone glucocorticoid and the sex hormone testosterone. The monkeys lived in the Amboseli National Park in Kenya and were divided into five groups. The researchers ultimately found that the samples that were taken from alpha males contained significantly more stress hormone than was present in those samples that were taken from lower-ranking animals.

It's likely that this phenomenon occurs within all hierarchical social structures, with stress burdens increasing in accordance with rank position. In humans, more work and more responsibility automatically equate to more stress. In dogs, it's not rank itself that causes stress, as a dog has no understanding of ranks. What prevents your dog from relaxing is rather his sense of responsibility.

If you want to take away your dog's leadership responsibility and the stress associated with this, you need to reduce his scope for making decisions. You're far more capable than him of managing the relevant tasks, so be sure to follow through with your intentions. Taking over responsibility means exactly what it implies: You need to take over the tasks for which your dog previously felt responsible.

When you take over responsibility, your dog will have more free time and less work. He'll then be able to have fun on a far more regular basis and will actually be able to play. He'll also be able to relax more often and more intensely and will similarly refrain from undesirable behavior.

The more manageable a dog's territory, the easier it is for him to monitor this territory and the lower the stress that the territory will cause him. You can use body language to let your dog know which areas of responsibility you claim inside and outside of your home. He'll hand over responsibility for these areas once he's learned that they belong to you.

---

[5] L. R. Gesquiere: *Life at the top rank and stress in wild male baboons*, Sience, Vol. 333, July 15, 2011

'Social stress can be reduced by the regular practicing of routine acts – including setting limits – and therefore establishing clarity. Responsible lead animals have demonstrably higher stress levels than lower-ranking animals if they take all of their duties seriously, e.g. recognizing and defending against threats. Young animals can live a largely carefree existence under the supervision of their elders, even though they occasionally have to be proverbially knocked back into line. Whoever has a framework for what they can and can't do also suffers from less stress.'
(Günther Bloch, Elli H. Radinger, 'Understanding Wolves, For Dog Owners', Page 41, 2010)

9.1 At home

If you want to take away your dog's obligations within his inner territory (your home), you need to reduce his scope for making decisions to an absolute minimum for the length of the exercise. If he previously made all of the decisions, he now needs to learn that he no longer has to make any decisions. You'll take away your dog's scope for making decisions and claim this responsibility for yourself. The only decisions that he'll be allowed to make are those that concern his bed area. The rest of the house will be your responsibility from now onward.

Choose a bed area for your dog that's surrounded on at least two sides, e.g. in the corner of a room. In this location, your dog should be exposed to as few of the other happenings that go on within your home as possible. You'll ideally choose a place where he's never had a fixed bed area in the past.

His bed area should be appropriate to his size and can be a large dog blanket, a basket, or a special dog bed. It should be clearly separated from the floor so that he knows where his area ends. A normal blanket isn't sufficient for this purpose.

It's now your job to make this bed area a paradise for your dog. He shouldn't prefer to spend time anywhere else.
The area needs to be appropriately equipped and neither too soft nor too warm. In the future, you'll satisfy all of your dog's needs apart from those that

Taking responsibility

concern his bed area. He shouldn't have access to toys, as everything positive – including play – needs to come from you and occur with you. You'll now decide when, where and for how long he plays.

Your dog shouldn't have any property of his own (stuffed toys, bones, tug ropes etc.) until he's recognized your rules.

It's important that he always has access to water in his bed area. When he's recognized the boundaries of his area, he won't think to run to the kitchen to drink. It's therefore important that he has access to water in his bed area right from the start.

He shouldn't wear a collar in his bed area unless it's required for exercises that are currently taking place within the home. He shouldn't experience any punishments, sanctions, bans or commands in his bed area. He should view this place in solely positive terms, so you need to refrain from any kind of negative interaction here. Limiting his free space already constitutes a form of negative interaction, but he'll only consider your action in this manner if he's outside his area. As soon as he's back within his part of the territory, the negative interaction ends and positive interaction follows.

Your dog needs to see his bed area as an absolutely safe place. He mustn't be exposed to danger here under any circumstances, whether from children, other pets, falling objects, visitors or other dogs. Keep all danger away from him and this area. He'll then see the area as secure in future and will retreat here if he's uncertain or afraid.

The area should be located where your dog can be separated to the greatest possible extent from hustle and bustle within your house. Storage or office rooms are particularly suitable, as you won't enter these rooms on such a frequent basis. Also position his bed area where he's never laid down before.

In familiar areas, your dog will have already learned to recognize routines that allow him to anticipate what will happen next. As an example, when he sees you put on your shoes, he knows that he'll soon be going outside. He'll normally react before you've even finished getting ready. He recognizes this and many other routines from his current bed area, as it's from this current bed

Taking responsibility

area that he learned the routines in the first instance. If his new bed area prevents him from immediately recognizing the same signs, he'll have to learn these signs anew. He'll find it difficult to learn new rules if he remains in a familiar area for the exercise, as he'll then first have to forget the routines that he knows.

Let your dog know what belongs to him and what belongs to you by showing him who controls which parts of the territory. The only decision that you have to make here is where your dog is allowed to stay. If he's no longer allowed to enter your area, he won't be able to monitor, defend or even mark this space. This simple exercise allows you to take away all of his duties.

Lead your dog to his bed area and throw him a few pieces of food as a welcome gift. From now on you'll claim all of the territory outside of his bed area and won't tolerate him entering your territory. He'll immediately learn that only you make the decisions for your part of the house.

He'll at some point want to enter your area, whether out of habit or in direct response to an event. You need to stop him from doing this as soon as he tries to leave his place. Stand in front of him and block his path to show him that he isn't allowed to enter your territory under any circumstances. You'll also need to turn toward him in a challenging manner and look straight at him. You may even have to move toward him so as drive him back into his own area. It's all about controlling the situation and making it clear that you won't tolerate him entering your territory without your request. The most important part of this exercise is learning to follow through with your decisions when you deal with your dog.

The more energetically your dog tries to get around you, the more energetically you need to use your body to drive him back to his place. You should only contain your dog with your body language. Don't use visual or audible signals on any account. Don't say 'No', 'Leave it', 'Stay', 'Sit', 'Down' or send him back to his bed area with a command. You need to work without using either gestures or your voice. All competing stimuli that your dog encounters during the exercise will only hamper his learning and direct his attention away from the real goal. You're far better off using your verbal

Taking responsibility

energy for watching him and then containing him at the correct moment. You'll then be taking a hands-on role and so making it clear to him where his area is located. Stay calm but firm at all times. If your dog withdraws to his area, stop your containing efforts at once and reward him for this behavior. Throw some food into his territory without saying a word.

A dog will quickly learn what's meant by your body language if you block his path and so stop him from claiming anything for himself. You can see how resources are managed in this way within a wolf pack. If a wolf isn't allowed a certain resource, he'll be prevented from reaching it, pushed away from its location or have his path blocked.

Dogs use their physical presence to fend off rivals from their property, and they'll typically use aggressive behavior as an additional measure to underline their claims.

It's levels of freedom that differentiate animals' rankings within a pack. The more freedom a pack member claims for himself, the higher his position within the pack hierarchy. If your dog has the greatest level of freedom and maintains control over the entire territory, it's therefore clear how he sees his position within your family. We can use simple body language to show our dogs those freedoms that we claim for ourselves and those freedoms that we leave to them. This will show your dog that it's you who makes the decisions within the territory. Your physical containment will also show him that you're willing and able to enforce your decisions. Your dog will only submit to you when he's had this experience. If you don't manage to follow through with your rules or decisions, he won't have any reason to submit to you, to trust your decisions, or to surrender his resources to you. He'll instead perceive you as a weak social partner, and no dog will entrust a weak social partner with his security or the responsibility for his territory.

Your dog will initially respond with confusion if you're successful in preventing him from entering your territory. If he subsequently looks at you and withdraws his behavior, reward him for this response. Always acknowledge and reward your dog for watching you attentively, regardless of this exercise. Eye contact will then become a universal alternative that your dog can seek out if he's uncertain or requires direction. Be careful not to unconsciously acknowledge begging while you do this, however.

Now is the sole exception as to when a reward should not be given out of your hand. It should instead be placed or thrown onto your dog's bed area, as this will help him to connect the food experience with his bed area. If you feed him out of your hand, he'll associate the reward with you or with your hand. He may then want to follow your hand, and this makes the exercise unnecessarily complicated. If your dog remains lying down, he'll be rewarded with food right from the outset. Happiness should rain down. It doesn't matter if you're working in the kitchen or are in any other way occupied: Don't forget to reward your dog. Don't say anything, as vocalizations will also increase the complexity of the exercise. Your dog learns in a situation-specific manner, so he'd now have to process your vocalizations in addition to the actual exercise. The fewer stimuli he needs to associate, the easier the exercise will be for him and the faster he'll recognize the new boundaries.

Consistently prevent your dog from entering your territory over the coming hours and days. Continue to contain him solely by using your physical presence to drive him back, and always try to contain him at your earliest opportunity. If he manages to walk around your home for a few minutes before your get him back into his area, he won't understand where the boundaries of his area lie.

Expose your dog during the exercise to all of the stimuli that would normally cause him to leave his area. You can practice these situations by ringing the doorbell, for instance, or by preparing food in the kitchen or having family members and visitors enter or leave your home. Practice each situation individually and repeat them at short intervals.

When he's spent a long time relaxing in his area, it'll eventually be time for a walk. Put his collar and leash on in his area and begin the walk here. He should only follow you when you have the leash in your hand and are walking away from his place. This routine should become a ritual over the next few days. After your trip, bring him back to his place and remove his leash here. Continue to avoid speech in any form.

Taking responsibility

If you can't react quickly when your dog enters your territory over the next few days, drive him back immediately and consistently as soon as you've noticed where he is. If you come back from shopping and notice that he's in your territory, bring him back to his area before your unpack what you've bought.

Everything that occurs outside of your dog's bed area will now be controlled by you and not him. When he adjusts his control behavior, he'll learn that doing so doesn't have negative implications for him: He'll even receive rewards for his lack of action. He'll very quickly realize that it's more worthwhile to remain in his place than to constantly monitor everything and everyone. This is ultimately a task that he doesn't enjoy.

If you remain consistent with the exercise, your dog will gladly hand over responsibility to you within just a few days. He can now relax in his paradise and return to this area if he senses danger. After a while, he'll no longer see any sense in controlling anything over which you've taken responsibility.

If your dog exhibits very pronounced control behavior, he may literally fight for his old territory – the majority of which you've now claimed for yourself. He'll defend his freedoms and may be very forceful in doing so. You should only practice with a muzzle if your dog demonstrates aggression, and you'll need to accustom him to wearing a muzzle in advance.

Place food in the muzzle so that he's occupied with this new piece of equipment for a while and so considers it in positive terms. Ideally give him all of his food solely from the muzzle. He'll then have less difficulty in accepting the muzzle in future.

In dogs with pronounced control behavior, any aggression or vocalization behavior that may be present will recede on a gradual basis. Your dog's stress levels may increase during the first few days, and he may also become more vocal during this period. This is completely normal and positive, as it means that your dog will have already learned and recognized that you manage your part of your home for yourself. He isn't absolutely sure about this, however.

He'll only gain certainty when he sees that what happens in your home has no effect on either him or his bed area.

A dog will normally recognize his new territorial boundaries within a few days. If his control behavior has been established over several years, however, it'll take longer before he gives up his habits.

> **As a rough guide:**
>
> No. of exercise days = Dog's age x 2

If you still haven't made any progress after this period, your dog isn't taking you and your containments seriously. You should work on how you're containing him and check whether you're really being consistent (see Page 129, "Success through consistency").

Your dog will almost never settle down at first, and will instead remain very vigilant while he lies in his area. He'll try to carry on with his monitoring tasks even though he's no longer allowed into your territory. But you'll soon notice that this behavior changes and reduces, and he'll eventually stop acting in this manner altogether.

If your dog is to accept his bed area, the reward that you give him needs to have a high value. He should have developed such a strong food drive that he considers your acknowledgement as an adequate alternative to his control behavior (see Page 161, "How do I build up food drive?").

You need to continue actively containing your dog until he's recognized your claim of ownership over your territory. This occurs when he's submitted to your decision. When he's understood what belongs to you, he'll accept this state of affairs and will behave accordingly. He won't enter your territory unless you request him to do so, even if there's food right in front of his nose. If the food's in your part of your home, he won't touch it.

Taking responsibility

Your dog will tell you when the exercise has come to an end. If he shows complete disinterest and continues to relax in his place when he's faced with the stimulus that previously drove him to leave his bed area more than any other, he's understood the limits and the exercise can stop.

He should be given all of his day's food as a reward for his behavior, and he should eat this food either in his bed area or while you're out on a walk. You can change this manner of feeding when he's recognized his bed area's limits. I personally recommend continuing to feed him in the same manner, as your dog will then know that whatever's in his territory belongs to him. If you give him a bowlful of food on the kitchen floor, he may bolt it down as quickly as possible because whatever's in your territory belongs to all pack members. He knows that you also have a claim to that food, so he may swallow it as fast as he can before anyone else can do the same. From experience, dogs that eat their food in their places also eat in a much calmer manner. They similarly learn that everything in your territory belongs to you and that no one ever challenges this situation.

Containing sensitive dogs
You should be careful when using physical containment if your dog is easily startled or is fearful. You may even need to avoid using physical containment at all. Such containment presents your dog with a threat. He'll instinctively meet it either by retreating or fleeing, and this will normally see him return to his area.

All forms of containment amount to negative interaction for your dog. It's therefore important to be consistent at all times during the exercise, as doing so will keep the exercise as short as possible. When I take on a new dog, the whole process is finished and the dog recognizes his boundaries within 20-30 minutes. I can look forward to positive interaction with him from then on.

Unlike a new dog, your dog has already claimed ownership within your territory. If a new dog enters a group, he hasn't yet claimed anything for himself. He'll initially behave in a reserved manner, watching to see who makes the decisions before taking direction from them.

Your dog already has a position within your family, so he needs to give this position up before he can recognize his new position. The training will therefore take much longer than if a new dog were to move in with you.

You can show a very sensitive or easily scared dog his new bed area by leading him around your home on a leash. Active physical containment could unsettle such a dog and upset his trust in you. It's less a question of physical presence in this situation than it is of trust and whether the dog will hand over responsibility to you. It's often sufficient for him to learn that he's safe in the area in which you've placed him.

Use a short leash without a loop at the end for this exercise. Such a leash will prevent your dog from getting caught up anywhere. Leave the leash on his collar for as long as you're in the house, and you can then guide him back to his place at any time. Lead him back with the leash if he enters your territory, and refrain from making any comment. The whole process needs to be conducted calmly and without causing the dog any stress. Don't tug at the leash, but rather accompany him back to his area and show him how he needs to behave. If he lies down out of fear, you can also carry him back to his area.

Watch him when he's back in his place. Reward him if he looks at you or demonstrates any behavior that indicates his recognition of the situation.

It's also important to practice all situations that give your dog cause to leave his area. It's only when he's learned an alternative behavior for every situation that he can withdraw to his territory in a relaxed manner and leave the work to you.

Containing dogs with low control behavior

If your dog shows only limited signs of control behavior, it's often sufficient to give his bed area positive associations. If he's developed sufficient food drive, only give him his day's food within his bed area. Feed him at irregular intervals, and later only when he shows you desirable behavior. Refrain from any form of vocalization and concentrate on correct timing when giving rewards. Also be sure to only provide your dog with acknowledgement for staying in his place, and not for searching out his place of his own accord.

Taking responsibility

Create positive moments for your dog while he's in his area. Searching games occupy him and allow him to associate his area with positive experiences. Guide him to his place when you return from a walk, and always collect him from his place when it's time to go out. You'll then create routines from which he can take direction.

Practice staying

If your dog's going to stay in his bed area when you're not present, he needs to learn that you can still control situations when he can't see you. Over time, he'll come to learn that his lack of action has no negative effects on him. He'll then stop demonstrating his control behavior. If your dog no longer sees any necessity in doing something, he'll stop doing it. Control equates to stress for your dog, and he doesn't enjoy this.

Gradually move away from his bed area and praise him by throwing him food. He's only allowed to take this food if it lands in his territory. Then increase the time between rewards and slowly move further and further away from his area. You can later leave the room for a certain period and close the door behind you, or at least move to where your dog can't see you. If he stays in his place, go directly up to him from time to time and reward him. If he becomes uncertain and leaves his area, you've probably moved on too fast. In this situation, you'll need to go back a step in the exercise. Remain patient and don't overwhelm your dog. It can take hours for some dogs to remain in their places once you've moved out of view.

If your dog stays lying down when he can't see you, you can increase the periods of your absences and eventually even leave the house. You always need to progress in small steps so that he has sufficient time to learn. It's better to repeat a familiar situation than it is to impatiently demand the impossible. You're almost certain to experience steps backward at some point, as progress will only occur in a strictly linear fashion in the absolute minority of cases. This shouldn't give you cause for concern. Your dog is only human (please don't take this literally!), so some days in his life will be better than others. You'll also have some days during which you can make yourself understood by your dog more effectively than on others.

If you want to teach your dog to observe boundaries and rules, the training will only end when he recognizes the boundaries and has learned the rules.

I like to compare this exercise with climbing a mountain. If you want to be successful, you need to reach the peak. If you stop halfway up, you'll eventually end up back down in the valley and so may as well not have started in the first place.

The most important aspect of the exercise is consistency. If you practice for two hours today and no hours tomorrow, your dog will never learn what you really want from him. Take several consecutive days to train with him, including nights if necessary. If you set down a rule, it needs to apply constantly, 24 hours a day.

My dog's learned it!
If your dog remains calm and relaxed in his place when faced with all of those stimuli that formerly caused him to seize the initiative, he's recognized the new ownership situation and sees his place as somewhere secure.
When he's learned which areas belong to you, you can readily grant him multiple bed areas or a wider overall territory. You can also move his place just as easily as you can provide him with new places. He'll find it useful if you can simply take his place with him when you enter unfamiliar surroundings.
Practical experience has shown that it's useful to be able to provide your dog with a new place wherever he's supposed to lie. If you want to show him that you're providing him with new places, lead him to a new place instead of his old place when you return from a walk. He may return to his old place of his own accord. If this occurs, respect his decision and don't force him to remain in the new place. He'll become accustomed to the new place with time. A place could be a chair, the couch or the bed. Once your dog has recognized your ownership of the home territory, there's no problem in him lying on the couch or spending the night on your bed.

If you only want him to lie on the couch at a certain time, you can use a discriminatory stimulus to let him know when this is allowed and when it isn't. You could spread out a blanket to represent his place, for instance. He'll then learn that he can only enter that area when the blanket has been spread

Taking responsibility

out. If the blanket isn't there, it's a no-go zone. The blanket is the discriminatory stimulus in this example.

Allow him to choose if he wants to leave his territory, but remain consistent if he's supposed to leave your territory. If you want to send him back to his place, lead him back as you did before. You should also retain sole control over his food and manner of feeding. Only you should decide whether to continue feeding him in his territory, to call him to where you'll feed him, or to bring him to where you'll feed him. From experience, a dog will eat food that's located in his own territory more calmly than he'll eat food that he finds anywhere else.

The garden

We consider a garden as belonging to our outside space, but a dog considers it as part of his inner territory. If your dog guards your garden and barks at passers-by from the garden fence, you need to show him that you'll take on those tasks that he feels responsible for in the future. You do this in exactly the same way as within your home. First you establish a bed area or define another space that's solely for him in the garden. He should still be able to notice those stimuli that cause him to charge at the garden fence, for instance. He should therefore have a clear view of the garden fence so that he can see passers-by, visitors or unfamiliar dogs.

If he reacts to a passer-by and wants to run to the fence, contain him straight away and drive him back to his place. Praise him if he stays in his place by throwing food, just as you did with the exercise in the house. You need to continue this exercise until he shows no more desire to get up from his place when passers-by walk alongside your fence.

9.2 Control in the outer territory

If you also want to relieve your dog of his tasks while he's away from your home, he needs to learn that you make the decisions here as well. He similarly needs to know that you'll continue to bear responsibility for his security and that you're up to this task. He'll ultimately learn that he's safe even despite not carrying out his own control tasks, and that you're in a position to protect him from any dangers that he may face.

If he's going to learn these things, you need to keep him on the leash and close to you for the entire duration of the exercise. You need to be a team, and there shouldn't be any reason for you to ever walk separately from one another. If you walk several meters apart, you can't influence your dog, protect him, or react to his fears or uncertainties.

What does the leash mean to your dog?
Most dog owners consider it a punishment if dogs have to walk on the leash. If we humans see a dog on a leash, we immediately feel the need to release him. We project our need for freedom and independence onto the dog (see Page 62, "Empathy"). We wouldn't like to walk on a leash, so we assume that it must be torture for the dog, as well.

Dogs aren't humans, however. A dog sees far more threatening situations that need to be coped with in everyday life than a human. We've learned to take care of our safety, and we can ensure it to a certain degree. We face practically no life-threatening or serious dangers that we can't control on an everyday basis. A dog sees his surroundings as much less secure. It's not just other dogs that pose a serious danger: It's often also traffic, construction sites, aircraft, in-line skaters, playing children and large crowds.

A dog considers many of our everyday situations to be serious threats, and he'll often see danger in a situation that we humans consider to be entirely harmless. We know that a car doesn't pose any danger to us, and the same applies to in-line skaters, motorcyclists, bridges, fireworks and crying children. These things nevertheless represent real dangers for a dog. You have the opportunity to provide him with security when he's on the leash. In actual fact, most dogs feel much safer being correctly led on a leash than having to face the daunting situations of our civilized and technological world alone. Most dogs would rather avoid a confrontation with another dog and remain safe than face the constant risk of having to defend themselves.

If your dog constantly walks ahead, you're unconsciously giving him a huge amount of responsibility.

If your dog walks several meters ahead of you, he's forced to resolve any conflicts by himself. There's no one else there to manage situations for him. From his perspective, you shirk responsibility by walking so far behind. Don't see the leash as a punishment, but rather as an aid.

The walk
Before you consider setting limits for your dog and taking over responsibility from him while he's away from your home, you first need to give him the opportunity to build up trust in you. Trust is an especially important basis for a relationship with dogs that are fearful or that demonstrate shyness toward people.

If you want to win your dog's trust, you need to show him that when you're outside of your home, you still don't present any danger and you also still want to share in his life. Do this by always staying close to him during your walks. If he pulls away from you on the leash, stay with him and follow him. Explore what he finds interesting and important alongside him. Follow his paths and watch what he does. If he glances at you questioningly, is uncertain, looks around the area aimlessly and doesn't know what to do next, make a decision on how to proceed. Use a brief tug on the leash to show him the new direction, or motivate him to follow you with a piece of food. You'll then show him that you know what to do.

He'll realize that you're always with him when there's something to discover and that you share in his experiences. He'll therefore develop a strong sense of a common bond between you. Avoid talking to him or giving him commands. Instead, watch him attentively and find out when and where he feels comfortable, in which situations he's uncertain or afraid, and when he becomes aggressive.

Show your dog that he's safe on the leash. Always keep him on the side that's separated from danger. If a cyclist approaches you from the right, for instance, keep your dog on the left side. If you meet an unfamiliar dog that's walking on the left side, take your dog behind your back and onto your right side.

Leashed dogs often encounter misunderstandings with other dogs, as their ability to communicate using body language is severely restricted when the leash is attached. Their limited freedom of movement means that they're frequently only able to show incomplete gestures and signals that are easy for other dogs to misinterpret. If your dog wants to show submission to another dog, for instance, the leash can prevent him from doing so. The other dog may then be quick to misinterpret what he's showing as provocation.
You should therefore avoid all contact with other dogs while your dog's on the leash. Misunderstandings even occur regularly among dogs that know one another when leashes are involved, and these misunderstandings have the potential to end in violent scuffles. Always stay between your dog and an unfamiliar dog until you're certain that the unfamiliar dog poses no danger and that your dog really wants to interact. If the other dog doesn't leave you alone and continually tries to get past you to reach your dog, counter him with a short but forceful step. Most dogs will then immediately take flight. Contact between two dogs should only take place once the initial tension and excitement has faded.

Avoid contact with other dogs for as long as your dog remains attached to his leash.

New territories

Many owners are constantly on the lookout for new places for their dog to let off steam. They do this in an effort to provide them with varied lives. Dogs spend their entire lives in a single territory when in the wild, and they won't normally leave this territory if there's sufficient food. A dog knows his territory and it provides him with security. We may find it boring to always move around the same places, but these places are home for our dogs. They feel safe here, and they know all of the smells in the areas and their rivals. Winning your dog's trust involves taking him to areas that he already knows on a more regular basis, and not constantly exposing him to new stimuli and dangers.

Walking on the leash

If we're going to control the risk that's posed by our domestic predators, it's absolutely vital that they become accustomed to walking on the leash. It's not in a dog's nature to walk on a leash, so they need to learn how to do this.

Time that your dog spends on the leash is a constant learning experience. He won't automatically implement what he's learned while on the leash once he's let off it, and the same situation also applies in reverse.

A leash isn't a towrope, so it's not intended for pulling your dog around. Its sole purpose is to safeguard him against third parties; when your dog's on the leash, you can determine the direction in which he walks. The leash isn't meant for pulling him away from sniffing or marking, for dragging him behind you, or for inflicting pain on him with powerful tugs.

If your dog hasn't yet learned how to walk on the leash, you first need to identify why he pulls on it or what he considers to be more exciting than walking alongside you. Give him as much leash as he needs to no longer pull, and then watch what he does. Many dogs will want to examine smells from other dogs in more detail. You can see where dogs sniff during winter particularly well when the ground's covered in snow. It's frequently feces from other dogs or footprints from other dogs or humans that will arouse their interest. But isn't it extremely unlikely that they'll take a liking to these smells?

There are certainly thousands of smells in a dog's world that are more fragrant than the smells that others leave behind. This means that there must be another reason to take such a strong interest in these smells that they'll pull on the leash and accept the choking pain from their collars in order to reach them.

Why does your dog sniff in the first instance if not for pleasure? Scents contain a huge amount of information, and especially those scents that come from other dogs. They tell him who's been in what place at what time, whether another dog is making any ownership claims over the territory, what rank that dog considers himself to hold, and much more. This information is of survival-

Taking responsibility

critical importance for your dog. When he meets other dogs, he immediately knows which dogs he needs to submit to, which dogs are claiming which resources, and which dogs rule the territory that he's currently moving through. His security depends on how he behaves during confrontations with unfamiliar other dogs. If he already has information about his rivals, he can adjust to a meeting in good time and thereby avoid conflicts. If he doesn't have this information, he may react insecurely or inappropriately, behave in a provoking manner, or end up 'putting his foot in it' in a way that triggers a conflict.

Your task is now to take this important information away from your dog. If he can't smell other dogs' scent markings or odors, he won't have the opportunity to develop his own problem-solving strategies. Without the information, your dog is helpless and so forced to rely on you (see "A blind man among enemies", Dog Training in Practice, R. Labjon, 2012). You now have to show him that he can rely on you.

He won't need the information if he learns that you're able to keep him away from danger. He'll then trust in you and seek protection from you if he needs it. If he recognizes your claim to the territory and feels safe with you, he'll only rarely sniff around and will also discontinue his marking behavior.

It's common to hear or read that a dog needs to sniff around. People say that dogs live in an olfactory world and communicate with one another using smells, so you shouldn't prevent your dog from sniffing under any circumstances. In reality, a dog has no need to sniff. All he actually has is a need for security, and it's this that leads to his needs for information. A dog collects the information that he needs to identify dangers or rivals from smells. The communication that takes place via smells has nothing in common with a human conversation or reading a newspaper. The information is instead of survival-critical importance, so a dog requires it to satisfy his need for security. He doesn't sniff around because he enjoys doing so, but rather because he has to. He wouldn't otherwise know what's happening in his territory, who's present in it, and where dangers lurk.

He won't require this information if he learns to rely on you. If he continues to obtain it, however, he won't have any reason to take direction from you or to discard his own conflict-solving strategies. He'll carry on keeping his own solutions to problems in mind, and he won't care about what you think of these solutions. In future, it needs to be your territory instead of his.

If you watch wolves roam around their territories, you'll see that they all walk with their heads held high instead of acting like vacuum cleaners with their noses constantly close to the ground. They can afford to act in this manner because they know that they can rely on their leading animals. These leading animals bear the responsibility for the safety of the pack.

If you want to take the information away from your dog, actively use your body to prevent any attempt that he makes to sniff at a scent. If he wants to inspect other dogs' markings, use your leg to push him away from that location and claim the area for yourself. If he accepts your containment, step back slightly from the area, let the leash go loose, and watch if he tries to return to the area to sniff at it once more. If he shows no signs of wanting to do so, use the leash to give him a quick indication as to where you're heading and then continue with your walk. If he tries to sniff at the area despite your efforts, begin the containment process again.

If your dog accepts your containment and drops his intention to sniff at the other dogs' marking locations, reward him by giving him a piece of food from your hand.

Your dog will need to defecate at some point during your walk. He'll sniff here too, and you of course shouldn't prevent him from doing this. You therefore need to learn to differentiate between whether he's looking for a place to defecate and whether he's monitoring his territory. Most dogs will announce when they're about to defecate via individual signs that all owners will recognize in their own four-legged friends. It's usual for a dog to lift his tail and undertake a wide-ranging but perfunctory search for an appropriate defecation spot. In contrast, a dog that's controlling his territory will be highly concentrated and will take his time to check individual locations in particular detail.

Taking responsibility

Note that if a dog has a low territorial ownership claim or is in an unfamiliar territory, he'll tend to defecate somewhat away from other dogs' pathways. He'll usually flee into shrubbery or high grass. This is an attempt to avoid provoking other dogs with his smell. No other dog should notice his presence if at all possible. His feces reveal a lot about him that he doesn't want to share with just anyone. Defecating off the beaten track is a form of preventive measure for avoiding conflict.

If your dog recognizes your ownership claim over your territory, he may also defecate away from you so as not to provoke you. You should respect this behavior and not contain him if he does this.

A dog pulls on a leash for two reasons: He's compelled to do so by tasks for which he feels responsible, and he also doesn't have a reason for remaining with his owner. You therefore need to consider what reason you give your dog for staying alongside you.

Make yourself the center of your dog's life. He needs to feel more comfortable with you than he feels anywhere else.

Make yourself into the greatest attraction for your dog. If he learns that you can satisfy his every need, he won't have any reason to leave your side. It'll then be completely irrelevant for him whether he's walking next to you with or without the leash. If he gets everything at your side that he'd otherwise have to fetch from elsewhere, there won't be any need for him to move away from your side. He'll then be able to walk as if he were on a leash even if there's no leash actually involved.

Use your dog's food drive to become more interesting for him. Learn to use food in a controlled manner so as to reward desirable behavior. You can't use food as a reward for as long as your dog considers monitoring his territory or marking to be more important than food. Food won't be a genuine alternative to what's he's otherwise doing. You'll therefore need to develop his food drive (see Page 161, "How do I build up food drive?").

Before you set out on a walk, place a piece of food in your hand and move it past your dog's nose so that he can smell it. This will increase his expectation.

Hold the food in your left hand if your dog should walk on your left-hand side, and in your right hand if he should walk on your right-hand side. Then pass the leash behind your back and hold it in your other hand so that your feeding hand is free for giving rewards. Your dog will now be standing behind you and to the side, looking in the direction that you're about to move. Next pass your feeding hand either behind your knee or behind your thigh, depending on the size of the dog. He'll then be able to get to the food without breaking his walking rhythm or needing to jump up. Your dog should be standing behind you, trying to get at the piece of food with his nose and so driving forward into your hand. Now move onward and ensure that he continues to drive forward while following the speed of your steps. Give him the food once you've completed a few steps. Repeat the exercise at short intervals until he's learned that he can take food from your hand if he walks behind you and to the side in the way that you require. Don't acknowledge him from your side, but rather behind your body. In the future he'll walk about one head length ahead of you, as his wide field of vision allows him to keep an eye on the place where you'll reward him.

You can now gradually increase the amount of time before you release the food. After a few attempts, your dog should refrain from pushing toward your hand and instead walk attentively behind you until you give him the food. Such encouragement is only necessary on the first few attempts to get him on the move. If your dog is already following you, this encouragement is no longer required.

Your can later increase the difficulty of the exercise and only reward him if, for example, he establishes eye contact with you and walks next to you as desired. Your rewards determine those behavior patterns that you'd like to encourage in your dog. You therefore also need to be careful that you only reward desirable behaviors.

During the first few attempts, you won't be able to avoid rewarding him if he claims the reward with his behavior. If he shows learned behavior in order to demand a reward, you'll know that he's understood the lesson. With time, however, you should refrain from acknowledging progressively demanding behavior and instead make your own decisions about when to give food. As

Taking responsibility

soon as your dog's learned that you'll give him food, he'll be glad to walk by your side.

Claiming territory

At the start of this exercise, you need to find a nearby green space where your dog will usually relieve himself straight away. You should visit this place and allow him to relieve himself here at the start of every walk and, at least initially, also at the end of every walk. This will be the only place that he's allowed to relieve himself for the duration of the exercise. You should only allow him to urinate away from this green space as an exception, and only then if this urination isn't the result of marking behavior.

When you arrive at the green space, position yourself at its edge and give him a long leash. Allow him to sniff around and relieve himself in peace. Start your walk if he doesn't relieve himself after a few minutes, and then give him another opportunity when the walk is over. Keep your first walks short until he's regularly relieving himself in the place that you've designated.

A dog with less pronounced territorial behavior will often leave responsibility for the territory to you if you remain close enough to him while he's monitoring territory markers. Follow him and stay so close to him that you're almost touching his shoulder with your leg. He'll need to carry out his checks far ahead of you if the checks are to make sense for him, as only then will he be able to recognize dangers and enemy territorial boundaries in good time and so protect you as his vulnerable social partner. If you remain close to him all times, this work will cease to make sense and he'll happily hand over the task to you.

As you're now behaving differently from usual, your dog may initially be somewhat confused and so give you quizzical looks or glance around the area in an erratic manner. He has no idea what will happen next in this moment, so he's waiting for information from which he can take direction. Reward his behavior with food and take away his current uncertainty. After you've praised him, take charge and use the leash to show him where you're about to head. He'll then learn that you'll take responsibility in uncertain situations and that he can take direction from you.

As soon as you're on the move once more, contain him whenever he tries to sniff at other dogs' marking locations. Use your leg to coax him away from the place that he's currently investigating without making any comment.

If your dog has demonstrated marking behavior up to this point, you need to prevent him from doing so in future by claiming the scent locations for yourself. Dogs usually only mark in places that they've already extensively sniffed. If your dog doesn't have any opportunity to sniff, he also won't mark. If he does mark, simply claim the place for yourself and use your body to coax him away from that location. Prevent him from claiming this place for himself.

By preventing him from claiming territory, you let him know that you're the only one with the right to assert such claims. If he recognizes your claims, he won't mark in your territory.

The more places within a territory that a dog claims through urine markings, the greater his area claim will be within that territory. If his marking behavior is limited to just a small place within the territory, e.g. to the green space that you visit at the start of your walks, he'll end up developing a far less pronounced ownership claim.

Most dogs demonstrate a very high willingness to submit to humans and will generally be very quick to respect human ownership claims.

During long walks, your dog may want to relieve himself without marking. If all he wants to do is urinate, he won't spend long looking for a suitable position before he starts. You can assume that he wants to claim an area for himself as soon as he begins to closely examine a potential urination spot.

Don't pull on the leash if this occurs, but instead seek out a confrontation with him and use your body to take him in the direction that you want to head.

He'll initially be somewhat confused. He'll look at you quizzically, to which you can respond by acknowledging him with food. Repeat this exercise until he stops marking of his own accord. After you've repeated it several times, the territory will belong to you. Your dog won't want to control an area that doesn't belong to him, so his control behavior will also show a marked decrease.

If your dog learns that you claim all territory markers across diverse situations, his marking behavior will similarly subside to a noticeable degree when you're in unfamiliar territories.

If a dog has a very pronounced controlling urge or shows aggression while he's on the leash and so strongly pushes forward, you can use active containment to prevent him from reaching those places that he wants to control or in which he becomes aggressive. Your dog will then learn that from that moment on, only you will control the situation ahead. You won't tolerate him taking over control, and you'll use active containment to prevent him from carrying out his tasks. Start by determining the boundary that your dog should observe, as this will help him to differentiate between what's your responsibility and what's his responsibility. Such a boundary might be your shoulder line. If your dog crosses this line, he'll be met by containment. From now on, don't allow your dog to impede on your responsibilities or become involved with situations that are occurring under your control. Your boundary won't just split the territory into two areas of responsibility: It'll actually split it into a safe and an unsafe area. Following the shoulder line, the area behind you is safe while the area in front of you is unsafe. The ultimate goal should be for your dog to stay in the safe area behind you while you go on ahead.

Your shoulder-line forms the boundary between the safe and unsafe areas. Your dog should only remain in the safe area behind you in future.

It isn't taken for granted in the wild that a leading dog will always walk on ahead, however. Quite the opposite, in fact: Other animals will usually take the lead, especially when it comes to hunting. But when a threat arises, the pack will pull back and allow the leading animal to take charge.

"Nisha led the group (...) very often, but she remained in constant contact with the leading male, Storm, who would naturally pass by her in dangerous situations and take over charge of the pack."[6]

The pack knows that the leading animals are best placed to assert themselves when conflicts approach, so they'll gladly allow these animals to go ahead during such situations. Other animals will only retake the lead when there's no danger in sight. It's therefore not important if an animal walks ahead; what's important is whether he takes the lead.

For dog training, this means that it isn't mandatory for you to always walk ahead. Your dog will still rely on you and your decisions. If you allow him to walk ahead of you, this area should be absolutely safe. This can prove to be extremely difficult in practice, because you can never be sure that a cyclist won't shoot around a corner or an unleashed dog won't suddenly appear in your path. I therefore always walk ahead, even when my dogs are running free. They're only allowed to be in front of me if we're all taking a break and I'm certain that they're safe.

Using your body for active containment provides a simple method for quickly teaching your dog how he should move. It should be used with caution on sensitive and fearful dogs, however. You can rapidly scare a sensitive dog with your body language to such an extent that he'll be scared to be close to you in future. This naturally isn't what you want to achieve. If you're uncertain about whether your dog might react in an overly sensitive manner, employ a slow approach when getting a feeling for your containment method.

---

[6] Bloch G. and K. Timberwolf, Yukon & Co., *11 Years of Observing the Behavior of Wolves in the Wild*, Mürlenbach/Eifel, 2002.

Taking responsibility

Begin by gently coaxing your dog off his present course with your leg if he tries to press on ahead of you during a walk. It'll then become clear how your dog reacts to you. If you have a smaller dog, simply place your foot in his path. You'll be able to see how he deals with your containment and if he stops at your boundary. Watch your dog at all times and try to establish eye contact with him. He'll try to catch your eye as soon as you contain him, as he'll want to ascertain whether or not your action was intentional. If he seems startled, you'll know that your containment was already too severe. In contrast, if he ignores you and continues to walk on, you'll need to change your containment method and employ a more forceful approach.

A particularly good approach for preventing forward drive in a fearful or easily scared dog is placing your hand on his chest to stop him before you gently push him back. Then take your hand away and watch to see if he accepts your containment. If he carries on walking ahead, stop him with your hand and coax him back once more. Repeat this exercise until he stops walking ahead, and only then continue with your walk. You can already begin using this containment method while you're at your front door.

Behave in a calm manner during the exercise and avoid making sudden movements with your arms. A prerequisite for this form of containment is that your dog shows absolutely no aggression. If he does, there's a risk that he'll end up biting your hand or arm.

You can also actively contain your dog with your body by lunging into his path as if you want to trip him up. He'll withdraw his behavior if he sees that he can't get past you, and you then need to praise him for this response. If his urge to get past you doesn't decrease, use your leg to drive him in the opposite direction in a somewhat more vigorous manner.

This type of containment is particularly effective if you can't turn toward your dog for some reason, e.g. you need to keep an eye on other dogs that are approaching from ahead. Your won't turn your body language directly toward your dog as you'll be facing in a different direction, so you should use this containment method to offer him protection, to control a threatening situation, and to physically prevent him from becoming involved in such a situation. He'll then learn that you face up to danger and that he no longer has to do this.

The most effective method for actively containing your dog with your body is direct, face-to-face confrontation. Start by holding the leash behind your back and gripping it tightly with your right hand if your dog's supposed to walk on the left. Your back will act as a fulcrum if you have a strong dog, allowing you to better control his forward drive. Keep your dog so close to you that he can't walk with his nose any more than half a step ahead.

As soon as he pulls ahead and crosses this boundary, use a vigorous twist to place yourself in front of him, containing him and counteracting his forward drive. If he establishes eye contact with you and so ceases his forward drive, acknowledge this behavior immediately. Your dog will learn that you're the only one who controls the situation ahead, and that there's therefore no reason for him to push forward. You're now claiming the freedom that your dog previously claimed for himself. If he doesn't cease his behavior, strengthen your behavior by pushing in the opposite direction until he gives up. You need to boost your behavior if your dog doesn't relinquish his urge to get ahead.

If your dog is to understand your actions, it's incredibly important that you raise your claim against him with a direct confrontation. If you can impose your decision on your dog, he'll understand after just a few repetitions that you now make all of the decisions in the territory and that he no longer has any freedom for making decisions here himself. Use your body language to express your will. If you just pull on the leash, he won't know what you're trying to tell him. On the one hand you're backing down and shirking responsibility by leaving him in charge, and on the other hand you're stopping him from carrying out his tasks. No dog will understand this state of affairs.

It's only through direct confrontation that your dog will understand what you want to achieve with your containment. Your active physical containment isn't about punishing him if he crosses the boundaries that you set, but is rather about showing him where he can move without being exposed to danger. Your containment is only limiting him from one of many potential actions. He can still move around freely within the boundaries that you set, and all other actions also remain open to him.

Even if your dog walks behind you and doesn't cross your area of responsibility, he may still sense interesting smells to the left and right of his path that cause him to pull on the leash so as to examine these marking locations. You won't usually have the option of containing him in good time when this occurs. Instead, stay close to him and follow him. If he stops to smell at something, coax him away from the scent location and praise him if he accepts your containment. Once he's left the territory to you, he won't need to break away from your side any longer.

The most important thing for your dog isn't the territory per se, but rather control over it.

If your dog has already had hunting success within his territory and has therefore learned to control prey, i.e. the food resource, it may be more worthwhile for him to continue controlling this area than to accept a relationship of dependency with you. In the case of doubt, he'll choose the easiest and most comfortable path for satisfying all of his needs.

You communicate with your dog via body language. This doesn't involve reducing your body language to mere facial expressions, as you actually communicate actively with your whole body. Show your dog what you want to achieve with your actions. Don't be afraid of harming him in the process, as you won't normally touch him at all. The containment has more of a psychological effect and is comparable with a set of threatening gestures.

If you want to stop your dog from becoming involved in a very stressful situation that might also be presenting you with intense challenges, stand straight in front of him and take him behind your back on a very short leash. The short leash should reduce his freedom of movement and so stop him from intervening in the situation. If an unleashed dog comes toward you, for instance, keep your dog behind you and position yourself between him and this unfamiliar other dog. You may have to shield your dog like a bodyguard. A forceful step toward the other dog will normally result in a quick diffusion of the situation. If the other dog becomes aggressive, don't be afraid to kick him and use all possible means of defense. An attacking dog can pose a danger for you as well as for your dog. You should be prepared for such a moment and have no reservations about inflicting damage on the attacker. Pepper spray can help to protect you both in the case of doubt.

Think like a mother who wants to protect her child. What would she do if an aggressive dog zeroed in on her child? You bear the same responsibility for your dog as a mother does for her child.

The fact that you claim a territory for yourself isn't sufficient to make you a pack leader. Your dog may have recognized your claim to the territory, but he still doesn't know if you can control conflict situations and provide him with security. He'll learn to trust you if you come through a situation such as the one described above, so search out danger and don't try to avoid it even if doing so seems simpler. Use every opportunity to show your dog what's within you and that you're able to protect him from harm.

If you use your body to actively contain your dog, you need to act just as forcefully as him. It's no use to him if you harass him without any motivation. He needs to recognize an extreme change in your behavior. He's previously seen you as vulnerable and has never considered that you could defend yourself. You now need to change this perception, and he should come to realize that you're superior to him. You don't need to treat him aggressively or violently to achieve this realization. You simply need to act correctly in important situations. You're the CEO of your pack and are more intelligent and experienced than your dog: He just doesn't know it yet. Physical violence and aggression aren't required. You have time on your side, and consistent and determined actions will show your dog that you're up to the task of leadership. He needs to sense that you take this task seriously. If he's hanging on the leash with his front legs lifted off the ground, you need to react with an equally forceful reaction if you're going to drive him back and stop him from carrying out his intention of resolving the situation for himself.

He won't recognize your behavior as containment if you demonstrate too little commitment. He won't understand what you want from him and that you're

Taking responsibility

making a serious claim to the territory. You want to take away freedoms that he's previously enjoyed. He considers freedoms to be of survival-critical importance, so he'll only give up responsibility for them if you can show him that you're more able than him to handle conflict situations.

If you can't control situations that your dog considers important, he won't trust you to secure resources or ensure his safety. If you can convince him that you're up to the task and also offer him food as an attractive alternative, he'll be glad to hand over responsibility to you and leave the work in your hands.

Reward him if he acts as you want and walks alongside you of his own accord. Praise him more regularly at the start so that he associates closeness to you with something positive and therefore gives you more attention. If he continues to show the desired behavior on a regular basis in the future, only reward him after he's walked next to you for a longer period.

If your dog hands over responsibility to you, he'll appreciate his surroundings in a much more relaxed manner and will also be able to enjoy experiences without the constant urge to control them. He'll know that he can rely on you. You'll similarly notice that he soaks up smells much more calmly, is less tense, and is far easier to recall.

He may walk behind you without any enthusiasm for the first few days. He first needs to become accustomed to how you've taken over his tasks. Help him to rediscover his walks and to fill them with happiness and fun (see Page 285, "Keeping a dog occupied").

You shouldn't contain him if he pulls away from an alarming situation out of fear. This action isn't a result of his territorial behavior and so can't be altered by containing his freedom. You instead need to reduce your dog's fear and provide him with security and confidence (see Page 225, "Managing fear").

You can use containments to counteract all stimuli that motivate your dog to drive forward. He has no property of his own, so there's no reason for him to want to press ahead. To make it easier for your dog to understand your active physical containments, it's initially useful to practice in surroundings with few stimuli. He'll then encounter few distractions and so will be able to concentrate on you. Practice on a large and empty supermarket car park, for instance, or on a remote paved footpath where there are few other dogs around. These places will usually smell less of other dogs and so will provide your dog with less distraction.

Be aware that your dog can recognize a clear difference in your behavior when you're containing him.

When everything's okay, behave calmly and move in a slow and relaxed manner. If your dog crosses a boundary, react forcefully, decisively and spontaneously. If you find it difficult to behave in a calm manner because you're too tense, make the effort to consciously move in slow motion and only change this behavior if your dog crosses into your area of responsibility.

If you have a dog with an especially strong food drive, it's helpful to start off without using any rewards and to instead concentrate solely on the containment. The food will cause your dog to enter a highly excited state, and this will make it difficult for him to remember the experiences that he's just gained.
Begin by making multiple short round trips during each of your walks. You'll then see if your dog's behavior changes at a specific place on the route and if he's recognized your ownership claim.

If you're confident with your containments and your dog reacts well to them, you can then extend your walks and show him that you'll also take over responsibility in unfamiliar territories. Take him to an unfamiliar area for this purpose, as he needs diversity in order to generalize what he's learned. He'll only trust you in a situation that you haven't ever practiced once he knows that you behave in the same way across diverse surroundings.

Also walk down a shopping street or through a mall with the same intention. You initially need to use every possible opportunity for practice. The more opportunities you use to prove yourself to your dog, the more trust he'll end up having in you.

9.3 angers and unfamiliar territories

Ensure that you're the first to enter unfamiliar territories and potential danger zones when you're out and about with your dog in new areas. It's your task to protect him from harm, so you need to take the lead when going through doors or up staircases that aren't familiar to him, and also when crossing streets. It's up to you to decide when a situation is safe. Glance at your dog frequently, as he'll then know that you have everything under control and are checking up on how he's doing. You should only allow him to move freely around an area once you've judged that area to be safe. If you behave in a consistent manner, your dog will soon learn to trust in you and your decisions.

9.4 Recognizing the boundaries

When you restrict your dog's freedom of movement, you need to continue doing this until he's learned to stay within the boundaries that you've set. The more consistently you enforce your rules with your dog, the faster he'll learn these rules.

When you're out walking together, always leave the leash loose so that you can see what decisions your dog makes. If he decides to stay next to you, you've done everything correctly. If he decides to move away, you know that you haven't yet reached your goal.

The exercises can only end when your dog has handed over responsibility to you and placed his trust in you. His behavior won't change if you stop the training before this point or fail to impose the necessary consequences.

He'll only be glad to stay within his area once he's recognized your boundaries and independently decided to show the desired behavior. He'll then know that he's safe with you, and will for the first time have discarded his old behavior and handed over responsibility to you. He'll now be able to wholeheartedly enjoy his newly won leisure.

9.5 Success through consistency

You need to win your dog's trust and convince him of your capability before he'll hand over his ownership claim and responsibility to you. This requires the consistent observance, monitoring and assertion of your rules.

A dog needs to know what's allowed and what isn't. A rule that's established today also needs to apply tomorrow. If you don't accept one of your dog's behavior patterns today, you also can't accept that behavior pattern tomorrow. Exactly the same applies in reverse: If you tolerate a certain behavior pattern in the morning, your dog will be unsettled if he's punished for that same behavior pattern in the evening.

He won't be able to trust you if you keep dangers away from him today, but he then has to defend himself again tomorrow.

If you want to take away responsibility from your dog, you need to be aware that you're doing this forever.

Don't confuse consistency with severity or toughness, however. Neither a particularly tough crackdown nor exceptional severity will help your dog to learn. It isn't his fault if he doesn't learn something: You simply haven't yet found the correct way of teaching it to him.

You should always remain friendly and calm. You're the pack leader from now on, but your dog doesn't yet know this. You don't need to become aggressive toward him for this reason, as he simply needs time before coming to accept your decisions.

Consistency means adhering to established rules and creating fixed rituals and procedures from which your dog can take direction.

1.) In future, you should decide when, what and how much your dog eats. You should control the food resource. Your dog will only do what you expect from him if it's worth his while to act in this manner. Control his food and his food drive. If you feed him too much, he'll consider food as far less of a reward.

Taking responsibility

2.) You need to decide when and for how long to leave your dog with prey (toys). You control the resources that satisfy his needs. If he learns to satisfy his own needs, e.g. by killing prey or misusing you as a ball-throwing machine, your status in your relationship with him will lower and your influence on him will follow. Need satisfaction should come solely from you from now on.

3.) You need to decide the areas in your home in which your dog is allowed. If he has decision-making authority over a territory, this territory also belongs to him. Show him that you claim the territory and that you bear responsibility for it. Give him his own territory in which he's safe and feels secure. He'll withdraw to this area during uncertain situations and leave the work to you.

4.) Your dog should never be successful when demanding need satisfaction. If he can win food by begging, for instance, he has control over food. You'll lose your influence over him, as he'll have found a strategy for controlling food. He can then decide when food is available, and there's no longer any need for him to meet your expectations.

Your dog controls his own drive satisfaction if he's successful in demanding actions from you. On the other hand, you increase your status if you control his need satisfaction and he's only able to experience drive satisfaction through you.

5.) You need to walk ahead, and your dog needs to follow. You should be the first to enter new territories or unfamiliar danger zones so that you can recognize threats in good time and protect your dog from risks. This means that you need to go before him through doors, up stairs and into rooms. He can go ahead if you know that he's safe from danger here, but you need to decide when it's safe for him and when potential dangers exist. Your dog will then learn to trust in you and will have no reason to show defensive aggression or to develop his own strategies for warding off dangers. He'll instead take direction from you during uncertain situations.

6.) Be there for your dog when he seeks out your help. Show him that you're able to protect him and offer him security in conflict situations. He can then decide whether to become involved in a dangerous situation or to remain in safety with you. If he doesn't have this choice, he'll find his own ways of coping with critical situations. The independence that he'll develop as a result may reduce both your status in your relationship and your influence over him.

7.) Always place yourself between your dog and danger. You're then always there for him in threatening situations, and you also show him that you're ready to face up to conflict. It's only when you're between your dog and danger that you can use your body language to show him that you're offering him protection. He knows where you are and whether you're close enough to him to intervene in a situation. If you stand on the far side from danger or are too far away from your dog, he'll automatically feel obliged to intervene in the conflict himself. He'll perceive you as having withdrawn from your position of responsibility.

8.) Always remain with your dog. You can't offer him protection if you're several meters away. He'll then be forced to recognize threats by himself and to defend against these threats if necessary. There similarly shouldn't be any reason for him to run away from you. It's only when you're together that he'll be able to develop a sense of a common bond in your relationship. You'll experience things together that he perceives as positive, and you'll also protect him from anything that might cause him harm.

9.6 Attention – The importance of eye contact

If you're going to train with your dog, he needs to pay attention to you. Don't expect him to be attentive, however, if you're not attentive yourself. Experiments have shown that a dog's behavior is strongly dependent on his owner's behavior.[7] If the dogs in the studies were watched attentively, they'd normally follow a command in the correct manner. If they weren't paid any attention, they'd follow the command inadequately or even not all. This shows

---

[7] Schwab C., Huber L., J, Competition Psychology, Aug. 2006.

Taking responsibility

that a dog is well aware of whether you're paying him attention or are distracted by other things.

A dog has to learn willingness to pay attention. If he doesn't pay attention to you independently, he needs to learn that it can be beneficial for him to look at you. Sit in front of him, take a piece of food, and place it down before him. Take another piece of food in your other hand and hide this hand behind your back. If your dog wants to take the piece of food that's in front of him, cover it with your hand and claim it for yourself. He'll then try to get at it. Only take your hand away when he backs off. As soon as he tries to take the food again, cover it up once more. He'll at some point realize that the food belongs to you and that he's not allowed to take it. Before he reaches this realization, he'll look quizzically up at you. Reward him for this look with the food from your other hand. Be careful to only reward him for eye contact, and not if he looks at your shoulder or at the hand with the food. When he's learned that he receives food for looking at you, practice this lesson in different surroundings. Your dog needs to successfully learn in different situations so as to generalize the behavior (see Page 175, "Situational learning and generalization").

You can also train eye contact as an individual exercise. Hold a piece of food in each hand and then pass both hands in front of your dog so that he can smell the food. Now stretch your hands away from one another. Your dog will be uncertain about which hand he should follow. His uncertainty will cause him to look at you at some point. Praise this eye contact straight away with the food from one of your hands. Repeat this exercise until your dog understands that he only receives food if he looks at you.

10 What dominance means

'Dominance' is derived from the Latin word 'dominatio' and means 'control'. Control isn't bad in principle, but many people are quick to equate it with military obedience and oppression. Control is only actually bad if those over whom it's exerted have needs that are left unmet.

Control means power, although power is also associated with considerable responsibility. If someone exerts control in a responsible manner, this control may even be an advantage for those over whom it's exerted. The controller makes decisions that benefit the welfare of his subjects. It's only when every individual's needs are met that they all recognize the control and are glad to submit to it. Only then will the control endure on a long-term basis.

Dominance necessarily requires not only someone to exert control, but also someone to recognize that control. This is exactly where most misunderstandings arise. Subordination won't endure on a long-term basis if it's claimed through force. It'll only really occur if it results from free choice.

Dominance also exists among dogs. The leading animals control their pack, for instance, with the male leading animals normally being dominant over the female leading animals. If both leading animals are responsible rulers, they'll remain in their positions for their entire lives. They're then dominant over the other animals – and not because they demand this dominance, but rather because the pack wants them to act in this manner and because all pack members take direction from their decisions. The other animals trust them. If a leading animal were only concerned with his own benefit and couldn't satisfy the pack's needs, the pack would probably kill him.

There's no dominance in the wild that's enforced through violence. Dominance's biological purpose is to increase the chances of survival for all, and not just for the leading animals.

There are various forms of dominance among dogs.

Formal dominance

Formal dominance is determined by an animal's rank within the pack. This type of dominance exists on a long-term basis and is permanently recognized by all low-ranking animals. Formal dominance only exists within an animal's own pack, so it plays less of a role during day-to-day meetings with other dogs outside of the animal's own social group. Dominance only exists here in situational terms.

Situational dominance

No dog is dominant in all situations. Dominance among unfamiliar dogs doesn't exist on a permanent basis. It's always connected to a specific situation.

When dogs meet during a walk, this meeting usually constitutes a confrontation between unfamiliar animals that are first and foremost rivals. Dogs remain rivals even if they know one another. They don't have a clearly defined and long-lasting relationship like animals within a pack, so formal dominance can't exist between them.

If a dog controlled a resource at one point, it's in his nature to protect this property. If he didn't consider the resource as important, he wouldn't have taken possession of it in the first instance. The greater a dog's ownership claim, the more vigorously he'll strive to dominate rivals that pose a threat to his resources. He'll enact this dominance by trying to assert his claim to his resources over others. If another party doesn't pose any threat to his resources, he equally won't see any reason to fight with this other party.

If control is to be exerted, there always needs to be something to control. No dog wants to dominate another dog without a reason. He may want the other dog to recognize his claim to control over a territory, for instance, or his ownership claim over prey or food. If neither dog has any property of his own, neither will want to compete with the other. In an ideal situation, the human will control all property and so remove all motivation for a dog to enter into competition with others.

Conflicts often occur because the areas that surround our homes normally contain several dogs that claim ownership over one and the same territory. The more similar two dogs' claims, the more strongly they'll compete for the respective resources.

It's not in a dog's nature to constantly force others into submission. Doing so on a regular basis can be tiring, unnecessarily using up energy and always carrying the risk of injury. This is why submissive dogs are quick to show signals of their submissiveness. Injury-causing fights are then avoided to the greatest possible extent both within and outside of a pack.

11 Tips for owning multiple dogs

Many dog owners are faced with the decision of whether to adopt a second dog. Multiple dog ownership presents a range of questions that require consideration before a domestic pack is enlarged. There's a vast difference between owning one or two dogs. On the other hand, there's almost no difference between having two or twenty dogs live in your pack.

It isn't important how many members there are in your pack if you've thought about and fixed the relationship structures within your social group. Everyone in the social group has their own set place and knows who makes the decisions in which situation and who leads the group. It's common for owners to only begin thinking about their relationships to their dogs when problems arise within their families. If the dogs are to find their way within their social environment, it's important to show them at an early stage the position that they occupy within the group and the freedom for making decisions that they possess.

The greater a dog's freedom for making decisions, the greater the leadership responsibility that we bear for him. The nature of our relationship to individual dogs is critical for distributing roles and tasks within the community.

There are different relationship models for this purpose, and all are justified in certain circumstances. A dog finds his place within a pack based on his relationships to the other group members. He'll see himself as a lower-ranking animal if he's weaker, not very assertive, and has to constantly submit in confrontations with other social partners. The same animal will see himself as having an equal rank to the other animals if he no longer has to assert himself in competitive situations and so has the same freedom as every other pack member.

A dog's role is only valid within a certain group. If an alpha male enters an unfamiliar group, for example, he may find himself with considerably less freedom for making decisions and so also a lower rank position. This means that there's no single alpha male or alpha bitch. A leading animal's position is only valid within his social group, as it's only here that everyone recognizes his role. If his social environment changes, he may quickly find himself at the bottom end of the hierarchy within his new pack. You can only determine the leading animal within a pack when you consider the pack in its entirety.

The sense of belonging that a dog feels within a group also determines how comfortable he feels in this community. He'll feel less comfortable and more often frustrated if he's constantly ostracized and bullied than if he's treated as being of equal rank and value and with the same care as the other animals.

I'd now like to present some relationship models and clarify their effects on a dog.

Linear hierarchy
The linear hierarchy is the classical hierarchy model that also predominates in nature. There are set structures and freedoms that provide information on an animal's respective rank. Interaction between animals occurs almost exclusively within their own hierarchy levels, and never with animals of lower ranks. As an example, a leading wolf would never groom an omega animal or invite this animal to play.

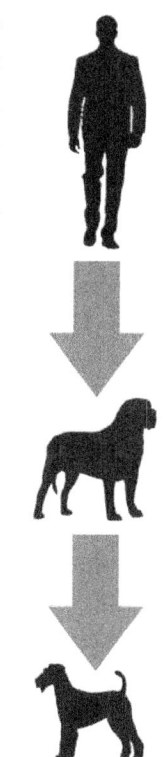

This fixed ranking structure often leads to frustration and dissatisfaction among lower-ranking animals, and especially among those animals at the very bottom of the hierarchy ladders. This frustration and dissatisfaction often causes the affected animals to migrate.

The linear hierarchy form is still present in dog ownership today, e.g. in relationships among sled dogs. There's a clear team leader here, but it isn't the human. The musher (sled driver) will normally have the most intense relationship with the pack's leading animal. All of the lower-ranking dogs will primarily have a strong relationship to the leading animal and not to the musher, as they need to follow the leading animal and not the human who will stand behind them on the sled. If these dogs took direction from the handler and not the leading animal, the human would be forced to run ahead if the dogs were to pull the sled.

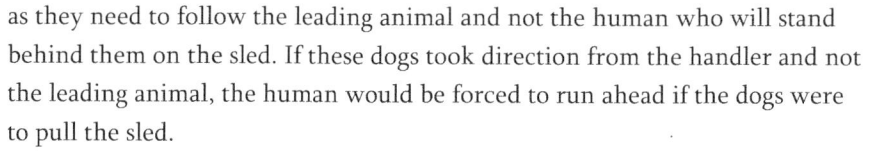

Circular hierarchy

This hierarchy form has flexible ranks and is characterized by there being no fixed rankings between group members. All members have roughly equal ranks in their relationships with one another, and no individual member feels responsible for the group. There's no sense of togetherness, and every animal looks out for himself first and foremost. A circular hierarchy form is common if multiple unrelated animals have to temporarily live together in a group, e.g. in animal shelters, some kennels, rescue centers or among street dogs. A linear hierarchy will develop at some point if the same animals have to live together for a longer period. A flexible-rank hierarchy causes enormous stress for each animal due to the lack of a long-term rank structure from which they can take direction. Efforts are therefore normally made to form a fixed rank structure.

It's often impossible to form such a fixed rank structure, however, because the composition of the group is always changing. New animals will frequently join the group while others will leave. The remaining animals are then left constantly stressed because of their regularly altering relationships to the other animals. They also feel uncertain due to the constant risk of having to defend their freedoms against someone new. Freedoms will normally change when the group's composition changes, and this often leads to conflicts and serious disputes.

A human will normally play no role within these groups. He doesn't make any claim against the dogs for his own freedom, so the pack doesn't recognize him as a leading figure. It therefore isn't surprising that there are often reports of animal care staff being bitten in enclosures. The human has been seen first and foremost as a rival. A dog doesn't care that we've created his present situation. He judges a social partner in accordance with this partner's behavior. If we humans behave like omega animals and fail to secure our own freedom for making decisions, the pack will treat us in line with this behavior.

The wolf expert Dr. Dirk Neumann felt these effects when he was attacked by a pack of wolves in an enclosure in Hanau in the mid-'90s. He deliberately set out to have no influence on the group's rank structure, and this meant that he also had no freedom for making decisions. The wolves tolerated him until one day the leading wolf perceived him as a rival. The other animals in the group joined the leading wolf in the attack, so it's a real wonder that Dr. Neumann managed to survive the situation.

A similar event occurred in a Swedish zoo in June 2012. An eight-strong pack of wolves attacked a female keeper, and she unfortunately didn't survive the incident.

An animal keeper will usually interact with animals in positive terms, and this establishes a bond between the keeper and the animals. All that this means, however, is that the animals are less inclined to become hostile toward the keeper than they are to people with whom they have no relationship. The keeper doesn't automatically become a leading animal even if he feeds the animals. If one of the animals sees the human as a rival, e.g. during the mating season, he'll treat him in a corresponding manner.

Radial hierarchy
I believe that this hierarchy form is the only sensible option when owning multiple dogs. It makes the human central and gives him the greatest freedom for making decisions, and it also provides him with a positive relationship to each individual animal. The animals all have relationships to one another, but there's no rank structure among them. They don't own any property, so they similarly have very limited freedoms for making decisions. Since they don't need to defend or expand freedoms that they don't have, competitive behavior doesn't develop among them. The human instead decides who is entitled to which freedoms. He makes all of the decisions and bears the responsibility for the entire pack. He alone is responsible for recognizing and satisfying each individual's needs.

Tips for owning multiple dogs

The attentive reader will have noticed that we give the dogs the role of omega animals in this hierarchy form. Like in the wild, an omega animal has almost no decision-making authority within our pack. Such a state of affairs quickly leads to frustration and then migration when it occurs in the wild. We naturally don't want this to happen, so it's important to understand that this frustration doesn't arise from a low rank or a lack of decision-making freedom. It's instead dependent on whether an animal's survival-critical needs can be satisfied in his present social environment. An omega animal's life is ultimately dependent on the goodwill of the rest of the pack, but a pack can't control survival-critical resources like humans. It's only with great difficulty that a pack can satisfy its own needs, let alone do the same for or guarantee survival to its lowest-ranking animal. In an emergency, the lowest-ranking animal will be the first to succumb to starvation. As an omega animal's frustration is the understandable result of survival uncertainty, it's simple for us to prevent this frustration. If we can recognize and actively satisfy our dog's needs, we can even ensure that he feels happier in his role as an omega animal. As well as protecting him from frustration, we can also develop our bond and strengthen our relationship with him – and all despite him not having any decision-making freedom of his own. It's almost as if he's on permanent vacation with full pay.

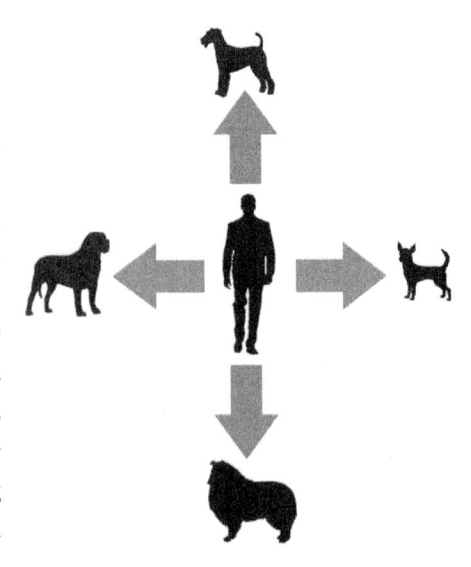

As this hierarchy form means that the dogs don't have any of their own property or areas of responsibility, it also removes all motivation from them to establish their own ranking structures. In consequence, no competitive behavior or aggression will develop among them.

If there's rivalry between dogs, it's down to the human to resolve these conflicts. He's responsible for peace within the group, and he alone makes decisions as to whether and which interactions are permitted between social partners. This decision-making power doesn't just concern interactions between dogs, but also interactions with other family members, and with children in particular.

We need to immediately suppress negative interactions such as rivalry or competition. Our interventions will allow each individual pack member to rely on the fact that we're able to recognize hostile disputes and prevent them if necessary. If we prevent all hostile confrontation among the dogs, all that remains to them is peaceful interaction. The dogs can then begin to establish positive relationships with one another. Competitive behavior would make the establishment of such relationships impossible, as rivalry and competition only end in a positive outcome for the party that manages to prevail against the other.

When you live alongside multiple dogs, you need to note that you can only establish relationships to the individual animals, and not to the group as a whole. This is also why interactions should only ever involve two partners, regardless of whether they concern a dog and another dog or a dog and a human. It doesn't matter whether it's feeding, affection or play: You should only deal with one dog at a time instead of trying to please them all at once. You'll then prevent competitive behavior or aggression from developing, e.g. over food. You'll decide which dog you're dealing with, who gets how much food, and when each dog is allowed contact with another dog. When an interaction takes place between two social partners, whether dog or human, both partners should see the interaction in positive terms and as representing added value. If your child strokes one of the dogs in your group, you should ensure that that dog also wants to be stroked at that moment. If he doesn't want to be touched or hugged, your child needs to learn to respect this desire. It's your task to recognize your dog's mood and, if need be, also to keep your child away from your dog. You're otherwise acting against one of your dog's needs. Doing so is negative for your relationship, and it may equally lead to your dog using his own means to let the child know when he's not content. This is exactly why most dog bite incidents involve children. They can't recognize a dog's needs and so also can't respect these needs. It's therefore your task and your responsibility to recognize what needs your dog has.

In a study from Dr. Vikram Durairaj of the University of Colorado, he and his colleagues analyzed data from 537 children who were treated in a pediatric clinic for dog bites between 2003 and 2008.

Durairaj and his team found out that 68% of the children were under five, and the vast majority of the children were under three. More than 50% of the bites had occurred when the dogs were manhandled, cuddled, frightened or had been accidentally stepped on by the children. The children were normally bitten in the face, with the doctors diagnosing facial fractures, torn eyelids, and injuries to the tear ducts and eyeballs.

What's scary is that most of the children who were bitten knew the dogs that attacked them. The dogs usually belonged to the families or to their friends or neighbors. The data suggests that children have a 50% chance of being bitten at least once during their lives. If a bite does occur, there's an 80% chance that it'll be to the face or neck.

Limiting freedoms

Before you walk the whole pack together, every dog should know his role within the group and should have left leadership responsibility up to you (see Page 95, "Taking responsibility").

You can't freely use your body for active containment if multiple dogs are present or are being taken on a walk at the same time. Most dogs will find it difficult to identify which dog you're targeting with your containment attempts. All of the dogs will react in the case of doubt, even though most of them will have been behaving in an absolutely correct manner. This can create uncertainty within the group and throw already learned and established behaviors into question for individual dogs. Each dog should therefore learn those areas of responsibility that you claim and those that are left to him on a one-to-one basis. Communal walks and other communal activities can only be considered once every dog has left the leadership responsibility to you and is able to manage without containments.

As with containments, you should also refrain from punishing animals within your group. If the pack recognizes your sanction against an individual pack member, the other dogs may join you and attack the punished dog. This pack dynamic is virtually impossible to control and can lead to serious harm for both you and your dogs.

A new dog
Before you consider adding another dog to your domestic pack, you first need to answer why you're obtaining this new dog. If you want him for yourself, pick him out alone. If you want him for the pack, they should also have a say in which dog enters the group. You should bring the dogs together and observe which new dog is best accepted by your pack.

Unfamiliar dogs should only be brought together away from your home and on neutral turf. If you have several dogs, each one should be introduced to the newcomer without the others being present. You need to be at the center of every meeting, and not just in proverbial terms.

You should always be between the two dogs, closely observing how they react to one another. Don't allow them to make direct body contact. Most dogs will look for the anal region on their first meeting or will want to sniff at the other dog's genitals or face. Dogs that haven't yet learned to take direction from humans will normally display a very strong urge to smell one another. This isn't about greeting the other dog, but rather about establishing who's there and whether or not they present any danger. When they both know that the other dog doesn't present any danger, they'll leave one another and continue on their individual paths. If it emerges that one dog poses a threat, however, a power struggle will develop. It'll be almost impossible to predict the outcome of this power struggle or to influence its final result.

By stopping the dogs from approaching one another, you prevent them from gaining sufficient information to decide whether the other dog poses a threat. They then won't have any reason to become aggressive and will instead be forced to rely on you – which is exactly how they should behave.

If both dogs recognize that you make the decisions, they'll know that you're able to maintain peace between them and guarantee each one's individual security. This applies whether or not they make contact.

If both dogs make it through the first few minutes of the meeting and recognize your position, go for a walk in your territory for a short while. You still need to remain between the dogs, always observing them closely. Take a break if one dog's interest in the other decreases, allowing both dogs to then move around without constraint. Continue to watch them, but this time allow them to make contact. Separate them immediately if display or competitive behavior develops after the sniffing, however. This will show them both that you recognize critical situations and don't allow such behavior to occur.

Allow the dogs to decide if they want to make contact, and don't try to encourage them with any actions. If they make the decision of their own accord, you'll know that they actually want to make contact.

Dogs will only compete to claim freedoms or resources from another dog. If you claim every resource for yourself, they won't have any reason to compete over anything. If they continue to compete, their behavior will quickly show you which dog is trying to make which ownership claim. In the case of doubt, continued competition means that you need to work on your position.

Playing or competing?
If you want to promote positive relationships between your dogs, you need to consciously decide when they're allowed to interact with one another. If you want them to build up a bond with one another, you should permit positive interaction and prevent negative interaction.

Play is a very positive interaction among dogs, for instance, and it's very beneficial for building up a positive relationship. It needs to be play, however, and both parties need to see it in this manner.

If two dogs play together without an object, you should ensure that there are frequent role reversals. Neither dog should be in a permanently inferior position or should force the other dog to submit. You should also intervene and end the activity if one of the dogs shows aggression (e.g. growling, barking, fur standing on end) or fearful behavior (e.g. trembling, tail between legs, escaping).

Tips for owning multiple dogs

When two dogs play with an object, they're in most cases not actually playing. The object is usually a reason for competitive behavior, with each dog trying to win possession of it. The only dog that will see such an interaction as positive is the dog that can call the object his own when the interaction ends. You should be particularly cautious that the object doesn't trigger a competition.

If you have multiple dogs and you ignore competitive behavior, individual dogs will be able to make permanent claims to resources, and so to property. Rankings may then develop over the long term, leading inferior dogs to become frustrated and superior dogs to take over responsibilities that actually fall within your remit.

Other competitive situations that you should control include competition over food and claims for bed areas. You need to decide who gets how much food at what time, and even whether there's food at all. All dogs should be given their food in their place, and no dog should search the others' bowls once they've finished. Each dog only has a claim to what you leave in his territory.

You similarly need to decide who can claim which bed areas. If a dog wants to claim a bed area that's already occupied, you should immediately step in if the other dog clears his place or doesn't want to be visited. You should allow a dog to lie down in an empty bed area, however. You should equally allow dogs to share a bed area, lie together or lick one another if they choose to do so. These are positive forms of interaction that strengthen the bond between animals. This is also how dogs show their affection for both one another and humans.

12 Learning through conditioning

12.1 Conditioning vs. training

If our dog is to 'function' in everyday life, we expect him to immediately show the desired behavior when we present him with a command, to submit to us as if by magic, and to recognize existing problem behaviors and stop new ones before they develop. It's generally claimed that very obedient dogs are well-trained dogs. In actual fact, both training and subordination are fundamentally different from conditioned obedience.

Any dog can learn commands, regardless of his position within his social group. He'll still be a long way off from being trained, however. Learning commands and their desired behaviors is the result of pure conditioning. Conditioning is a learning method and not a training method. Leading animals can be conditioned without the need for any training to take place, for instance. Lions and tigers in a circus ring have learned to perform tricks on command, but it's not possible to live alongside these animals because they haven't submitted to humans. Conditioned actions are nothing more than dressage. The dog demonstrates an action because it's worth his while to do so.

Conditioning refers to the learning of stimulus-response patterns from originally spontaneous behaviors. The frequency of a behavior is permanently altered in relation to its pleasant or unpleasant consequences (amplifiers). This learning method is carried out in the same way for all dogs.
A connection is established during the learning process between an action and its consequences. Whether or not a behavior will be shown on a more frequent basis depends on the nature of the consequences. If the consequences have a rewarding effect, the behavior will be shown more frequently. As soon as they have a negative effect, the behavior will be shown less frequently.

In practice, we differentiate between two types of behavioral conditioning.

Conditioning active behavior

An active behavior such as sitting or lying down is conditioned by means of stimulus-response patterns. This is where a stimulus triggers a conditioned response. Auditory or visual signals are normally used for this purpose.

When conditioning an active behavior, it's crucial for the reward to follow soon after the action has been shown. This allows the dog to connect the action with the reward.

Two methods are predominantly used in operant conditioning today. These are conditioning with positive reinforcement ("learning by success") and conditioning with positive punishment, whereby the term 'positive' refers to the addition of an unpleasant consequence. We add a positive consequence to positive reinforcement by rewarding the desired behavior, e.g. with food. The dog will then show this action on a more regular basis in the future or will demonstrate it when given a command.

In positive punishment, the dog is exposed to a stimulus that he considers as negative when he shows undesirable behavior (positive = adding a negative stimulus). The dog will then avoid that behavior in future because it's followed by a negative event. Examples of negative stimuli include pain and unpleasant noises.

If positive reinforcement is to work, the dog needs to want the reward that's used as an amplifier. He needs to do everything that he can to receive that reward. In an ideal situation, his desire for the reward should be stronger than any alternative.

If food is to be seen as a reward, you need your dog to have a pronounced food drive (see Page 161, "How do I build up food drive?"). If your dog hasn't developed any desire for food, he won't do anything to satisfy such a desire. He then won't consider food as a reward, meaning that food can't be used as an amplifier for positive behavior.

Learning through conditioning

How do I give rewards in the correct manner?

If a reward is to be connected with a behavior, it's incredibly important for that reward to be given soon after the desired behavior has been shown. Your dog should receive immediate acknowledgment if he responds to a command in the correct manner. The sooner he's rewarded, the easier he'll find it to connect his behavior with your command.

Complex exercises should be rewarded in steps. Acknowledgment is then important whenever your dog shows either the right basic approach or even just minor progress in his learning.

A dog will only effectively and permanently learn things that he's worked for himself. Be careful to only present him with an offer when using any type of reward. He needs to want the reward, because if he doesn't want it, it isn't a reward. When he finds other things to be more important than food, it becomes especially critical to increase food's value and to investigate what else is holding his attention.

Your offer provides him with a decision-making opportunity: He can decide whether or not he wants the reward. He can then work for learning success by rewarding himself. Your dog's eagerness to receive the reward will equally show you when your acknowledgment loses value.

With a food reward, the quantity that you give isn't important. What's much more important is the frequency of the reward. The more often your dog is successful in what he does, the more quickly he'll learn. Every reward consolidates what's been learned. Reward desirable behavior with a small amount of food, and do this frequently. Every time he's rewarded for a behavior, he'll connect that behavior with the reward and make a mental note of this connection. Crucial to success are stimulation of the taste buds and the smell of the food, not the fullness of your dog's stomach.

We often tend to wait for our dogs to make errors during training, as we can then correct their behavior with commands or punishments. If your dog independently demonstrates desirable behavior on an everyday basis, praise him for this without constantly giving him commands. Don't be sparing with the rewards, but rather with the commands (see Page 155, "Conditioning passive behavior").

Discriminatory stimuli

Dogs learn in accordance with the situation that they're in. A discriminatory stimulus (signal stimulus) indicates to a dog the potential consequence of a situation. Various factors can therefore cause a learned behavior to be shown only in the presence of the relevant conditional factor (signal stimulus).

If you only practice the 'Sit' command on the dog-training field, for instance, your dog will only perfectly respond to this command in that location. The dog-training field is a discriminatory stimulus in this example. If you give the command in a completely different environment such as a busy city, your dog probably won't carry it out immediately. The discriminatory stimulus then isn't present to build up his expectation for the reward.

The same issue applies to other learning environments, e.g. practicing with and without a leash.

Dogs are very good at differentiating discriminatory stimuli. They can feel which collar they're wearing, which leash they're being walked on, and whether or not they're on the dog-training field. Discriminatory stimuli can be consciously employed to practice behavior under specific conditions. If a behavior needs to occur regardless of situation, the learning needs to be generalized (see Page 175, "Situational learning and generalization").

Discriminatory stimuli can be used to engage dogs in place-specific behaviors. If your dog is only allowed to take food from the dog-training field and never from the street, for instance, you can use the dog-training field as a discriminatory stimulus: You can offer him food or search games while he's here and so interact with him on a positive basis.

The relationship that you build up with your dog through positive interaction is a prerequisite for efficient conditioning. If your dog sees you as a threat or rival, you won't be able to reward him. He may perceive your presence as something negative, so conditioning with positive reinforcement will be impossible.

Learning through conditioning

If you're going to successfully and permanently condition behavior patterns with positive reinforcement, i.e. learning by success, you need to know what a dog understands as success. It's therefore important to know your dog's needs. Only when he sees the prospect of his behavior leading to a benefit or a positive experience will he be glad to show this behavior and similarly keen to repeat it. You can use this simple learning method to make your dog show various behaviors on command. The method also allows you to teach him behaviors without him being consciously aware that learning is taking place.

Your dog will learn habits and routines that show him when drive satisfaction is likely without you having to consciously teach these to him. This often gives the impression that a dog is cheating us, tricking us, or shamelessly using every situation for his own benefit. In reality, he's only doing what he's learned.

You can't teach your dog not to do something. He can't do nothing on command or follow a command that doesn't require a final action. He knows that stop signals mean that he should refrain from something, but doesn't know how to act instead. This means that he isn't learning any behavior. Your dog should always know what action you expect of him when you use a command, as only then can he know how to behave in order to receive his reward.

The process for conditioning your dog with a behavior follows a simple pattern.

The stimulus (command) triggers expectation of a positive consequence (reward). The action that your dog then shows is simply his means of receiving the desired reward.

Let's consider begging as an example of the successful conditioning of an undesirable behavior. The triggering stimulus might be the smell of food on the table. This stimulus forms an expectation of drive satisfaction in your dog, as he's already experienced drive satisfaction in similar situations. Success for him is now satisfaction of his food drive. His begging (e.g. whining, pawing, barking) is made up of actions that have helped him to win drive satisfaction in the past or that are likely to help him in this circumstance. He was probably rewarded with food from the table when he showed these behaviors previously, so he's learned that these behaviors lead to success. He's also

Learning through conditioning

successful again this time, as you subconsciously reward his behavior with food from the table and so provide him with drive satisfaction.

This example doesn't mean that a dog can never be given treats from your food. I often give my dogs something from table, but never if they beg.

An example of conditioning a desired behavior can be seen with the 'Sit' command. The stimulus here is an auditory or visual command, which in turn creates expectation of drive satisfaction. Your dog then demonstrates the required action by sitting down, and subsequently has his expectation satisfied by being given a food or prey reward. The behavior is then strengthened, leading the dog to repeat this behavior whenever he notices the command in the future.

Both of these examples show the simplicity of conditioning either a desired or an undesired behavior. Although it may sound trite, the biggest problem for humans and dogs living together remains mutual understanding. You and your dog may as well come from different planets, so your means of communication are very dissimilar.

A dog doesn't know spoken language like us humans. Our dogs understand us by watching us in unclear situations, working out our intentions through our body language, and interpreting impulses from us that prompt them to demonstrate certain behaviors. These behaviors mostly serve the aim of need satisfaction.

In contrast, we humans feel the need to verbally communicate with our four-legged friends. We do this because it's how we've learned to communicate with our other social partners. It's not too simple for us to change our communication method; we first need to learn how to do so. We often speak to our dogs in full sentences and think that they understand us. If they don't get what we mean, we speak louder and express ourselves as if we were talking to a small child. A dog isn't a small child, so he won't understand what we're saying regardless of how often we say it in this manner.

It's best to put yourself in a dog's position by watching people who speak another language talk to their dogs. You won't understand a word of what

Learning through conditioning

they're saying, and you also won't be able to work out from their behavior exactly what they want their dogs to do. It makes sense that their dogs similarly won't understand what's required of them.

It's common for a dog to do something when we speak to him, but if his action isn't what we want, we're quick to say: "He knows exactly what I want him to do". No, he really doesn't. A dog won't do what he's supposed to do if we can't let him know what we want.

> **We humans claim to be the most intelligent creatures on Earth, so rather than expecting our dogs to learn our language, we need to learn their language instead.**

Here's a short example to make clear how a dog learns from your body language.

You see a married couple in the distance. They're arguing, but you can't hear what's being said. You can assess the situation correctly because you're able to subconsciously notice indications of rage or aggression in both people. These indications include hand gestures, head movements, stooped posture and abrupt or threatening hand movements. Many of these indications present you with an overall picture of the situation. You haven't heard a word, but you still know that the people are having an argument. You can assess the situation correctly without needing to hear what's being said.

Your dog reads situations in exactly the same way. In the wild, dogs communicate almost exclusively through body language. A dog's perception is therefore directed much more toward our body language, whereas humans have learned to pay most attention to spoken language.

Dogs use their whole bodies to be understood. Everything is used for communication, from the ears right down to the tail. They instinctively notice many more signals in their counterparts than we humans notice in ours. They don't just notice posture: Your dog will register movement patterns, speed, rhythm, breathing, hand movements, eye and mouth movements, foot position, head posture, vocalizations and body odor. He'll then connect the overall picture that's afforded by all of these impressions with the prevailing situation. If he finds himself in the same scenario in the future and was previously rewarded for behavior in that situation, he'll now repeat that behavior once more. If he has a choice between several actions, he'll ultimately opt for the action that promises him the greatest benefit.

The stimulus that your dog needs to demonstrate a successfully conditioned behavior should ideally always be the same. This is one of the most difficult tasks given its evident complexity. You should always behave clearly from your dog's perspective, as he considers a 'Sit' in a normal voice to be a different command from a 'Sit' that's yelled. It's not just the volume that's different, but also the manner in which you behave. You're usually angry when you yell and will subconsciously show this anger through your body language. Your movements will become more frantic and impulsive.

Your dog can't understand the content of the word 'Sit'. All he can do is associate your behavior, body language and vocalization with what you want him to do.

A command doesn't just consist of an auditory or visual signal, but is rather the overall picture of the respective situation. The more similar a command's overall picture, the more easily your dog will learn that command. You should therefore pay attention to maintaining consistent body language and speech. Use clear terms that you preferably don't employ on an everyday basis. Think up your own commands, perhaps by saying the words in a foreign language or by only using a visual sign. Your dog will then have a clear indication as to when a command is addressed to him.

Use canine commands instead of human commands. A human command such as 'Stay here' will always carry emotion because it contains content, a call or a desire. It's particularly in critical situations that emotionally laden commands will lead to your dog not doing what you expect of him, as it's in such situations that your signal will be different. Our emotions determine the correct execution of a command, not the command itself. If you use the phrase 'Kumbaya' instead of 'Stay', for instance, the command will carry less emotion because you're not using it on an everyday basis and it doesn't have any

Learning through conditioning

meaning for you. The term acts purely as a command – like a switch on a television – and not as an expression of your state of mind.

As years go by, your dog will eventually learn that twenty different behavior patterns from you all really mean 'Sit'. Until this occurs, unclear signals will always cause him uncertainty.

If your dog masters the 'Sit' command within your home, this doesn't automatically mean that he'll immediately act in the same way when outside.

Your dog learns in accordance with the situation that he's in. As well as watching your behavior, he also observes external circumstances and has to bring all of this information together with your command. If the environmental stimuli change, he may have to relearn a command that he already knows so as to remember it in the new situation. He'll only generalize your signal when you've practiced the behavior in a variety of situations (see Page 175, "Situational learning and generalization").

A behavior that you desire for your dog doesn't need to consist of just a single movement. He's actually able to learn complete movement patterns if doing so means that he'll find success. On the one hand, this presents you with the opportunity to teach him complex behaviors such as fetching. On the other hand, he can also learn actions that you don't want him to demonstrate.

Always praise your dog immediately, because once he's laid down, for instance, there's the risk that he'll get back up again a short while later. He's learned that he's given a reward for lying down, and not for staying in that position. If he wants to get a reward, he now needs to get up so that you can place him back down and then acknowledge his successful completion of the command. He doesn't want to annoy you with his behavior, but he's only learned what you've taught him – even if the result isn't exactly what you'd intended. Your dog learns complex behavior patterns, intervals and routines to find success. Even after you've acknowledged a behavior, he may show that behavior again so as to demand further acknowledgement. You should consequently always watch him carefully and differentiate between desired and undesired behavior patterns if he demands a reward. Avoid rewarding him if he's demanded the reward, even if the behavior that he demonstrates is fundamentally correct in that moment. Consider that your dog isn't doing what he's doing for you, but rather because he has a goal: His need satisfaction.

Conditioning passive behavior

You can also condition passive behavior. The dog won't perform any action here, but will instead simply behave as your desire.

If you're sitting in a café and your dog is lying in a relaxed manner next to your chair, for example, his behavior corresponds to your expectations in that moment even though he isn't actively doing anything. If you want him to show this passive behavior on a more regular basis, he'll gladly do so if this action benefits him. You should therefore praise your dog when he behaves in a way that you desire. He'll then choose to demonstrate this behavior again in the future, even if he might be more distracted at that time.

It's not important for the reward to follow straight after the action with this form of conditioning. Your dog can always be rewarded for what he's doing if he continues to demonstrate the desired behavior. When you're next in a café, he'll then find it advantageous to lie next to your chair and remain in this position.

There are also known stimulus-response patterns with passive conditioning. The stimulus in this instance isn't an auditory or visual signal, but rather a reference point such as a table, the floor of a café or background noise. If your dog notices one of these stimuli, he'll face a decision about how to behave. If lying under the table brought him a benefit previously, he'll now be glad to lie under the table once more. He'll also find it easier to choose the desired behavior than he did in the past.

The conditioning of passive behavior has a considerably more far-reaching influence on a dog's behavior patterns than is perhaps obvious at first glance. This is because everything that he does, every behavior that he demonstrates, and every option that's awaiting a decision in his head are all influenced by the size of the advantage that he can potentially obtain.

Learning through conditioning

If your dog lies in the middle of your hallway from where he can see the whole house, for instance, he's chosen this position because it provides him with the greatest advantage over everyone else.

There are three factors that influence his decision once again: Stimulus, response and advantage. The territory, so your home, is the stimulus. He's then faced with the decision as to which lying position to choose.

Even if the floor is less comfortable than anywhere else, this position is where it's easiest for him to monitor the whole house. He never needs to get up and always has a clear picture of what's happening in his territory. He'd certainly like to lie somewhere more comfortable, but monitoring his territory is currently more important to him. He therefore has the option of constantly getting up from a comfortable place or positioning himself so that he can see everything with only minimal effort.

12.2 It's not what you say, but rather how you say it

If you want to condition your dog to perform an active behavior pattern when he's given an auditory signal, you place yourself at considerable danger of conveying emotions through your voice. Whether your dog carries out the command will then depend on your mood and not on the command itself. If he recognizes from your voice that you're rather hostile, for example, he'll find it more difficult to respond to a recall command than if you always give your command with the same pitch. Experienced dog trainers are able to give auditory commands that always sound the same and exclude moods and feelings. It's otherwise unimportant whether you use a loud, soft, deep or high voice. What's crucial is that the command always sounds the same to the dog.

Avoid giving your dog commands in whole sentences. Use short or succinct words or sounds instead, and ensure that they don't appear in your everyday speech. This will make it considerably easier for him to recognize and distinguish between your commands. Remain natural and calm at all times, and use a consistent tone to show that you have everything under control – especially in critical situations.

12.3　Using rewards for learning success

Behavior needs to be rewarded if your dog is to recognize and repeat it. When you acknowledge a behavior with a reward, the frequency with which your dog will independently repeat this behavior will increase. Acknowledgement doesn't teach your dog what's right and what's wrong, however, as he has no moral or legal understanding. He doesn't care about whether a behavior is right or wrong from a human perspective. He equally won't question a behavior so long as it remains worth his while to demonstrate it. Rewards simply influence the probability that a dog will demonstrate a behavior pattern in a manner that we desire.

You should always be the one to acknowledge your dog for a desired behavior. You should be the center of his world, and he should associate everything that's positive with you. This is also why you should always be close to him when you give him rewards. If he learns to reward himself, the rewards that you offer will lose their value. A dog can reward himself by satisfying his prey drive, for instance. The best example of this is a ball game. The throwing of the ball triggers his chase and prey drives. When he's a long way away from you and 'catches' his prey by grabbing the ball, he ends up rewarding himself. He may possibly bring the ball back to you, but only so that you can throw it again and he can reward himself once more. Such behavior is often interpreted as an invitation to play, but your dog really wants to play with his prey and not with you. If the ball could move by itself, he wouldn't need you at all. It isn't you providing him with satisfaction here: He's providing his own satisfaction by grabbing the ball at a long distance away from you. It'd be very easy for you to be replaced by a machine.

A dog sees a reward as everything that satisfies a need. We often use strokes or appreciative slaps on the back as rewards. Before you acknowledge your dog with touch, however, confirm that he really perceives touch as a reward. Many dogs consider being touched by a hand as neutral, and some will even avoid such touches. In these instances, you first need to show your dog that a touch is a positive experience. Connect touches with positive experiences so that you can use them as rewards during your everyday dealings with him.

Learning through conditioning

Touch as a reward

A dog feels a touch in very different ways depending on the situation. If he's 'on the job' and busy with territory monitoring, marking or dealing with other dogs, your touch may not interest him and may even disturb him. You'd probably also find physical closeness to be rather annoying if you were faced with it while managing some difficult tasks at work. Once your dog has finished for the day and completed all of his tasks, he'll then be able to feel your touches in a positive manner.

Don't assume that your dog likes your touches at all times and all over his body. You similarly won't always find other people's touches to be pleasant. Only he knows how he perceives human touches. Unlike for humans, caressing doesn't satisfy any of a dog's needs. This form of body contact doesn't exist with other dogs in the wild, let alone with other species.

You can nevertheless be certain that he doesn't feel touches in the same way as us. You can see whether he perceives them in a positive manner if, for instance, he demands more touches when you stop stroking him. But don't confuse his attempts to reassure you with an invitation. A dog will often display reassurance signals when you stop stroking him, e.g. after a greeting. Your dog has learned that you're in a friendly mood when you stroke him, and he therefore understands this moment clearly. If you stop stroking him, he'll become uncertain and may begin to show reassurance signals once more. He isn't looking to be touched at this point, but rather for a sign to let him know that everything's okay.

If your dog reacts to your touches with reluctance or uncertainty, you can try to condition his negative emotion into a positive emotion. He'll then see your touches as something positive in the future. You'll need to do this by connecting touches with the experience of drive satisfaction. Feed him from your open hand, and while you're satisfying his food drive, begin to stroke him in an ever-increasing manner. He'll then connect the feeling of his food experience with your touch, and will later perceive your touches in a positive light.

12.4 Why do we praise our dogs?

Our dogs similarly don't recognize the spoken word. They don't require verbal recognition or praise because they haven't developed a need that can be satisfied in this manner. This also means that language can't be used to reward them.

So why do we constantly praise our dogs?

Praise that's given to our dogs when they demonstrate a desired behavior can't be equated with praise that's given to a human. We understand praise as meaning social acknowledgment, appreciation of our performance, and confirmation of our social position within the community. It satisfies our human need for recognition. Our dogs don't possess this need.

The verbal praise that we direct to our dogs is a conditioned acknowledgment, and it triggers expectation of a reward within them. Our praise announces the reward.

It's only our reward of food or prey (toys) that satisfies a dog's expectation. If you don't provide him with the expected reward, you fail to satisfy his needs and so interact with him in negative terms.

Your verbal reward will eventually lose its meaning if you fail to provide him with his expected reward for an extended period. It isn't your verbal praise that's the reward, after all, but rather the food or the toy. Your dog will subsequently lose his motivation for carrying out the associated action. It's no longer worth his while to demonstrate the behavior when you demand it.

Your dog will be just as glad to accept your reward if you give it to him without a verbal announcement.

12.5 Food or toys as rewards?

Whether you use food or toys as rewards shouldn't depend on your dog alone.

Food has many advantages over prey (toys) as a means of reward. A dog considers his food drive to be of much more significance than his prey or chase drives. This is because food is the primary goal of his drive to hunt prey.

All dogs can be fed, but it isn't advisable to promote every dog's hunting drive for the purpose of using prey as a reward. Food drive is simple to promote and monitor, and food itself is simple to give out in regulated amounts.

Prey and chase drives require more from a dog because they place him into a stronger state of excitement. When you want to work on new exercises, you'll now have to reduce this excitement level so as to gain his full concentration. The dog will therefore become more difficult to control and more easily distracted. Hunting drive similarly can't be given out in regulated amounts once it's been triggered.

Prey and chase work can additionally lead to your dog no longer limiting his prey-catching behavior to his toys. It won't take long for him to generalize the stimulus triggers if you promote the behavior with throwing games that use various prey items such as sticks, kongs, balls or food bags. He then won't differentiate between a ball, a hare, a deer, or maybe even a child's arm. If he learns that he can satisfy his drive with anything that moves, he won't care what the object is.
Your dog can quickly become a danger to other animals and humans if you have no control over his hunting drive.
You should only reward learning successes with prey if you've recognized this consequence but still consciously want to promote hunting drive in your dog.

It's important for conditioning that you control the resources that you use to reward your dog. This means that acknowledgment should only come from you. If you're using food as a means of acknowledgment, give it to him from your hand. If you're using prey and you want to prevent the development of your dog's chase drive, use multiple prey items and place them into his mouth instead of throwing them. Once again, all you're doing is offering a reward. If he doesn't want to accept it, you can't praise him in this manner.

If you offer your dog prey, it's often necessary to develop his prey drive in advance so that he builds up the necessary expectation. Use a new prey item for every exercise. Your dog will soon ignore the prey item from the last exercise once you awaken his interest in the new item.

If you throw prey items away from yourself as a means of acknowledgment, be aware that he won't associate these items with you because he's chasing and grabbing them by himself. This means of acknowledgment promotes independent and self-rewarding hunting. His bond to you and dependence on you will then be less pronounced than if he were only to receive rewards directly from you and when close to you.

12.6　How do I build up food drive?

If you want to motivate your dog with food, he needs to see food as a reward. You can increase food's value by deliberately building up his food drive.

Food drive is inborn and is critical for your dog's motivation to eat. A dog can't exist without food drive.

Food drive can be separated into two components. The first is appetite, which is the sheer desire for food regardless of actual hunger. Appetite develops in the limbic system and, as a cognitive-motivational event, is strongly influenced by sensory perceptions. A food's appearance, smell, taste, temperature and consistency all play important roles as a result. Since appetite isn't controlled by the body's hunger center in the hypothalamus, it's possible to want food even when you're not hungry. The same reason explains how you may not want a certain food even when you are hungry.

Dogs with little or even no appetite and sheer desire for food will only eat when they're genuinely hungry. The feeling of hunger is unpleasant, so a dog that feels it will be far less picky than a dog that only feels his appetite. Hunger is the need to eat to be full.

Learning through conditioning

If your dog has a constant urge to eat, ask yourself whether he's feeling genuine hunger or just his appetite. We humans tend to eat more than is necessary because we have appetite but no real hunger.

A dog with a less pronounced food drive will usually have either very little or no appetite. He'll only eat when he's hungry, so he won't want food if he's already full up. It's only when he feels hunger that he'll develop an urge for food and be prepared to do something to satisfy this need.

If you want to build up food drive in your dog, reduce his daily food ration or give him his entire daily ration during exercises. You can also introduce a fasting day for him before you begin to train with food. You shouldn't do this if your dog is still growing.

If you currently have fixed feeding times for your dog, you can now give these up. His food drive will automatically increase if you feed him at irregular intervals. Since there are then no fixed feeding times from which he can take direction, he'll begin to take food whenever it's given.

You're not in control of the food resource if it's the clock that determines when food is given. Your dog will soon learn his feeding times and will demand food from you when these times come around if you don't stick to the schedule. All that you're then determining is when his fixed feeding times occur and how much food is given out. It's completely normal for most creatures to manage without food for a certain period. A healthy dog can manage for three weeks without any food at all. A permanent surplus of food is actually unnatural for a dog, and this is important because his metabolism controls many biological and hormonal processes that are directly related to how much food he consumes.

Irregular feeding times are far from unnatural for a dog. He also doesn't have to eat until he's full at every meal. In the wild, prey doesn't run past and place itself in a bowl every morning at 7 am and every evening at 6 pm. Regular feeding times are just as unnatural for a dog as they are for a human.

Adjusting your dog's feeding habits will strongly develop his food drive. You can then use this drive so that he sees food as a reward and is motivated to demonstrate desired behavior.

The stronger your dog's urge for food, the more prepared he'll be to do things in return for food.

You'll soon realize what value your dog places on food if you offer it to him during his daily walk. If territory monitoring and marking behavior are more important to him than accepting your offer, his urge for food isn't yet sufficiently developed. The same applies if he doesn't respond to your recall command despite having learned that every recall is rewarded with food: Food doesn't yet hold the significance for him that it should. In the wild, a dog would drop everything if he knew that you'd provide him with food in abundance.

Only your dog can decide whether or not he wants food. If he doesn't, he currently has access to too much food. You should therefore reduce his amount of food or stop feeding him altogether until his food drive has developed. Food should be his highest priority, as he'll then see sense in demonstrating behavior in return for the prospect of a reward. The more value your dog places on food, the more easily and quickly he'll learn and the keener he'll be to demonstrate learned behavior. If he places no value on food, you'll be lacking an important means of interacting with him on a positive basis.

You should proceed with particular caution if you want to develop food drive in a dog that demonstrates fearful behavior. Dogs won't accept food while they're afraid, so their food drive can't be developed while they're in this state. Fear will often also reinforce a dog's control behavior, making him refuse food and become difficult to motivate while he's in unfamiliar areas. If you have such a dog, train him in familiar surroundings where he isn't afraid and first help him to overcome his fears (see Page 225, "

Learning through conditioning

Managing fear").

It's important not to overlook what you can feed your dog for motivational purposes. A dog will usually prefer food with a stronger smell to food that's dry. The richer a food smells, the more popular it will normally be with a dog. Most people therefore choose wet food over dry food. If you can't tempt your dog with prepared food, boiled chicken meat or cheese will generally help you along. You can use cheese in small amounts during exercises, but it shouldn't constitute the main part of his daily food ration.

It's very difficult to develop food drive in some dogs to such an extent that the drive provides them with a real alternative to undesirable behavior. Dogs with a pronounced hunting drive that have had prior hunting success may never completely enter into a dependent relationship with humans, for instance. These dogs have learned to reward themselves and provide food for themselves via their self-conditioned behavior. In other words, they've learned to control the food resource. There's no reason for them to give up this privilege and enter into a situation of dependence. Wolf hybrids act in a similar manner. These crosses often have very strongly pronounced primal drives that usually make submission impossible – regardless of the fantastic treats that you hold before their noses.

12.7   Developing prey drive

If you want to use prey (toys) to reward your dog during training, it makes sense to encourage the drives that increase his desire for prey.
Prey games are usually sufficient for encouraging his chase drive. A flirt pole is generally very good for this purpose.
A flirt pole is a rod with a cord attached to one end and a leather rag tied to the free end of the cord. You can encourage your dog to hunt for the leather rag by moving the rod. Always practice outdoors and in distraction-free surroundings. Prey games can trigger competitive behavior, so there should be no other dogs in sight.
The leather rag serves as the prey replacement. Start by standing in a fixed position and slowly turning in circles while dragging the flirt pole's prey in front of your dog. He'll normally begin to hunt the leather rag at this point.

Constantly increase his desire by pulling the prey away before he can grab it. You'll proverbially drive him up the wall after just a few minutes.

His drive will now have reached such a point that he'll see the prey as a reward. A dog's prey drive will always be accompanied by a certain level of aggression that needs to be built up if he's to catch prey in the wild. This aggression causes adrenaline to be released.

Adrenaline is a stress hormone, and it acts like a stimulant within his circulatory system. When your dog is exposed to adrenaline he'll become wide-awake, belligerent and more tolerant of pain. This highly driven state of excitement will only reduce on a gradual basis, so most dogs remain ready to hunt and are difficult to calm down for a long while after an exercise has ended. Such a state of excitement isn't advantageous for all exercises. The long duration of your dog's excitement will also cause him to quickly associate a situation with a drive trigger. His prey drive may then subsequently develop when you simply approach your training area or find yourself in a similar situation. This excitement is often interpreted as pleasure, but it really causes a dog stress and is just an expression of his learned expectation. He's preparing for the hunt as soon as he detects signs that a chase is imminent. His concentration is equally likely to suffer a result of his excitement, as he'll tend to be fixated on prey instead of on humans.

12.8 Is acknowledgment a sufficient reward?

If you don't have any prey or food to hand, the question arises as to whether acknowledgment also constitutes a reward for a dog.

If your dog has recognized your leadership role and has submitted to you, he'll be eager to please you as his leading animal. He'll want to avoid provoking you simply because he knows that you're superior to him. In a dog's world, disobedience is a form of provocation. It's therefore possible to motivate your dog without food or prey merely due to the fact that he doesn't want to provoke you.

Such motivation isn't a truly positive means of interacting with him, however. His expectations are fulfilled if he responds to your commands, but these expectations weren't of anything positive. He's responded to your commands only with the expectation of not provoking you and so thereby avoiding penalties.

Learning through conditioning

Whether your dog's efforts to please you are sufficient to act as rewards in any situation is strongly dependent on his character and his willingness to submit. It'll certainly be easier for him to follow commands that he's learned in this manner when he's surrounded by few distractions – versus when he's affected by numerous external influences, e.g. street traffic, playing children or strange dogs.

12.9 How do I reduce rewards?

Once your dog understands what behavior you expect of him, it's time to gradually reduce the frequency of his rewards. When doing this, be aware that he can perceive your actions as a punishment if he's suddenly no longer rewarded for demonstrating a correct behavior. It's therefore important to reduce the rewards in a slow and incremental manner. Vary the intensity of the rewards for behavior patterns that are important to you. In future, a recall signal should be more intensively rewarded than a 'Sit' command that's given in an unimportant situation. The prospect of drive satisfaction will then be sufficient for your dog to demonstrate a desired behavior when he's instructed to do so. You should nevertheless retain the reward in between 80 and 90% of cases.

If you fail to give a reward for a long period, your dog will at some point cease to see any point in following your command (see Page 242, "Extinction"). The frequency with which he'll show the learned behavior will then decrease.

Acknowledge desired behavior randomly and without any discernable pattern. You'll then maintain the necessary level of expectation in your dog on a permanent basis. This form of acknowledgment is referred to as 'random intermittent reinforcement'.

Intermittent reinforcement is one of the most effective techniques in operant conditioning. It's therefore also an important element in the conditioning of your dog. As he now won't be able to reliably anticipate reinforcement, he'll try harder to demonstrate correct behavior and will be markedly less likely to forget behavior that he's already learned.

Learning through conditioning

Vary the form in which you give rewards. Use food or touch on an alternating basis to acknowledge desired behavior.

I reward every command when I work with dogs. This method doesn't follow intermittent reinforcement, but it has proven effective because the dogs can rely on always receiving a reward. To balance matters out, I don't use commands very often at all.

A command is nothing more than an announcement of food. If I use hundreds of commands each day, I need intermittent reinforcement so that my rewards don't lose their value. If I only use three commands each week, each command is like winning the lottery for the dog. No one would pass up that reward.

12.10 How does a dog learn new commands?

Now that you know how to motivate your dog, the next question concerns how you can get him to demonstrate desirable behavior.

Your dog learns in the most efficient manner when he can acquire the necessary learning experiences independently, voluntarily, and without violence or pressure. The first thing that your dog should learn is that you'll satisfy his needs if he demonstrates the behavior that you demand. He'll only develop a willingness to learn once he's gained this experience. I'd always start off with the simplest of all commands: The recall.

Recalling your dog

There shouldn't strictly be any reason to recall your dog. If he doesn't return to you voluntarily, you need to urgently work on your status and your relationship with your four-legged friend. You should first consider the following questions: What does my dog find more interesting than me? What reason does he have for running away from me? What should induce him to come over to me?

It's helpful in some situations if your dog will gladly – and primarily always – return to you when he's given an auditory signal. Examples of such signals in this context include 'Come', 'Here', and simply the dog's name. Always use one

Learning through conditioning

and the same command when you recall your dog in future, and only use this command for this purpose.

Begin by training your dog somewhere with few distractions, e.g. in your home. When you first start, it'll usually be sufficient to crouch down when your dog is a few meters away from you. As you don't normally crouch down, he'll generally come over to you of his own accord because he's interested in the situation. Reward him as soon as he reaches you. Once you've repeated this exercise a few times, he'll connect your posture (crouching) with food and so come running over to you as soon as you bend your knees. You've now successfully conditioned a behavior to your body language. You can subsequently introduce an auditory signal to the exercise. Always give the signal when you crouch down.

Embed this experience through constant repetition. As you do so, gradually increase your distance away from your dog. If he no longer wants to leave your side, ask a partner to hold him on a leash so that you can get further away. An incredibly strong expectation will now build up within him when you crouch down. Your partner should hold him back for a short period and then release the leash so that he can run to you. The holding period will increase his willingness to act and the speed with which he responds. Over time, you'll be able to slowly reduce your body language and instead focus the exercise on the auditory or visual signal.

Practice the exercise in different situations with gradually increasing levels of distraction. If your dog has already developed other pronounced drives, the incentive to return to you will need to be much stronger than anything else, e.g. the prospect of hunting success. The incentive has to be very strong because your dog will be faced with a decision as to which need to satisfy. He'll have to back away from drive satisfaction that might be right in front of his nose, and instead come all the way back to you so as to first satisfy his food drive. If his chase drive is very pronounced, for instance, your recall will always need to present him with the prospect of winning the jackpot.

It's not possible to condition a reliable recall signal in all dogs through reward alone. A dog that's already had hunting success will have learned to satisfy his

Learning through conditioning

hunting drive by himself. It'll then be difficult for you to condition a reliable recall signal with positive reinforcement.

Note that behavior patterns that are solely conditioned with positive reinforcement will never be carried out with 100% reliability. Your command is simply an offer to your dog that he can accept if he wants the reward. If other things are currently more important to him than the reward, he won't accept your offer and your command will fade away into nothingness. You should therefore never rely on a command, especially when faced with critical situations.

You can condition additional commands if your dog knows that benefits may follow when you demand behaviors.

If you want your dog to learn new commands, use the prospect of a reward to playfully encourage him to show you a desired behavior of his own accord. Do this by moving with the reward in your hand and inviting him to move as well. He should follow the hand that contains the food. You can use this method to prompt him into displaying certain movements and actions.

For the 'Down' command, take a piece of food in your hand and let your dog smell this reward. Now begin to move with the piece of food still in your hand. Your dog will instinctively follow the piece of food with his snout. Next place the hand with the food onto the floor in front of him. Close your hand around the food as you do this. He'll try to get to the food with his snout, and at some point he'll lay down his legs so as to better reach the food. You can reward this behavior as a preliminary stage in the 'Down' exercise. Your dog will later lie down fully, and you should immediately reward him for doing this by releasing the food from your hand. Repeat the exercise until your dog understands that he'll receive food for lying down as soon as your food-containing hand points toward the floor.

You can encourage desired behaviors equally well by watching for when your dog demonstrates these behaviors in everyday situations. If he sits down by himself when you reach a set of traffic lights, for instance, simply reward this behavior if you want him to do the same going forward. It'll then only take a

Learning through conditioning

few repetitions for him to gladly sit down whenever you reach street crossings in future, and to do this without being given a command.

You can introduce visual and auditory signals to an exercise once your dog is more certain about carrying out a command. Use as few auditory signals as possible. Your dog will then be significantly more attentive toward you and will establish eye contact far more often with you than if you were to bombard him with verbal commands. It'll be more difficult to gain his eye contact and attention if he's already learned to react exclusively to auditory signals. From his perspective, the prospect of a reward only exists when you give him an auditory signal. It therefore makes little sense for him to make regular eye contact with you or to look around for you. In reality, you can completely dispense with auditory signals in everyday life with just a few exceptions. It's possible to give your dog any command that he needs to perform in your immediate vicinity with visual signals or just your body language. A prerequisite here is that your dog has no visual impairment.

You can use your dog's natural appetitive behavior to refine behaviors. If you hold back an expected reward, he'll repeat the associated learned behavior and include slight variations in the repetitions. He'll also show variations on what he's already learned if you change your posture somewhat. You can then decide which version of the action you want to encourage by only releasing the reward when he behaves in the way that you desire.

It's incredibly important to correctly assess the period for which you can hold back the reward without your dog demonstrating a completely different behavior. If you hold back the reward for too long, he'll change to an entirely separate behavior because he won't have found success with what he's already shown. He may demonstrate a behavior that you've rewarded in another exercise.

He may also interpret your holding back a reward as a punishment. This can make him uncertain and cause him to question what he's already learned. Practice actions that he's already mastered in these situations, as these behaviors will help him to regain his self-confidence.

Before you begin an exercise, set down very clear criteria for what your dog must do to successfully complete the exercise and so receive the reward. Always use the same scale to assess his performance on an exercise. He'll find it difficult to please you if you reward several factors on a single exercise, e.g. speed, attention, exact execution and just giving you a sweet look. He won't ultimately know why he's received his reward.

Don't ask the impossible of your dog and don't expect miracles. If you want him to come to you, praise him as soon as he's with you. He'll then have successfully completed the exercise. Don't expect him to also sit or lie down right from the start. These are all separate exercises that should be gradually trained and built on top of one another.

Conditioning makes mental demands of your dog. It can therefore be very tiring for him, just like it is for us humans. Mental occupation is important for maintaining a dog's mental capacity, because – again like in humans – areas of his brain that aren't used or needed are subject to degeneration. His mental fitness will sooner or later decrease if he isn't provided with mental challenge.

Fetching

You can train your dog to fetch so that he learns to return objects to you. The exercise consists of many small individual components that together make up what fetching really is. All complex training exercises are realizable if they're split up into individual components that are then trained separately.

Begin the training at home if possible (within your home or in the garden) and only move further afield once your dog has mastered the exercise. Numerous unexpected stimuli could otherwise disrupt your training or even render it impossible.

Fetching is a very complex task for a dog, so you need a training area where he won't face any distractions. He should have straight, empty routes ahead of him.

Kneel down and direct your dog's attention to the object that's to be fetched. This could be a wooden retrieving dumbbell, a prey toy or a food bag. You

Learning through conditioning

should typically start out by using objects that he likes to hunt, play with or have in his mouth.

Throw the object a few meters in the direction that you want him to run. Your dog's task will now be to simply chase and grab the prey item. If he doesn't yet have a pronounced chase drive, you'll need to activate this drive before beginning the fetching exercise (see Page 164, "Developing prey drive").

Once he's seized the prey item, the next challenge is encouraging him to bring it over to you. Test out various stimuli that normally cause him to come to you. Take a piece of food in your hand, for instance, and offer it to him while you crouch down. Show him that he can take the food from you. If he comes to you with the prey item in his mouth, swap him for it by offering the food as an alternative. If he drops the prey on his way to you, hook him up to a long leash and give it a gentle pull to show him where to head with his catch.

It's not unusual for a dog to drop what he fetches before coming back to you. You mustn't forget that you're a competitor for his prey and so he first needs to learn that it's advantageous for him to bring such items to you. The more difficulty your dog has with individual steps in the exercise, the more often you should repeat and reward partial successes.

Only use commands once your dog has understood the exercise. It doesn't matter whether you choose auditory or visual signals, and the actual signals that you use are unimportant. All you should ensure is that your signals are clear and easy to distinguish from one another. If you're already using 'Come' as a recall signal, for instance, don't use the same signal when you want your dog to bring something over to you. You might instead choose to say 'Bring' or another common auditory signal such as 'Fetch'. The normal command for telling a dog to drop a prey item is 'Leave it'.

Practice without any vocalizations before you condition commands. This will allow your dog to focus solely on his own and your actions. The more stimuli he encounters during an exercise, the more difficultly he'll have in understanding what the exercise involves. Instead of using vocalizations, direct your energy toward observing him and praising him at the correct moments.

12.11   Everyday life without commands

You need to refrain from using commands as much as possible if your dog is to become well integrated into your everyday life.

Reduce the number of commands that you give on a daily basis and instead concentrate on acknowledging desired behavior that he's already demonstrating of his own accord.

Is he receives rewards for behavior that he's already showing, he'll gladly and frequently show this behavior in future even without being given a command.

The difference between this behavior and a command is that a command provides your dog with no choice. He has to obey because he doesn't want to provoke you. If he demonstrates a behavior independently, he's the one making the choice to act in this manner.

How did you feel as a child when someone constantly ordered you around?

> *'Come in! Take your jacket off! Sit down! Take the trash out! Leave that alone! Lie down! Be quiet!'*

Don't command your dog to do anything that isn't urgently required. I'm sure that you wouldn't want to be treated any differently.

Be clear about what you expect from your dog. If he's supposed to sit down at every street crossing, it's more than sufficient to reward him for correct behavior. You don't need a command for this purpose. Stand at a set of traffic lights and watch your dog. If you need to wait for a while before you can safely cross the street, he'll sit down at some point of his own accord. All you need is a little patience. When you come to another street crossing, wait until he demonstrates the desired behavior and then reward him for doing so straight away. If he doesn't act in the correct manner, hold food in your hand and use this hand to direct him into showing the movement that you want to see.

You can use the same approach in every other situation that you frequently encounter during your everyday life. Whether you meet acquaintances on the street, walk past other dogs, have cyclists ride toward you, sit in a restaurant or anything else: Your dog will gladly, voluntarily and often show behavior that you acknowledge. You can even condition him as to when and where to relieve himself. Every dog does this independently at some point in any case. If you provide acknowledgment at the right moment and condition the behavior to a signal, your dog will later watch out for your indication before relieving himself.

You should nevertheless always consider whether and why you require behavior from your dog. If you don't have a reason to demand behavior, refrain from using commands. Why does your dog need to sit down at street crossings, for example? Do you sit down at every intersection? Of course you don't – so why should he?

In reality I use just a single command for each dog. This command is the dog's name. If a dog hears his name, he knows that he can collect food from me. I only call the dogs very occasionally, so this command also works if I ever have a real reason to require it.

12.12 Acknowledgment using a clicker or 'Good boy'

Clicker training is based on a method of using a conditioned amplifier to acknowledge desired behavior and announce a reward. The clicker is a bridging signal: It connects a desired behavior with a reward. You operate a clicker by pressing down on a small metal plate to make a snapping sound. A clicker allows you to precisely acknowledge desired behavior. It was first used more than 30 years ago to condition dolphins, as it allowed exercises to be acknowledged without the trainer being particularly close to the animals.

Before you begin with clicker training, you first need to condition your dog to this form of acknowledgment. He needs to learn what effect the clicker's sound has on him. Teach this to him by simply pressing the clicker and then immediately offering him food. Repeat the exercise until he's understood that he can collect food from you whenever the clicker makes a sound. Don't push the food onto him, but rather create an offer for him. He can then decide whether or not to collect the reward. He needs to want to collect the reward whenever he hears a click.

Learning through conditioning

Once you've successfully conditioned the clicker, you'll be able to confirm desirable behavior in the exact second that it occurs. Follow this confirmation in the usual manner with food from your hand. It's no longer essential for the reward to immediately follow the desired behavior, as the acknowledgment will now have already been given by the clicking sound.

You'll need to try a clicker to see if it helps you in attaining better learning results. The most important part of acknowledging correct behavior is timing. You need to recognize the right point at which to give a reward, and a clicker can't relieve you of this task.

You can also condition a different auditory signal instead of the clicking sound, e.g. saying 'Good boy' or giving a whistle.

You'll often subconsciously allow a vocalization to slip out when your dog does something correctly or you're pleased with his learning success. Such vocalizations serve the same purpose as a clicker in this respect.

If you want to use a vocalization as a conditioned amplifier, ensure that you're always using the same vocalization or sound. Dogs have excellent hearing, so there's no need to shout this praise. If your dog doesn't respond to your vocalization, the issue lies with the reward's value and not its volume.

12.13 Situational learning and generalization

Dogs learn in various ways, e.g. via observation, imitation (learning from a model) and conditioning. Learning via observation and imitation are most common during puppyhood, whereas learning via conditioning takes place throughout a dog's life. Dogs always learn via conditioning in situational terms. If a certain situation is advantageous for them, they'll remember that this was the case.

A command announces a positive situation by arousing expectation of a reward. A dog sees a command as being made up of a variety of different stimuli. In addition to auditory or visual signals, your dog will also notice environmental stimuli that influence his current learning experience. These

Learning through conditioning

environmental stimuli could be the outside temperature, the weather, the time of day, the surface he's standing on, the location, your clothing, smells or noises.

When you train in different situations, the environmental stimuli alter depending on your surroundings. All that stays the same is the auditory or visual signal. Once you've repeated an exercise a few times under various conditions, your dog will learn that it's sufficient to respond to the auditory or visual signal if he wants to achieve success – and that the environmental stimuli aren't parts of the command.

12.14 Less is more

Learning success will become evident more quickly if you start out by limiting the stimuli that your dog has to process to the stimuli that concern the exercise. His learning experience will otherwise require him to process stimuli such as speech, environmental noises, traffic, smells, joggers and other dogs in addition to the actual task. He then won't be able to concentrate on the exercise because he won't yet know where to direct his focus. He needs to learn this beforehand. He'll include the entire situation in his learning experience, so the fewer additional signals he has to process, the easier it'll be for him to learn what you intend.

Your dog will be far more attentive if you use less language. You're forced to work actively with your body when you don't use your voice. You then automatically focus more closely on having clear body language, and this in turn makes you easier for your dog to understand.

12.15   The 'No' command

If you want to condition a stop signal, you first need to consider why you actually need this command. There's no such thing as a universal command for everything that we don't want. The 'No' command doesn't mean anything to a dog because it doesn't require him to demonstrate any particular action. While we expect him to stop doing something when we give this command, he isn't capable of doing nothing. He doesn't do anything without a reason, and he sees sense in the behavior that we find undesirable. He therefore won't understand why we want him to stop this behavior. 'No' doesn't teach a dog why he should stop what he's doing, but rather to avoid or suppress that action.

Imagine a small child at Christmas time. He's standing in the living room doorway and can see the Christmas tree and lots of gifts. He can't wait to start unwrapping, so he runs toward the tree, full of anticipation. There's suddenly a loud shout of 'No', and the child stops.

This is unfortunately where the story ends, because the 'No' command hasn't accomplished anything else. The child has stopped what he was doing, although he doesn't know why he's needed to do this. The command similarly hasn't reduced any of his motivation for unwrapping the gifts. It's instead just prevented him from satisfying his need, and has therefore constituted a negative interaction.

How can the story pan out differently if the 'No' command isn't used?

Imagine the situation again. The child is standing in the living room doorway, but he now knows that the presents under the tree belong to his parents and not to him. He won't have any motivation to run up to the tree, and no command will be necessary to prevent him from doing this. He instead sits down on the couch and is given one gift after another by his parents. His needs are met and a positive form of interaction takes place – all without the use of a command.

Learning through conditioning

Discard the 'No' command and instead take away your dog's motivation for developing problem behaviors. You then won't need any command to make him refrain from undesirable actions.

12.16   How can I cancel commands?

A dog should continue to perform a command for as long as that command remains valid. If he doesn't know the duration for which it should remain valid, he'll make his own decision about when to cancel the behavior that it requires. He'll only show this behavior again when it makes sense for him to do so. As an example, he may decide to cancel the 'Stay' command after three minutes if you don't cancel it for him. He'll then learn that he can decide when to cancel this command's behavior. His reliability for following the command in future will subsequently depend on his level of interest. Your dog will ultimately end up making decisions about matters over which you should really hold the decision-making authority. If you don't hold this authority, commands such as 'Stay' will make little sense.

You shouldn't just aim to induce a desired behavior when you give a command. You should instead aim to determine both the start and end of that respective action.

The start of a desired action will always follow soon after the command has been given. If the action needs to be performed for a set period of time, the end of the required behavior should also be marked with another command. This second command can be universally valid, so you don't need to establish something new for each exercise. The signal should be associated with an action so that your dog can identify what you expect from him.

We distinguish between commands that are valid for a set period of time (Time commands: 'Sit', 'Down', 'Stand') and commands that are only valid for a moment and so have no end point (Moment commands: 'Here', 'Go', 'Jump', 'Fetch').

It makes sense to use a moment command to cancel a time command. An exception arises if you want your dog to sit after he's been lying down, although you'll still need to use a moment command to finally cancel the sit. Examples of commands for cancelling a time command include 'Come' and 'Here'.

Practice cancelling time commands after gradually longer periods, as this will teach your dog to continue demonstrating the commands until you provide him with cancellation. If he cancels a time command of his own accord, give the command again and reduce the amount of time that you wait before providing cancellation.

12.17 For how long can I train?

Your dog can remain attentive for a long time and has the capacity to train for hours. As a working animal, he previously had to maintain a high level of concentration and carry out tasks over extensive periods.

The length of time for which he remains attentive and focused depends solely on his motivation. If he's motivated, he'll be glad to train for a very long while. You're responsible for his level of motivation, and therefore also for when he loses interest in exercises or begins to find other things more important.

Dogs continue to learn throughout their lives. No dog is ever too old to learn or be trained. An older dog will even be especially grateful if you show him that you're taking over responsibility for the pack and so allowing him to sit back during his sunset years.

13 What your voice means to a dog

We humans talk all day long. We speak to our friends, our partners, our birds, our plants, and especially our dogs. Humans can use language to convey a lot of information to other humans, but not to our dogs.

Our speaking abilities differentiate us from all other creatures. Richly varied language could only follow in the wake of anatomical changes over the course of human evolution. Ancient skulls prove that our palates only finished arching and our larynxes only finished lowering around 100,000 years ago. Our ability to understand language as well as to speak is similarly the result of our evolutionary development.

What your voice means to a dog

Language allows us to point out our experiences to other people when we undertake joint actions. Linguistic communication therefore contributes to the creation and advancement of community. Humans don't have to go through every essential experience first-hand, as we can instead share in other people's experiences.

Animals communicate through means such as body-language signals, scents, sounds and their colorings. The corresponding signals are usually fixed, so signals within the animal kingdom can't be readily combined to establish new meanings.

When we talk to our dogs

We can only guess at how our dogs perceive our spoken words. It's nonetheless a fact that they can't understand syntactical language.

They remain unable to understand the contents of words even if we associate these words with actions or objects. All they do is associate the words with a sequence of tonal sounds.

They interpret our vocalizations in accordance with the meanings that these vocalizations have within their worlds.

Dogs don't use their voices unless necessary. Something's wrong if a dog makes a sound. He'll bark as a warning of danger, for instance, or because he wants to drive rivals out of his territory. If he's stressed, he'll whine or whimper and show his readiness for aggression by growling.

If a dog hears vocalizations from a social partner, he'll immediately assume that something is wrong if he can't work out what these vocalizations mean.

It's likely that dogs interpret our language as richly varied barking. Quiet muttering can also be interpreted as growling and so can cause a dog to feel uncertain.

If a dog hears vocalizations that he doesn't understand, he'll become more alert and his threshold for demonstrating protective aggression will lower. If he's already uncertain about how to assess a situation that he may just have observed, our vocalizations can help him to reach a decision on this matter. If we look at the same situation and express ourselves with our voices, he'll tend to assume that the situation is dangerous rather than positive or neutral.

Some dog owners even manage to directly trigger uncertainty with their voices. It's common for people to talk to their dogs in situations when the dogs are already uncertain. If they subsequently become more uncertain, the owners continue to talk to them but with a louder tone of voice. It's almost as if they're pouring oil onto a fire. The dogs will assume that their owners are now also overwhelmed by the situation. Who can solve the problem if both parties are in a state of panic?

If you always remain calm and never need to use your voice in conflict situations, your dog will see you as being much more confident than he could be in these same situations.

If you absolutely want to talk to you dog, you can use your voice for purposes such as initiating and finishing routines. Your voice will then provide him with a clear indication of what's about to happen. What you say must always be the same and must equally be used in a consistent manner. If you always use the words 'Let's go out' before you go outside with him, for instance, he'll at some point run to the door of his own accord whenever he hears these words. He'll know what's about to happen – although not because he understands the content of your words, but rather because you've used your voice to announce a routine. You can refrain from using your voice just as well, however. Your dog will still recognize the signs that are associated with an imminent walk.

14 What a dog can and can't do

Evolutionary barriers prevent your dog from developing or responding to human feelings. If you want to assess what a dog can do, you first need to recognize what he is. Judge his actions in accordance with their nature, purpose and biological function. Emotions also have a function, although these functions differ greatly between types of creature. Don't judge behavior patterns from a gesture or a facial expression, but rather observe the situations in which your dog shows these behaviors and then consider what purpose they may have among dogs. Don't attribute your dog social competence or a human ability to think. He isn't a human, after all.

14.1 Can a dog cry?

A dog can generate increased tear fluid that flows like tears in humans. Unlike in human tear fluid, however, no hormones have been detected in canine tear fluid. Hormones are chemical messengers that control emotions. They transmit information to the brain where feelings arise. As canine tears lack hormones, they're not an expression of an emotion and so can't be interpreted as crying.

14.2 Can a dog have a guilty conscience?

A dog doesn't have the necessary abilities to develop such a complex feeling as a guilty conscience. He has no sense of justice, and he equally doesn't understand anything about morals or ethics. He doesn't know the norms of human civilization. A dog associates an event with its consequence within just a few seconds. If he wrecks your home while you're at work, for example, he won't have a 'guilty conscience' when you return home. He doesn't know that humans consider such behavior to be incorrect. If he reacts in a submissive manner when you arrive, it's simply because you're behaving differently from normal.

14.3 Does a dog know love, faithfulness and allegiance?

A dog doesn't know love or allegiance on a human scale. He'll follow whoever can fulfill his needs. He only follows us because he's dependent on us. Would your dog stay with you if you stopped feeding him? Probably not. Dogs can also be disloyal at the end of their masters' lives. If a human is no longer able to satisfy a dog's needs, he won't stay with that human out of blind faithfulness.

Faithfulness in a relationship, on the other hand, is quite natural for a dog. Wolves will normally also live in fixed, fair and monogamous relationships. They certainly establish bonds with other social partners, although we'll probably never find out whether their associated feelings are comparable with human love.

14.4 Can dogs become friends?

Dogs consider unfamiliar other dogs to be first and foremost rivals for territory and food resources. Unfamiliar dogs are those that don't live in the same family, so every dog in the neighborhood. In the wild, animals from other packs would be mortal enemies. During the mating season, even siblings would become mating rivals.

Dogs will tolerate one another once they've become acquainted and made it clear that they don't endanger each other's resources. Actual closeness in a form that we'd call friendship is rare and dependent on the provision of sufficient resources. In most cases, a strong bond between two dogs can only develop if they've lived together for a long while and know one another well. If a situation ever threatens their survival or resources become scarce, they'll still revert to being mortal enemies.

14.5 Can a dog feel resentful or offended?

If you 'offend' your dog and offer him food a few moments later, he won't sulk in the corner and refuse the food. He can't become angry, feel offended, or resent your human misconduct. The feelings that we experience from insults are emotions that we've developed because of our need for recognition. A dog doesn't have this need, so he also can't feel these emotions.

Try not to be resentful if your dog chews up something that you prized and was expensive. This is a difficult task. If you notice what he's done after it's too late, you might even look at him with joyful expectation: He doesn't know that he's done something wrong, and far too much time has already passed for him to remember what he did perhaps an hour ago. Learn to deal with your anger immediately because your dog hasn't made a mistake. If you've provided him with ownership of an item, you also need to deal with what he does as a result.

14.6   Does a dog have a sense of time?

Dogs don't have any direct sense of time, as their perceptions are predominantly fixed around daily rituals. A dog can't determine whether two hours or twenty minutes have passed. There are no minutes and hours in his world. He doesn't know that his master left the house four hours ago and won't return until another two hours have passed.
Dogs take direction from their surroundings. They remember what's important to them and act in accordance with their biorhythms and external stimuli such as temperature, sun position, noises or our habits. They memorize everyday routines and take direction from them.

Time is a matter of subjective experience even for us humans. The length of a moment is perceived while it passes and also when we relive the same period in hindsight, remembering what we experienced and assessing it in temporal terms. A dog doesn't have the ability to recall the past. Notions of time are also subject to distortion. All individuals, including our domestic dogs, perceive time differently. For them, there's no other time apart from the present.

How a period of time is perceived depends on how boring or entertaining it's felt to be. A varied day may subjectively pass much faster than a day during which there's nothing to do.

14.7 Does a dog know what we can see?

If your dog brings an object to you, he'll normally place it down within your field of view. He knows whether or not you can see it. This has been proven in experiments in which human subjects have faced both toward and away from dogs. Your dog knows that you can't see him when you're facing away from him.

14.8 Can a dog learn through observation?

Especially young dogs learn through imitation. This involves taking direction from role models and it teaches them routines and their meaning, how to recognize dangers and enemies, and how to gather information about resources and other social partners. An adult dog will solve a problem more quickly if he can watch how the problem needs to be solved. It doesn't matter who or what he watches, and he won't directly mimic or copy the behavior that he observes. He'll instead use his observations to develop his own strategies. It's a real challenge for a dog to reach a piece of food on the other side of a fence, for instance. If you show him how he can reach the food by going around the fence, it'll be much easier for him to solve this problem himself. If a dog learns that he can pick up problem-solving behavior via observations, he'll copy actions more often and align himself more closely with the social partner who showed him the solution.

14.9 Can a dog understand communicative indications?

In a study, food was placed out of a dog's sight in one of two containers.[8] The dog needed to find the correct container to reach the food. If a human gave him an indication as to the correct container via pointing, the dog had no problem in selecting the right one. Without this assistance, he found it much more difficult to reach a decision. He therefore took more direction from the human's communicative gesture than from the smell of the food.

---

[8] Kaminski J., Tempelmann S., Call J., Tomasello M.: Developmental Science, 12.11.2009.

The more often a gesture provides a dog with an advantage, the more strongly he'll take direction from such gestures in future. The ability to interpret communicative indications distinguishes a dog from a wolf, as wolves are less able to interpret these signs. Primates are completely overwhelmed when it comes to interpreting human gestures.

14.10   Can dogs count?

Dogs were shown pieces of food consecutively as part of an experiment.[9] When all of the pieces of food were uncovered, the dogs were surprised if the total number of pieces didn't match the number that they'd just been shown. They examined these uncovered pieces of food for longer than they did when the number of pieces was correct.

14.11   Is it there or has it gone?

Dogs understand that things exist even when they can no longer see them. If you hide a piece of food behind several obstacles, a dog will look for that piece of food behind the obstacle that's masking it. If he can't see where the food is hidden, he'll check behind the other obstacles. He'll quickly lose interest if he's not successful, however. He doesn't understand that if he hasn't yet found the food, it must logically be behind the last obstacles that he hasn't yet checked.

14.12   Noticed a detour?

An experiment looked into spatial learning in dogs.[10] The dogs were only able to reach a piece of food by making a detour. They could solve this task after a few repetitions. The detour was then changed. Most of the dogs were unable to cope with the altered situation even after multiple repetitions. Dogs find it difficult to abandon spatial motor patterns that they've learned. They'll also only continue to look for a solution until they've solved a problem. After this

---

[9] Young R., University of Minas Gerais, West R., De Montfort University: New Scientist. 9.2008.
[10] Osthaus B., Marlow D., Ducat P.: Animal Cognition, 20.06.2010.

point, they won't make any further attempts to identify the best or simplest routes or to improve their strategies.

14.13   You human, me dog!

A dog isn't stupid. He knows that you're not a dog, and he doesn't expect you to act like a dog. Don't even try to do this, because it won't work. Many people think that you have to imitate canine behavior to be understood by a dog, but your dog won't understand what you're doing. He'd first have to learn what human gestures mean, as this isn't something that he instinctually knows.

14.14   Deductions, deductions

A Border Collie, Rico, appeared on a television show in Germany in 1999. 77 different words had been assigned to 77 different toys, and Rico was able to collect the correct toy from another room when given a command. He could ultimately differentiate between more than 250 different words. When he was told to bring an unfamiliar toy from the other room, he was still able to do this despite not knowing what the new toy was called. He'd work out that it couldn't be any of his familiar toys, so he'd bring the only toy that he didn't recognize. He made his decision via a process of elimination.

His ability to learn words was subsequently investigated at the Max Planck Institute for Evolutionary Anthropology.[11] It was established here that he was learning by so-called 'fast mapping'. Fast mapping is a form of elimination process that had previously only been evidenced in children.

14.15   Can a dog learn rules?

It's within a dog's nature to live in accordance with fixed rules. Rules, routines and boundaries simplify his life and help him to find his way. A dog can only follow rules that he understands and that are always valid, however. He needs clear, understandable rules and routines from which he can take direction. He can't try to understand our human world. From his perspective, the only

---

Bloom P.: *Can a dog learn a word?* Science, Vol. 304, Page 1605.

What a dog can and can't do

things that exist are those things that are chiefly determined by his territorial and social behavior. A dog lives solely in the present. He lives from experiences that influence his actions, but he can't anticipate the future from the past. He doesn't know that everything will be the same tomorrow as it is today, or that a visitor will be just as amicable tomorrow as he was yesterday. Rules and routines provide a dog with security and direction.

A dog doesn't understand why he should guard your property but allow visitors or the mailman to enter. If you've given him the task of guarding your property, you've left this task up to him. He'll claim the area for himself and will also defend it, considering everyone who enters this territory to be a potential threat. He can't differentiate between whom you deem to be desirable or undesirable guests.

He doesn't understand that he's allowed to monitor the territory outside but isn't allowed to pull on the leash. If he's going to recognize dangers or other dogs' territorial boundaries in good time, he needs to walk far ahead of you. He'll try to fulfill his tasks if he can't rely on anyone else to fulfill them for him.

If you hand over your home to your dog, you can't expect him to allow food to lie around on the table. The territory belongs to him, and this includes everything that's found within it.

He doesn't understand that he's allowed to hunt a ball but not a hare. If he's generalized the stimulus trigger that provokes his prey drive, he'll no longer differentiate between a ball, a hare or a playing child. His instincts compel him to satisfy a drive that's been provoked by a stimulus. If he's learned that he can satisfy this drive by hunting anything that moves, he won't distinguish between prey that you do and don't allow him to hunt.

He doesn't understand that he's allowed to mate but should also take on a subordinate position. Dogs that have had a litter are officially leading animals, because only leading animals are normally allowed to mate within a pack. It's usual for these animals to demonstrate more pronounced territorial behavior, and they'll often develop strong protective drives that can in turn lead to increased compulsions to control. Mating can cause behavioral changes in a dog that are very difficult to predict. He may end up defending his property more strongly, remaining more alert, and responding to threats in a faster and more aggressive manner than in the past.

He doesn't understand why he should bring prey to you once he's caught it. He'll only fetch prey once you've provided him with a reason for doing so and have made this action directly worth his while. Even Retrievers – named for their fetching behavior – won't usually bring back hunted prey of their own accords. It's not in a dog's nature to give up or share his prey.

Our dogs will never recognize us as leading dogs because we're not of the same species. They can nevertheless recognize the resources that we control and see that we're able to satisfy their needs. They'll then submit to us as if we were leading animals.

They appreciate that we're a different species. We should therefore endeavor to give them the same appreciation and accept them for what they are: Dogs.

15 Which dog is right for me?

Your dog should be a physical match for what he'll encounter during your everyday life. He should also possess character traits that suit your personality.

You should decide on his anatomical characteristics by considering your own desire for movement and action. If you go on extensive walks or hikes that last for several hours, your first choice shouldn't be a dog that has short legs or a short snout. There are nevertheless some smaller dogs that are just as willing as their larger counterparts to undertake such activities.

Canine character traits don't differ between breeds to the extent that many people assume. Dogs of the same breed can have very different characteristics. What's more important is closely examining a dog's origins and previous life experience, and also recognizing at an early stage any experiences that he may be lacking.

A dog's nature is primarily shaped by his experiences and not by his breed.

15.1 Why do we need pedigree dogs?

When most people adopt a dog, they're guided in their decision by their potential new family member's breed. The innumerable books about different breeds suggest that they all come with specific characteristics. Dog lovers subsequently believe that they can acquire particular features by obtaining a particular breed, much like choosing optional extras on a new car. In reality, a dog is and remains a dog. My experience tells me that there are more pedigree dogs that deviate from their breed characteristics than match them. Character descriptions for dogs are therefore a little like horoscopes: They apply to all and no dogs at the same time.

As an example, a German Shepherd with a breed standard-matching character needs to be well-balanced, unshakable, confident, absolutely at ease, entirely good-natured, attentive and trainable. He needs to demonstrate courage, fighting drive and toughness.

No dog will be born with these characteristics – not even a German Shepherd. A dog is an independent individual, and it's only his individual development that determines his nature.

Which dog is right for me?

Normal dog owners don't ever consider such issues. You'll usually have one or two dogs instead of a hundred, so if your dogs deviate from a breed standard character description, you're likely to see this as being something exceptional. All dogs are actually exceptional and very individual.

A dog's character isn't shaped by a description in a book, but rather by his social environment and his experiences. Various breeds may have their drives marked to different extents, with certain tendencies being encouraged or suppressed if a particular selection process has taken place. All that a tendency means, however, is that a dog will later be able to develop a specific characteristic that his breeder has selected. Whether he ultimately develops this characteristic is dependent on whether or not we encourage him to do so.

A tendency is like a chest: Its contents will stay hidden if it remains closed for a lifetime. It's only when we open it up that we find out what lies inside.

If your dog has a tendency to hunt, for instance, you should avoid hunting games if you want to control his hunting drive. Hunting games will encourage his hunting drive. If he's never given the opportunity to catch prey, his tendency to chase after prey will be greatly limited.

Most dog owners place more value on appearance, breed conformation and coat colorings than canine characteristics. They choose their dogs as if they were choosing a new car. A dog will subsequently tend to fulfill the function of a car by satisfying his owner's need for recognition. In the case of doubt, an owner who's interested in a dog for its own sake will prefer a healthy mongrel to an overbred pedigree. Dog breeding primarily fulfills a single purpose: The earning of money. It doesn't matter what happens to the dogs along the way.

This issue doesn't stop with breeders. They're usually just the starting point and are followed by breed-optimized food, breed-specific accessories, breed associations, and ultimately vets who fill their cash registers with pedigree dogs' health complaints.

The breeding of pedigree dogs inevitably leads to a loss of genetic diversity within individual breeds as well as substantially increased risks of genetically determined illnesses. Breed standards ultimately have to be met. An extremely limited population is essential if a breed is to retain its typical characteristics. A pedigree dog loses its breeding purity and so its value as soon as it's crossed with another breed or a dog that looks different. Pedigree dogs have on average two-year shorter life expectancies than mongrels.

Dog breeds originate from the time when animals were bred to complete certain tasks for which they were particularly suited. Dogs had jobs to perform. They had to herd sheep, guard the farm, help with hunting, or catch rats and mice. These working dogs were then bred among one another and so obtained common physical characteristics.

It's now increasingly common for so-called 'show lines' to be bred. The craze for the most beautiful dogs has led to the breeding of crippled and ill dogs for the sole purpose of producing particular appearances. An example of this phenomenon is the increased incidence of deafness in Dalmatians. There are even some illnesses that are named because of their frequent presentation in a certain breed.

Small breeds such as Chihuahuas, Miniature Pinschers, Poodles, Schnauzers and Yorkshire Terriers often suffer from knee or hip-joint abnormalities. They're also prone to gum disease, and their overly narrow pelvises can lead to problems when giving birth. Short-nosed dogs frequently have breathing difficulties and rhinitis, and throat and voice box complaints are similarly common. Shar Peis are especially susceptible to illnesses, with their primary problems being eye diseases and weeping eczema in their skin folds. Large breeds have increased incidences of hip and elbow dysplasia. German Shepherds, Saint Bernards, Retrievers, Mastiffs and Bernese Mountain Dogs are particularly frequent victims of hip and elbow abnormalities. Heart defects and conjunctivitis are also common among these dogs. Typical hereditary diseases for Border Collies include collie eye anomaly, progressive retinal atrophy, hip dysplasia and epilepsy.

An additional and generally underestimated problem is the selection of dogs for specific drives. Selection in the wild occurs via an entirely practical method: Whichever dogs are most successful in their living environments are also able to pass on their genetic make-ups to their offspring.

Which dog is right for me?

We humans interfere in this natural selection process because we want to develop particular drives or characteristics. Our actions ultimately cause imbalance in a dog's drives. Exaggerated drives come at the cost of a dog becoming more difficult to socialize. He'll behave in a completely anti-social manner within groups, perhaps by breaking off interaction with another dog so as to obtain drive satisfaction. If he has an extremely pronounced food drive, he'll immediately break off interaction with other social partners if he spots an opportunity to reach something to eat. He's also more likely to develop aggression toward rivals as a means of driving them away from food – something that a dog with conventional tendencies would never do. A dog that has a particularly pronounced prey drive will similarly leave his social partners to follow a track. In the wild, no animal with such exaggerated and entirely unnatural drives would stand any chance of mating and so furthering his genetic line. Nature ensures a harmonious balance of drives and doesn't tolerate extremes. These matters aren't important in human-directed breeding, however. The focus here lies on making money.

Dogs have long ceased to be working animals in our civilized world. They don't have to perform any real tasks and have essentially become out-of-work pets. So why do we breed sick pedigrees?

So-called 'breed standards' need to be fulfilled whenever a pedigree dog is bred. A breed standard designates a breed's fixed characteristic features as set out by the relevant breeders' association. Who needs such a list?

Definitely not the dogs. Only we humans require standardized dogs so that we can misuse them as status symbols. Why do we do this? Because status symbols are important for us in emphasizing our individualities. We care about the cars that we drive, how our homes are furnished, and which dogs are at the end of our leashes. Yes, we even care about the leashes.

We have a need for self-expression and individuality. Our dogs have to fit with us, as it's only in this manner that we can underline who we are. Someone who owns a Rottweiler would probably never consider owning a Shih Tzu, even though both breeds can make excellent dogs.

We want to display our inner selves and show our social environments just how unique we are. You can smile to yourself when we use cars or clothes for this purpose, but it becomes animal cruelty when we do the same with dogs. We don't build broken cars, after all. So why do we breed sick dogs?

15.2　A street dog

If you decide to adopt a dog that's grown up on the streets without much human contact, you need to reckon on him having developed an extremely high level of independence. He likely won't be able to establish a particularly strong relationship with humans. He'll probably only submit with great difficulty, as he's previously had to cope with every situation by himself and work out all of his own problem-solving strategies. He'll respond more poorly to commands and will only enter into a dependent relationship with significant reluctance. He's already learned to find his own food and defend himself. Such a dog will usually have considerable tolerance for other dogs, but

he'll also bite at an earlier point if he's faced with an appropriate threat. On an everyday basis, he'll see his own interests as having a higher value than your interests. Street dogs normally find it more difficult to take direction from human behavior. A street dog that's very independent and has a high level of self-confidence will similarly face greater challenges in becoming accustomed to walking on a leash. He'll often monitor what he passes and walk in all directions so as to satisfy his enormous need for information. He needs so much information about his environment so that he can follow strategies that he established during his time on the streets. It used to be exactly this behavior that secured his survival.

15.3 A dog from the pound

It's often difficult to work out the back-stories of dogs that come from pounds. These dogs may have previously lived in entirely different environments from those that will await them in the future. If a dog has never known city life, he'll probably become uncertain or even fearful when he's confronted with it. He may not be able to accompany you when you ride the subway, walk along busy streets or navigate large crowds. He may also be afraid of cyclists, disabled people, escalators, elevators, baby strollers, motorcycles or fireworks.

A puppy that learns to develop strategies for his own advantage will often be one of the most intelligent members of his litter. He'll also learn faster in the future as a result, making it easier for him to work out his own solutions to problems. He won't just learn what you consider to be right, of course, but rather what he considers to be important and correct. His intelligence will frequently keep him one step ahead of his owners. Such a dog will be quick to learn your routines and use them to his benefit. In future he'll be very independent and will have less interest in taking direction from you.

Dogs that are more cautious and fearful or that have learned to take direction from others are less prone to look for their own solutions to problems. You'll usually need a little more patience when teaching these dogs. On an everyday basis, however, they'll align themselves closely with a trusted person if they're provided with the right leadership. Their high levels of dependence and low levels of autonomy normally makes their bonds to humans stronger than are found with more independent dogs.

One of the biggest problems that arise in pounds is increased aggression toward other dogs. Dogs will often develop such aggression for the first time when they enter a pound environment, and this development will usually be the result of laws on how dogs need to be kept. The dogs don't have any means of avoiding or fleeing from a confrontation with a rival. A grating or fence

Which dog is right for me?

doesn't provide a dog with protection. Fearful or uncertain dogs are especially quick to find new ways of resisting rivals. It's in the pound that they learn to bark at or become aggressive toward other dogs.

If you want to adopt a dog from a pound, you should find out what experiences he's already gained and then work out whether you can deal with the experiences that he lacks. You should also know his previous position of responsibility within his family. This is because he'll demonstrate and initially maintain old, learned and proven behaviors when he reaches his new environment.

It's advisable to get to know a dog as a puppy if he's supposed to become a part of you and your family's life for a long period. You should establish contact with him at the earliest possible point. The sooner the young dog appreciates you as a social partner, the stronger the bond that he'll later establish with you.

15.4   A puppy

A dog's character traits are predominantly shaped by the learning experiences that he gains during his first few weeks of life. You should therefore observe the development of a whole litter and choose your dog in a considered manner. We often choose the puppy that comes to us of its own accord, as we then think that this puppy has chosen us. But why should a dog choose a human? He'd prefer to stay with his mother and siblings. A dog that has the courage to approach other predators (us humans) while he's a puppy is already very independent and has a high level of self-confidence. He's developed this self-confidence because he's already worked out his own problem-solving strategies. Such a dog will probably also tend toward independence instead of subordination in future. On the other hand, a cautious dog won't approach anything that's unfamiliar to him in future. If a puppy is afraid of everything and whimperingly retreats or looks for protection, he'll continue to fear many things when he's fully grown and may equally develop his own coping strategies. Many of these dogs can't escape or find security anywhere, so they end up learning that attack is the best method of dealing with dangers. If this development isn't counteracted, they ultimately become aggressive toward everything and everyone.

Puppies that learn to take direction from others will seek out someone to provide them with direction during their later lives. You'll then have the best chance of becoming the partner from whom they'll take direction going forward. Dogs that are cautious and reserved instead of fearful have less difficulty in accepting subordination. They appreciate the relief that you provide, but they similarly retain sufficient independence to develop their own characters and explore their surroundings with interest. You can develop a very intensive bond with these dogs – and with the right training, you can also establish strong mutual trust.

16 What is problem behavior?

We apply the term 'problem behavior' if we find one of our dog's behaviors to be objectionable. But a dog isn't usually behaving in an incorrect manner even if we won't tolerate what he's doing or judge his action to be inappropriate.

Dogs do what they've learned or what they consider appropriate and useful. They have no sense of justice and no morals, and they're equally unable to differentiate between right and wrong.

Problem behaviors arise from miscommunication and our misinterpretations of what dogs do. These issues are mostly caused by ignorance and untruths that have been propagated for decades.

We often try to combat the effects of a problem behavior without questioning this behavior's cause. If a dog pulls on the leash, we work on making him stop the pulling. We don't usually scrutinize why the dog is pulling on the leash in the first instance.

We tend to see problems as coming from within our dogs before we take responsibility for these problems ourselves. If there are problems that we can't resolve, we say that the dog is un-trainable or that the problems come from the dog's breed. In reality, we're the root cause of most canine behaviors.

Your dog doesn't have a problem; he behaves correctly. We usually look for ways of stopping the symptoms of problem behavior, but we fail to question what's actually caused these symptoms.

- Aggression is a symptom, not a problem
- If a dog pulls on the leash, this is a symptom, not the original problem
- Stealing food from the table is a symptom, not a problem
- Barking at passers-by from the garden fence is a symptom, not a problem

Actual problem behavior is only seen in dogs that suffer from mental or physical illness or that have had abnormal behavior instilled in them as puppies. If a dog behaves in an abnormal manner, he has a serious issue that behavioral therapy can't generally resolve. Such dogs may have been abused during their early development or may be responding to the pain associated with a medical condition.

A dog will live according to his own rules if he hasn't learned to submit to a human's rules. Your dog assumes that you're pursuing the same goals as him. He only knows his own world with his own rules and goals, and he doesn't know that we humans function differently. As he perceives the social group's ultimate goal to be the securing of resources, he'll take over tasks that you don't manage.

Animals complement one another within a pack, with every animal striving to compensate for pack shortcomings. This is how the community maintains its strength, secures captured resources and wins new resources. Dogs have used this strategy to ensure their survival for thousands of years.

Your dog doesn't know that your food source is the supermarket and not your territory – or that you secure your existence by going to work each morning and not by checking your territory for prey.

It isn't obvious to him that there are regular mealtimes on an everyday basis. We've learned to control our food resources, so it's been a long time since we've worried about whether we'll have something to eat. We can determine what and how much we eat, but dogs find these human privileges to be inconceivable.

> **Problem behavior doesn't arise from dogs' natures,
> but rather from mistakes that we make in our dealings with dogs.
> Humans are the source of every canine problem behavior.**

17 Explaining and handling problem behavior

If you want to understand undesirable canine behavior, you need to ask why – not what – your dog's doing. If you want to change problem behavior, you need to change this behavior's cause. If you want to change the cause, you need to take action.

Your dog won't change established behavior by himself unless you provide him with an acceptable alternative through your own behavior. He perceives his behavior to be correct and sensible; if he didn't, he wouldn't be doing what he is. He'll only change his behavior when he sees an advantage in taking direction from your rules. You're the guide who will show him how to behave in future.

17.1 Finding the cause

How do your establish what's causing your dog's behavior? You need to ask why he's acting in a certain manner.

Symptom: My dog pulls on the leash

Question	Answer
Why does he pull on the leash?	Because he wants to mark
Why does he want to mark?	Because he's claiming territory
Why does he claim territory?	Because I've surrendered it to him

Explaining and handling problem behavior

Symptom: My dog constantly barks at other dogs

Question	Answer
Why does he bark at other dogs?	Because he's aggressive
Why is he aggressive?	Because aggression is necessary for defending himself and protecting his resources
Why does he need to defend his resources?	Because I can't provide him with security and have surrendered the territory to him

Any of our four-legged friends' behaviors that we interpret as problem behaviors have their origins in territorial behavior. Such behaviors are also amplified by uncertainty and fear. Established territorial behavior can only be changed if you claim the territory for yourself and take over the responsibility for it (see Page 95, "Taking responsibility").

Problem behavior	Cause	Alpha Project Solution
Constant monitoring and marking	He feels responsible for monitoring the territory	Take over the responsibility and claim the territory for yourself
Barking at visitors	He's defending his territory and sees the stranger as a threat	Reduce his area of responsibility and take over responsibility for the territory; Show your dog where he's safe

Explaining and handling problem behavior

Problem behavior	Cause	Alpha Project Solution
Constant running around at home	He's monitoring what's happening in his territory	Reduce his area of responsibility and take over responsibility for the territory
Stealing food from the dinner table	Food that's in his territory also belongs to him	Reduce his territory and claim your home for yourself
Barking at other dogs while he's on the leash	He feels responsible for your protection and perceives the unfamiliar other dogs as threats	Show him that you're taking over responsibility for the pack's protection
Running up boisterously to other dogs or humans	He feels responsible for the pack's security and so runs ahead to check out the others' intentions	Show him that you're taking over responsibility for the pack's protection and that you're able to control the situation
Barking at cars, motorcycles, streetcars, wheelchair users, roller-skaters etc.	He's afraid and feels threatened by these things; He feels like he has to defend himself or he wants to drive these threats away	Show him that you're taking over responsibility for the pack's protection; Relieve his fears and create a safe area
Constant barking at passers-by from the garden fence	He's defending his territory and feels responsible for its defense	Reduce his property and take over responsibility for the garden

Problem behavior	Cause	Alpha Project Solution
Growling at you if you want to take away his food or prey	You've given him property that he's now defending	Show him that you control the resources, not him
Mounting visitors	He's uncertain and is relieving his stress with mounting behavior	Reduce his area of responsibility and show him alternative behavior patterns
Excited and unable to hold his urine when you return home	He's unsure of your mood toward him	Reduce his area of responsibility and show him where he's safe

17.2 Help, my dog has too much spare energy!

Various behavior patterns lead us to the conclusion that our dogs are bored or have too much energy to spare. On closer inspection, however, they'll often be showing compensatory behaviors as means of relieving stress. Stress suggests that they're actually facing too many demands instead of too few. Dogs are fundamentally unfamiliar with the concept of facing too few demands.

Whether your dog is over or under-challenged depends solely on the mental and physical strain to which he's accustomed. If he runs 30 km outdoors every day, he'll naturally demand the missing movement on days when he doesn't get this exercise. You can refer to a dog as being under-challenged in a situation like this.

Exhausting your dog as a means of changing his problem behaviors will work to a certain extent. The more intense the physical exertion that he's exposed to, the greater his subsequent need for rest will be. His need for rest will then take precedence and the problem behaviors will retreat into the background.

Your dog will become more resilient over time, however. At some point he'll reach a level of fitness that you can't keep up with, and physically exhausting him will then become almost impossible.

Mark Rowlands depicts this issue very vividly in his book when he recounts his attempt to counteract problem behavior in a wolf by tiring the animal out.

Trying to keep a wolf under control by ensuring that he's constantly exhausted is one approach. But even a moment's thought will tell you that it's not a very good one. (Mark Rowlands, The Philosopher and the Wolf, 2010).

Exhaustion work turns your dog into a top athlete. You'll no longer be able to exhaust him after a certain point. This is when problem behavior will reappear if it hasn't already done so, as you won't have addressed the behavior's root cause. It may not just be old issues that come to light now, either: Exhaustion work can also establish new problem behaviors.

The more activity and exercise a dog is accustomed to, the greater the intensity of activity he'll later demand if what he expects isn't provided to him. A lack of activity may lead him to search for alternative satisfaction. He'll then make his own decisions about what will provide him with satisfaction in that moment. It's more than possible that one or two pieces of furniture will fall victim to his urge for activity.

17.3   Relieving stress and providing rest

Changing problem behavior means avoiding stress and ensuring that your dog is able to rest. When you're at home, avoid constantly talking to him or encouraging him to perform actions. Simply leave him to his own devices. Dogs have a similar need for rest to cats, and both animals require exactly the same amount of sleep. Adult dogs need between 17 and 20 hours of rest each day, and this figure increases to between 20 and 22 hours each day for puppies and dogs that are elderly or ill.

Cats will retire of their own accord when they feel the need to rest, but dogs often won't do the same by themselves. Our domestic dogs have a natural ability to recognize their needs for rest, but they've also been bred to be eager and alert. They've consequently forgotten how to claim the rest periods that they require.

Sleep and rest are essential for our dogs. Sleep allows them to process current events, stress, tension and learning experiences. It's therefore our task to ensure that they get their essential rest. Establish a ritual of silence in your everyday life with your dog.

The effects of sleep deprivation were first studied in mice before research was extended to dogs and then humans. The dogs that were studied became restless when they entered the first stage of sleep deprivation. They became clumsy and agitated in the second stage, and then nervous and quickly irritable in the third stage. They next became aggressive and sickly. They became seriously ill if sleep deprivation continued into the fifth stage – and this illness would sometimes even become chronic.

Aggression is therefore not an unusual behavior for a dog within this context. It's instead a clear sign that he's overwhelmed. This is the final stage at which you can intervene before your dog suffers serious harm to his health.

Many illnesses can be associated with excessive demands because stress weakens the entire body. Overload can cause or contribute to cancer, allergies, organ failure and neurological disorders.

17.4   Problem behavior at home

If your dog has never learned which areas within your home he can claim for himself and which areas belong to you, he'll instinctively consider your entire home as his territory. He'll do the same if he can move around freely without anyone limiting his decision-making freedom. No one seems to be claiming the territory, so he'll take on this role and will secure the greatest possible level of freedom for himself. The problems that can arise from this situation are numerous and depend on the strength of your dog's territorial behavior. In the worst-case scenario, he'll become aggressive toward you or other family members if he perceives a threat to his property. This behavior can develop over a period of years (see Page 223, "Dangers can grow").

A number of signals point toward such a worrying development before your dog demonstrates signs of aggression. Marking within the home, defending toys, his feeding bowl or individual rooms, jumping up at people and barking at visitors are all clear indications that he sees his resources as being threatened. Many dogs will only need to see or smell another dog that's walking past a window in their homes to feel that their territories are under threat.

Reduce your dog's decision-making freedom and area of responsibility (see Page 95, "Taking responsibility"). If you limit his property, he'll only recognize his new space as his own and will acknowledge the areas of your home that belong to you. This learning experience will similarly force him to accept that you make the decisions about everything that's found within your territory. He won't have any access to your part of your home and so also won't make any decisions that affect this area.

17.5 Stress on the leash

If your dog already demonstrates undesirable behavior while he's on the leash, watch what he does and look for a reason for his behavior. Find out what he considers to be more important than remaining by your side. He'll usually be busy monitoring his territory or playing out rivalries with other dogs.

He has to behave in this manner if you've given him responsibility for the territory – whether consciously or subconsciously. The role causes him considerable stress, and he certainly doesn't enjoy pulling on the leash or becoming aggressive.

Managing the territory should be your job (see Page 95, "Taking responsibility"). Your dog then won't have any reason to check the area or develop competitive behavior. He won't want to monitor or defend anything that doesn't belong to him. If he learns that you're able to provide him with protection, he won't need to defend himself or become aggressive. Always pay attention during your walks so that you can recognize threats at an early stage and exert an influence over your dog in good time.

Your dog won't learn to walk on the leash if you pull on it or jerk it so that he's forced to walk alongside you. If you act in this way, he may come to see the entire situation of being on the leash in negative terms. Pulling on the leash can cause your dog pain or discomfort, and he may even respond by sitting or lying down and completely refusing to continue while the leash remains attached. If you ensure that he feels comfortable on the leash and secure in your presence, he'll want to stay alongside you of his own accord.

If you constantly tug on the leash to make your dog walk in the way that you want, he'll eventually develop avoidance behavior and may stop pulling. But he won't have understood why you're stopping him. He'll only have stopped pulling because doing so has unpleasant consequences or because you've demanded this behavior with a command. The only way he'll gladly and voluntarily demonstrate a desired behavior is if this behavior makes sense to him. If you're unable to provide your dog with security, he won't have any reason to remain by your side.

If your dog will only walk with you when he's commanded to do so, you need to ask why a command is necessary for him to act in this manner. If you force him to walk on a leash, his desire to monitor his territory will remain. Your command won't solve the problems that he has to face, so he won't submit to you. The same will remain true if you give the command more loudly. Your dog will learn to suppress his urge to monitor his territory, but he won't understand why he has to behave in this way.

17.6 Unwanted hunting

If you want your dog to give up unwanted hunting behavior, he shouldn't ever be successful when he attempts to hunt. Use your body to actively contain him as soon as you see that his hunting drive is building up (see Page 118, 'Claiming territory'). It won't normally take you long to realize when he has prey in his sights or has sniffed out a track. He'll position his ears forward, raise his head, stay silent, appear tense, and direct his gaze toward the prey or track. He'll remain at your side and won't enter your area of responsibility during this initial stage, but his mind will be exclusively focused on the prey. If he subsequently begins to give chase, you won't normally have any chance of stopping him. You should therefore disrupt the building up of his prey drive early on – even if he's walking alongside or behind you as desired when this disruption becomes necessary.

If you disrupt his plans at an early stage, he'll subsequently find it easier to let them go. If he later recognizes that you make the decisions within the territory, he'll also leave decisions about hunting up to you. If you contain his hunting attempts while he's still a puppy, he'll only demonstrate hunting behavior to a limited extend as he grows, and perhaps not even at all.

Most dogs have already forgotten how to hunt or are no longer able to perform all of the sequences required for successful hunting behavior. They may stalk prey and chase after it, but only very few dogs remain able to catch or kill what they find. They first have to learn the required sequences and gain a fair amount of experience before they can kill an animal. It's nevertheless the first stages of hunting behavior – up to and including the chasing – that give us problems.

A dog's hunting behavior is extremely complex and is divided into various sequences.

1. Tracking down (search behavior)	
2. Focusing on the stimulus (concentrating behavior)	Containment possible
3. Stalking	
4. Chasing	
5. Grabbing	Containment not possible
6. Killing	
7. Eating	

Explaining and handling problem behavior

If you first try to interrupt your dog once he reaches the chasing stage, he won't normally accept distraction by anything or anyone. His entire body is now focused on the hunt. Adrenaline flows into his blood, his pupils dilate, he becomes more tolerant of pain, his digestion grinds to a halt, his gaze locks on to the prey, and he essentially becomes deaf. A recall command will therefore be unsuccessful in most instances.

It's within a dog's nature to hunt, but this doesn't mean that hunting is an entirely instinctive behavior. An instinctive behavior is generally an inborn behavior pattern that doesn't need to be learned, e.g. eating or sexual behavior. A predator's hunting behavior is made up of various individual behavior patterns, some of which can be demonstrated from birth and others of which first need to be acquired. A dog needs to learn how the individual hunting sequences interact, for instance. Puppies will often mix up the individual stages, e.g. by killing prey before they lie in wait or creep up. You can also watch how puppies bark at prey and jump back and forth out of sheer uncertainty. They'll initially practice with insects or smaller prey animals so that they can learn their hunting techniques and train the necessary motor skills. Even creeping up on prey is an art that needs to be acquired.

A dog's search behavior can be referred to as an instinctive behavior, although all dogs still need to learn how to follow individual tracks in a targeted manner. Many dogs find it difficult to follow a scent trail without being distracted by other smells. A dog will tend to demonstrate rather untargeted search behavior if he never learns to follow a track, and his tracking ability will only improve if he succeeds in finding prey. His search behavior only becomes a hunting sequence once he's learned how to follow a track in a targeted manner. All of the individual hunting sequences are self-rewarding and become stronger whenever a dog is successful in his hunting attempts.

If you prevent a puppy from learning how to hunt and so don't allow him to attain success in any of the hunting sequences, he'll ultimately have a rather low overall motivation for hunting when he reaches adulthood.

17.7 Targeted aggression

Just as with hunting behavior, you should also contain your dog if he develops targeted aggression while he's on the leash. You'll normally be able to determine early on both when he's uncertain and against what he's becoming aggressive. He'll usually start by making himself seem large, focusing his gaze onto the threat, and altering his gait. Some dogs will also indicate an oncoming threat by raising the fur on their backs. You should react no later than when you see these signs, blocking your dog's way forward with a short but energetic step. If he doesn't give up his intentions, turn toward him and drive him back in the opposite direction. Be very energetic and decisive when you do this, as your dog is bracing himself for an altercation with what he perceives to be a serious threat. You should meet him with a corresponding level of resolve so that he abandons his plans and leaves the matter to you.

Tugging on the leash will only annoy your dog. Most dogs will equally have absolutely no interest in treats during such situations. You also wouldn't be interested in a chocolate bar if your wife waved it under your nose while you were preparing to defend your life.

17.8 When a dog bites

Biting is a dog's last resort for defending himself or a resource against a threat. Resources may include food, his bed area and his social partners.

It isn't wrong for a dog to bite, as doing so is a typical canine behavior. No dogs are born vicious, however. They'll only bite if they learn that this is their only option for warding off a threat. If a young dog learns that biting is his only means of surviving a confrontation, he'll bite sooner and without prior notice as an adult.

Confrontations between dogs can be split into ritual fights and serious fights. Ritual fights have a well-defined series of behaviors that are largely predictable for a dog's counterpart. They often consist of a stringing together of threatening or display gestures. Ritual fights can become serious or injury-inducing fights if a conflict can't be resolved via other means. The more similar both parties' claims, the greater the risk that a serious fight will ultimately develop.

This division of fight types is not usually very helpful on a day-to-day basis, as it's never possible to tell when a ritual fight will turn into a serious fight. We don't know the other dog's claims or interests, so we can't predict how the confrontation will proceed.

A serious fight will normally occur in an instant. No reassurance gestures will be accepted. The fight's purpose will be to seriously harm, incapacitate or kill the other dog.

The fight will solely be decided and ended through escape or defense. If no decision can be reached, the confrontation will only end when both dogs are fully exhausted or one of the dogs becomes unable to continue.

If you ever need to separate two dogs that are biting one another, it's important to know how this situation arose. If the aggression only came from one of the dogs, you can try to seize this dog's hind legs and push them over his head. You of course need to be physically capable of this action. The dog will subsequently lose contact with the ground and so control over the fight, and he'll then normally proceed to open his jaws. You can now separate the dogs. Pull the aggressor away from his opponent as soon as he's released his grip, and then – ideally with someone else's help – secure him with a rope or leash before you set him down.

You shouldn't ever attempt to separate two dogs by yourself if they've started biting one another out of rivalry or a struggle for power. Neither owner should try to grab his dog by the collar, either. You severely limit a dog's freedom of movement when you hold onto him. This restriction leaves him at his opponent's mercy without any means of defense, which will in turn increase his aggression level. The other dog also won't automatically end the fight now. He may take advantage of the held dog's helplessness by starting his attack once again.

Explaining and handling problem behavior

If more dogs are involved in a fight, they'll usually be united against a single target. It's very likely that you'll receive an injury if you try to intervene in such a situation, and you may even become the pack's target.

Don't intervene in a fight if you're uncertain about what to do or are afraid. Not intervening is difficult and requires deliberate restraint, as our protective instincts can induce us to act out of a desire to protect our dogs from injury. Pepper spray is the only really useful means of separating dogs that are biting one another while also remaining safe yourself.

You shouldn't punish a dog if he bites his owner, because he simply won't have done anything wrong. His only action will have been to protect resources that have been allocated to him or to defend himself against a threat. If you punish him or are violent toward him, the threat that he faces will increase and he'll become even more motivated to bite. You shouldn't consider competing with your dog, as you'll only ever lose. If a dog bites you and takes a firm hold, he won't readily let go. Vast amounts of adrenaline will surge through his body in this moment, making him extremely tolerant of pain. His jaws will clench and you'll have almost no chance of releasing them.

If you receive a bite from your own dog, you similarly shouldn't try to remedy this biting behavior. Your dog will have only bitten you because of what's gone wrong in the past. You should start off by showing him that you don't pose any threat and you should then build up a positive relationship with him (see Page 235, "Shyness toward humans"). If his shyness toward people was already pronounced when he was a puppy, you'll find it difficult to make him give up his aggression in its entirety. It's likely that only a few people will be able to establish a bond with him.

Once you can interact with him safely, it's now time to set boundaries for him, take away responsibility from him, and ensure that he follows your rules.

17.9 Begging

Your dog uses begging to demand that you satisfy his needs. Look out for behavior patterns that indicate begging. He may demand satisfaction of his chase drive or satisfaction of his food drive, e.g. at the dinner table. He may also demand strokes or something to do. He'll generally show behavior that he's learned by himself or reassurance signals that you've already rewarded. He'll look at you with a prompting gaze and reel off all of the submissive and reassurance gestures that you've rewarded in the past. If he's previously been able to demand need satisfaction by barking, for instance, he'll continue to show vocalization behavior as a means of begging.

Learn to distinguish between begging and behavior that's actually desired. Show your dog that you've recognized his prompting gestures and look calmly into his eyes. Avert your gaze after a while and deny him satisfaction of his need. He'll then learn that you've noted his begging but that it hasn't been successful.

If he begs successfully, you give him control over the food resource. If he's denied success, he'll at some point stop begging (see Page 242, "Extinction").

A dog that's praised with food for begging at the dinner table will quickly learn that he can demand food with his behavior. We're often unaware of the consequences of such actions. If he's learned to control food with begging, for instance, both his dependence on you and your influence over him will disappear.

You can try to discourage begging behavior that's already been established by conditioning alternative behavior patterns. Your dog can then continue to satisfy his drive, but only if he demonstrates a behavior that you demand. You'll subsequently regain control over food or a game. If he demands his reward in a vigorous manner, you might use a signal to send him to his place. He'll need to remain here until you reward him with food. You'll then retain control over food, and your dog will associate the reward with your signal instead of with his prompting behavior.

17.10 Garbage on the street

You should use containment to stop your dog from picking up leftover food from the street (see Page 118, "Claiming territory"). You won't normally know what he's picking up, and it could always be full of pathogens or laced with poison. It therefore makes sense to prevent him from picking up things that he finds.

You can achieve this result by using food as a stimulus to tempt him over the boundary that you set in front of your path. When your dog is walking by your side, stop and throw a few pieces of food onto the ground ahead. He won't touch this food if he accepts your boundary, but he'll otherwise want to run at the food without any further thought. You need to contain him in this moment and drive him back. When you've done this, allow the leash to become loose again so that you can see whether he's recognized your containment. Lead him slowly up to the food if he remains behind you. If he lowers his nose as you approach it, place your foot in front of him and stop him from taking what he wants. If he now looks up at you, give him something to eat from your hand. Contain him again if he subsequently tries to get at the food on the floor once more. He won't touch this food if he recognizes that you've claimed it for yourself, and will instead walk straight past it without trying to pick it up. He'll then have learned that he only receives food from you and never from the street. This is your territory, so everything within it belongs to you and not to him.

If you only practice this exercise on paved paths, he'll connect the exercise with this surface and so will continue to pick up anything edible from grass or sand. Dogs learn in a situational manner, so you should be sure to practice the taboo on various surfaces. He'll also find it easier to leave leftovers where he finds them if you provide him with an alternative that he considers to be of equal value.

If you want to play food games with your dog outdoors, you should allow him to pick up food on the surface where these games will take place – or else work with a discriminatory stimulus (see Page 149, "Discriminatory stimuli").

17.11 My dog isn't housebroken

It's in a dog's nature to keep his bed area clean. Puppies learn to be housebroken during their fourth weeks of life when they leave their nests to relieve themselves.

Puppies learn where they're supposed to go to the toilet when they're four weeks old. If they learn from the outset that this is on a natural surface, they'll continue to search out such surfaces when they need to go in future. If they learn to go within the home or on a concrete floor, they'll also maintain this habit with their subsequent owners. They simply won't have learned to do anything else. Take a close look at how your puppy was kept before you adopt him.

A puppy can't hold his urine for a long period during his first few weeks of life. He'll only be able to control his bladder once he's between 12 and 13 weeks old. You should take him outside as often as possible until he reaches this point.

You should give your puppy the opportunity to relieve himself outside at the following times: After meals; no later than half an hour after he drinks; shortly before he goes to bed; and immediately after he wakes up. He shouldn't eat anything less than two hours before he goes to bed. You also shouldn't initially wait any more than two hours between walks. Show your little friend his bed area, and then instead of allowing him to roam freely around your house, give him his own modest territory and remain close to it. If his territory is the same as his bed area, he won't want to dirty this space and so will become restless when he needs to relieve himself. It's time to go outside whenever you recognize these signs.

If a mishap occurs, it doesn't help to rub his nose in the mess or punish his behavior.

Your puppy would much rather relieve himself outside, but he can't tell you when he needs to go. It's therefore down to your powers of observation and how often you give him the opportunity to satisfy his need. If he suddenly starts to turn in circles and sniff while he's running around, for instance, he's looking for somewhere to go. It's then necessary to take him outside with the greatest urgency. Reward him lavishly once he's successfully relieved himself. Also reward him for indicating his need to you while you're inside.

17.12 Barking

Barking is an expressive behavior that mirrors a dog's emotions, e.g. fear, stress, aggression and expectation. You shouldn't forbid him from expressing himself with his voice in this manner.

When a dog uses his voice, he'll normally be doing so in a stressful situation. He'll never bark for fun. If we subsequently boss him around or shout at him as well, he'll first interpret our vocalizations in canine terms. He'll assess our sounds in accordance with the purposes that they serve among dogs, i.e. primarily as warning signals or as signs of our being overwhelmed.

The tenser our voices are at this point, the more threatening he'll perceive the entire situation to be. He'll subsequently become more stressed and his barking will become louder. You should instead remain calm, showing him that you have everything under control and that it's totally unnecessary for him to use his voice at all. He'll then refrain from his vocalizations.

Your initial approach to changing undesirable barking behavior shouldn't be directed at stopping barking. You should rather establish why your dog barks and what purpose he perceives his barking to serve.

You can differentiate types of barking based on their cause, e.g. fear barking, stress barking, aggression barking or learned barking. Certain triggering stimuli may equally lead to mixed types of barking, e.g. barking that's caused by both fear and aggression.

Barking out of fear

This type of barking is often high-pitched, hysterical and accompanied by whining. Other behaviors are usually also present, e.g. wandering around, running, scratching and attempting to escape.

You can avoid situations in which your dog demonstrates fear behavior. If he's afraid on a more regular basis, you can instead allay his fears with desensitization, counter-conditioning, and ideally by transforming his negative experiences into positive experiences (see Page 225, "Managing fear").

Learned barking

This type of barking is directed toward those social partners from whom a dog expects need satisfaction. It's mostly also associated with a prompting behavior. Your dog will have learned that he can control you with his behavior. Dogs will normally demand food or activities. You can stop your dog from barking by complying with his demand, but his motivation for future vocalized behavior will subsequently increase. He's attained success with his behavior, so he'll continue to bark in future – and perhaps even louder and at an earlier point. If you consistently deny him the satisfaction of any need that he demands through vocalization, he'll ultimately cease to see any sense in barking (see Page 213, "Begging").

Barking as a warning

Barking when the doorbell rings is an example of barking as a warning signal. Your dog knows that something is happening, but he isn't sure what this something is. His uncertainty about the situation prompts him to warn the pack of the potential danger.

If you want your dog to stop barking when the doorbell rings, you need to practice this situation. He should learn that the ringing is followed by either unimportant things that have no effect on him or by a familiar routine. If he learns that the ringing is followed by a familiar routine, he won't be uncertain in future because he'll already know how to behave.

Your dog will soon learn that the doorbell's ringing has no effect on him if the ringing occurs frequently and you behave toward him in a neutral manner. He'll learn this by himself on an everyday basis through constant repetition. You simply need to behave neutrally toward him and also normally in a general sense. You control everything that happens once the doorbell has rung. It makes sense for your dog to bark and point out the situation as soon as the ringing has an effect on him. You should therefore pay him no attention and so

Explaining and handling problem behavior

show him that the ringing is entirely unimportant. Visitors shouldn't pay him any attention either, including by touching him or speaking to him.

The most effective method for influencing your dog's vocalization behavior is to take over responsibility for your home and allocate him his own safe area (see Page 95, "Taking responsibility"). He won't see any further sense in barking once he's handed over responsibility for the wider territory to you. Most dogs will entirely stop barking within just a few days if this occurs.

Barking out of aggression
This type of barking is often marked by clear, loud barks and is accompanied by growling and the baring of teeth. The dog will also push forward and be tense and aggressive.

Such aggressive behavior can arise for the most diverse of reasons, e.g. territoriality, self-defense, food aggression, prey aggression or hunting aggression.

Aggressive behavior is often a strategy that a dog has learned to deal with his fears. He'll attack anything that he perceives to be a threat.

If you want your dog to stop barking out of aggression, you first need to remove the cause of his aggression. If the cause lies in his territoriality, you need to take over responsibility for the territory and make it clear to him that you're able to ensure his safety. There won't be any reason for your dog to become aggressive if he trusts you. He becomes aggressive as a means of defending himself, and this job should be your responsibility going forward.

Barking out of expectation
This type of barking arises out of an expectation of drive satisfaction. If a dog's expectation is too great, his stress levels will quickly build up before being subsequently relieved through barking.

You should avoid stress for your dog in general. Routines that build up expectations should be broken up so that no expectations develop. A sense of expectation arises in recurrent situations. The regularity of these situations makes your dog anticipate what's about to happen. If he regularly receives need satisfaction by chasing a ball or stick while you're out on walks, for instance, he'll come to expect imminent hunting whenever a routine indicates that you're about to go outside. The expectation in this situation can cause so much stress for your dog that he'll require a substitute action for the purpose of stress relief. This substitute action will often be barking.

If your dog learns that you'll satisfy his expectation whenever he barks, his barking will become learned barking rather than a substitute action (see Page 213, 'Begging').

Many owners recognize this phenomenon when they take their dogs out to run and play with a ball. Your dog may begin to spin around in your car several minutes before the open area is reached. The signs that the area is close are sufficient for him to develop an incredible sense of expectation. Reduce routine drive satisfaction and avoid routines that arouse expectations. Similarly refrain from associating experiences with single situations. Be aware that there may also be highlights for your dog within your home. These highlights don't always have to involve physical or mental activity: Rest, relaxation and sleep all satisfy your dog's needs as well.

Barking out of stress

This type of barking is mostly monotonous, stereotypical barking that is usually accompanied by additional stress-related behaviors.

If you want to stop this type of barking, you need to find out what's causing your dog stress and then avoid the stress-inducing situations. He'll often be overwhelmed by his tasks or won't feel safe. Take responsibility away from him and show him that you're able to carry on performing his tasks in future. Provide him with peace of mind and relieve his fears.

Barking at others

This type of barking is aggressive and is used to intimidate and chase away others. A dog will only stop barking in this manner once the threat has passed or the intruder has fled.

Barking isn't incorrect behavior. The dog is simply doing what he's learned, what makes sense from his perspective, or what's necessary to embrace the tasks that you've consciously or subconsciously given to him. He won't understand what's going on if you now punish him for this action.

Your dog doesn't bark to annoy you, and he also doesn't bark because he enjoys doing so. Barking is always stressful for a dog. He may bark to indicate lurking danger to his pack, to call his pack's attention to something, because he's stressed or anxious, or to chase away an intruder. Barking doesn't necessarily mean something bad: Pack members will merely interpret another member's barking as 'Heads up! Something isn't right!'

If your dog learns that you control situations and that he can rely on you, he'll gladly and voluntarily hand over to you responsibility for his security. He also won't bark any more, as doing so won't make sense.

If you punish your dog for barking, he'll think that he hasn't performed his task well. He'll then try to improve his behavior, and may end up barking louder and at an earlier point than before. He may equally stop barking due to fear of punishment, but this will promote avoidance behavior instead of solving the actual problem. His urge to perform his task will continue to remain within him, and his stress levels will rise further as a result. Punishing your dog for barking will mostly just create new problems that are very difficult to predict (see Page 223, "Dangers can grow").

If you want to change undesirable behavior, you first need to know what's causing this behavior. Once you've identified the cause, you can then offer your dog alternative behavior patterns to replace the undesirable behavior. Suppressing or punishing behavior can lead to the emergence of substitute or displacement behaviors that aren't predictable and can ultimately cause far greater problems.

17.13 Displacement behavior

Displacement behavior is a term from instinct theory. It describes certain behavior patterns that are seen as being unexpected due to their occurrence within behavioral sequences in which they serve no immediate purpose. These behavior patterns are interpreted as an expression of conflict: A previously observed behavior can't be continued, and the behavior that's shown in its place comes from an entirely different functional sphere. Displacement behavior can mostly be seen in situations in which a dog experiences stress and is attempting to relieve this stress. Stress in an internal conflict or tension that's caused by physical or psychological strain.

If your dog demonstrates undesirable behavior and you treat him incorrectly or in a manner that he can't understand, the worst-case scenario will see his undesirable behavior become reinforced. If you act incorrectly over an extended period, his undesirable behavior may become reinforced to such an extent that he'll now pose a threat to you.

If you forbid your dog from barking at other dogs while he's on the leash, your suppression of his protective drive will cause him considerable stress. His stress level will quickly build up further if the threatening situation doesn't change. He'll then use displacement behavior to relieve this stress. We can't influence or predict the behavior that he'll demonstrate in such a situation, but it wouldn't be unusual for him to bite objects that are in his immediate vicinity. These objects may well include a leg or an arm.

17.14 Aggression

All dogs have a natural potential for aggression that needs to be understood before it can be evaluated. Aggression is a secondary drive that assists a dog in satisfying his primary drives. If a threatening situation triggers a dog's protective drive, for instance, aggression will develop to help him defend himself against dangers or attackers.

Aggressive behavior can be classified into three divisions:

1. Aggression with prey behavior:
When hunting or bringing down prey

2. Protecting the external order:
Defending the young, one's self, the living area and the territory

3. Protecting the internal order:
Clarifying rank positions within a pack, both during play and emergencies

A number of indications develop on top of one another before a dog will seriously bite:

1.) A dog will initially demonstrate defensive behavior by trying to avoid the danger. He'll avert his gaze or flee.

2.) If avoidance doesn't work, the dog will bark so as to inform other pack members of the potential danger.

3.) If the threat increases, the dog will growl, bare his teeth or snap as a warning. Extreme caution is now being advised. These signals act as a final caution to the opponent of a serious confrontation.

4.) If the danger remains present, the dog will now attack and bite his opponent so as to eliminate the danger and avoid becoming the victim.

Your dog will endeavor to follow his instinctive drives. If you use punishments or command pressure to prevent his natural behavior in one of the above-listed aggression phases, he'll develop a high level of stress that he'll usually relieve with displacement actions (see Page 221, "Displacement behavior"). If these displacement actions don't suffice in offsetting his stress, he'll automatically skip to the next aggression phase.
He'll ultimately be left with only one possible action: To attack for his own protection.

Why does this happen? Your dog will carry out his task because no one else has taken over responsibility for his protection. If he's faced with a threat, he has to put up a fight even if there's doubt in his mind. He hasn't learned that he can take direction from humans when he's faced with danger. As you can see, it isn't your dog that has the problem here, but rather human behavior that allows his problem behavior to arise.

It's easy to change a dog's behavior once you understand it. Accept responsibility for your dog's protection and limit his area of responsibility (see Page 95, "Taking responsibility"). Don't allow him to become involved in conflicts in future. He'll at some point give up his aggression if it ceases to provide him with success and he also remains safe with you. He won't want to become aggressive if he trusts you with his safety.

17.15 Dangers can grow

Territoriality can be used as an example to describe how problem behavior can grow into a danger.

If your dog takes control over your home while he's young, he'll retain this control until someone takes it from him. A dog learns over the course of his life what's most difficult for him to control and which resource is most important to him. He'll then try to control these things. If he finds it difficult to control food, for instance, he'll try all the harder to defend this resource.

A dog may initially only growl if someone wants to take away his food bowl. He doesn't understand that we're not raising any claim to the bowl. He instead sees us as predators and so as rivals for it.

At some point you may pose such a threat to his food resource that he'll become aggressive toward you. You're his only rival for the bowl, and if he controls the wider territory, he'll also try to control the food within it. Over the course of several years, he may even bark you out of the kitchen where his food bowl lies. He'll determine who can and can't approach the prey.

Even if your dog is currently friendly toward other dogs, this doesn't mean that he'll remain friendly for his entire life. Dogs learn how best to avoid confrontations with hostile other dogs while they're puppies. They'll usually retain this behavior as adults. If your dog has learned that other dogs leave him in peace when he lies down, for instance, he'll be keen to repeat this behavior.

But a situation can still quickly escalate if you meet a hostile dog that doesn't recognize this signal. How will your dog then behave during his next confrontation with another dog? He probably won't lie down, as doing so hasn't provided him with reliable protection. He may decide to become aggressive at an early stage and to attack the other dog without warning. Behavior is always a mirror of experience, and your dog will continue to gain experiences throughout his whole life.

New problem behaviors can develop even if your dog is getting on in years. A dog's senses will usually weaken with time: His vision will degrade and his hearing will worsen. He'll still carry out his security duties if he's responsible for this task, although his ever-weakening senses may make him aggressive earlier on and over entirely inconsequential matters. He can no longer correctly assess many dangers, so he'll react to all stimuli that cause him uncertainty if any doubt exists in his mind. He may even perceive a threat if you trigger his light and shadow reflex. He'll bite if he can't recognize an associated danger – and if your arm has triggered the reflex, it may be your arm that ends up being bitten.

If an aging dog recognizes that security is a human responsibility, he'll most likely prefer to swap being aggressive for pulling back and knowing that he's safe.

Whether your dog barks, pulls on the leash or takes food from the table, all of these issues are symptoms and not causes. If you remedy the causes, you'll also remedy the symptomatic behaviors on a long-term basis. If you only eliminate the symptoms, your dog will continue to develop problem behaviors and will equally never be able to live a balanced and stress-free life.

18 Managing fear

Fear is a physiological response to an anticipated threat. What your dog considers as a threat will depend first and foremost on his previous experiences. A dog's character is shaped by his experiences, and particularly those experiences that he gains during puppyhood.

An important role is played by his relationships with humans and his siblings. If a dog has negative experiences with humans while he's a puppy, he'll develop a subsequent aversion to humans that may remain for his entire life. If a puppy is always last in line for milk and is constantly forced into submission by his siblings, he'll develop no self-confidence and so will be quicker to demonstrate fear behavior as an adult. These dogs will often avoid contact with other dogs and struggle with new things as they grow. They'll also show uncertainty, nervousness and a stronger fear of the unknown than their siblings.

Dogs with such negative experiences will frequently react with fear or anxiety when they're confronted with things that we see as being entirely harmless, e.g. construction noise, fluttering streamers, wheelchair users, statues, mirrors, children, vacuum cleaners, horses, lawn sprinklers and strangers.

Dogs can see threats in objects that we perceive as entirely harmless, e.g. fireplugs.

A puppy that grows up in surroundings that contain few stimuli will retain a lack of experience throughout his life. Unfamiliar situations may subsequently cause him to demonstrate fear behavior, with him attempting to avoid or sidestep these situations in future. If he can't avoid the situations, he'll develop his own strategies for protecting himself against the perceived threats. Wolves will also generally try to flee when they're confronted with threatening situations.

Managing fear

If a dog can't escape from danger, he'll be forced to develop his own strategies for dealing with a situation. Aggression will often end up being the only alternative that's left open for many dogs.

Fear and aggression toward other dogs usually develop during puppyhood. These traits are frequently caused when mistakes are made in bringing dogs together or when puppies gain negative experiences in poorly led puppy playgroups (see Page 23, "Puppy playgroups and dog re-socialization groups").

You can see how fear develops into aggression in many dogs if they're left alone with their fears. When a dog is on a leash, for instance, he may attempt to avoid an oncoming dog. If his owner pulls him back, he'll no longer have any means of escape. This constraint will often cause the situation to change, with the still-flighty dog now becoming aggressive. He may develop a pathological fear if his fear continues to increase or remains present for a long period. Such pathological fear will generally require treatment with medication.

18.1 How do I recognize fear in my dog?

There are a number of signals that can relatively quickly tell you whether your dog is afraid. These signals are instinctive behavior patterns and natural reactions to perceived threats.

- He's walking or standing in a crouched position – regardless of whether he's demonstrating escape or attack behavior.
- His ears are lying flat against his head and he's avoiding eye contact.
- His tail is lowered or held between his legs.
- He's panting heavily and raising his lips (dogs also pant to regulate their body temperatures when it's hot).
- He's trembling (dogs also tremble when they're cold).
- His heart and breathing rate have increased, which you can feel by placing your hand on his chest.
- His muscles have become tense and he appears stiff.
- His attention level is raised.
- He's urinating or defecating as a result of his emotion.
- He's drooling excessively, usually in combination with panting.

Holding the tail between the legs is generally associated with fear, but this action isn't a sign of fear by itself. More signs are always required if fear is to be identified. When a dog's tail is lowered, his anal glands are covered so that no odors can escape. This is a sign of his willingness to submit, as his odors can no longer cause a disagreement during a meeting with another dog. A dog that holds his tail between his legs wants to avoid confrontations and not provoke other dogs.

If your dog doesn't show any fear signals but instead feels uncertain, he'll mostly demonstrate this state with vocalizations such as whimpering, whining and short barks. He may also show his uncertainty by panting, frantically wagging his tail and moving around in a hectic manner.

18.2 Relieving fear

You should always build up a strong bond with a fearful dog before you consider setting him rules. He should first trust you and consider closeness to you as something positive. He should also see your home – or wherever he lives – in a very positive way. If he subsequently pulls away from the leash in a frightening situation, he'll gladly return to you once the stress has abated. If no bond exists, he won't have any reason to flee to you when a threatening situation occurs.

Avoid all forms of negative interaction from the outset and give your dog the opportunity to completely eliminate stress within his new surroundings. Refrain from brushing or washing him if possible, or find someone else to do these jobs if they're unavoidable. He then won't develop any negative associations toward you. If you have a foundation of trust, he'll tolerate much better the negative interaction that will necessarily follow when you establish rules and boundaries.

18.3 Fear during walks

If your dog demonstrates pronounced uncertainty while he's outside, begin by always following the same routes. Look for shorter routes and use them more frequently. Always follow them in the same direction and always make the same stops. Keep to the same routines as on the previous day and constantly remain close to your dog. You may find this process boring, but your dog will thank you for it and will develop more self-confidence on walks with every passing day.

If his fear or uncertainty is associated with familiar routes, you need to show him that he's safe with you and that it's fun to stay in your near vicinity. Associate going for walks with something positive by offering him food.

Your dog should now have sufficient self-confidence to explore new territories by your side.

He'll repeatedly be introduced to situations on walks that he perceives as frightening or unsafe. Repetition will help him to learn that the situations don't really pose any threat. The process is one of desensitization via familiarization, which in anxiety therapy is referred to as 'habituation'.

Habituation is a form of exposure therapy by which desensitization is achieved through a fear trigger. Exposure therapy is a classical method within anxiety therapy. It confronts the dog with a frightening object or situation and offers significant opportunities for rapid fear elimination. It also contains significant risks, however, and incorrect use of this method can consolidate or even strengthen a fear behavior.

There are various methods within this therapy form that differ in how the exposure to frightening situations takes place.

18.4 Habituation and systematic desensitization

The South African-American psychotherapist Joseph Wolpe first described the technique of desensitization in his 1958-published book, 'Psychotherapy by Reciprocal Inhibition'. He developed the systematic desensitization process for the reduction of fear behavior.

Wolpe assumed that physical relaxation is incompatible with physical tension. Exposure to a frightening stimulus while in a relaxed state should lead to conditioned repression of a fear behavior. Desensitization therefore aims to remove the association between frightening stimuli and fear behavior.

In human psychology, a distinction is made between in vivo and imaginal exposure – based on whether the patient is exposed to his fear in 'real life' or in his imagination. Exposure in the imagination (imaginal exposure) occurs when the patient is in a state of relaxation. He'll generally reach this state with the aid of a relaxation technique.

When the therapy is applied to dogs, exposure takes place in 'real life' (in vivo exposure). We unfortunately have no influence over what our dogs imagine, and this is why many techniques from human medicine can't be used on our four-legged friends. The basic conditions under which fear arises are nevertheless the same among all mammals. Exposure therapy can therefore be transferred from use on humans to use on dogs.

Desensitization is implemented over several steps. Observation is first used to determine the stimuli that trigger fear behavior in the dog.

These stimuli are then arranged into a hierarchical form, with each stimulus' position referring to the level of fear that it induces.

You can now introduce the dog to the stimulus that induces the least amount of fear. He needs to be calm and relaxed when the exercise starts. He'll then be led to the relevant stimulus until he begins to show slight signs of fear behavior. This position should be maintained until his fear begins to subside. If the situation is ended too early, there's a danger that his fear behavior will strengthen. This stage of the exercise is primarily about inducing a state of relaxation in the dog while he's exposed to the fear trigger. When he achieves this relaxed state, you'll know that he's processed the stimulus and now sees it as posing less of a threat.

The more isolated the dog's fear response, the better your chances of success with the therapy. If he's afraid of a vacuum cleaner, for example, it's easier to treat this fear than a more complex problem such as a fear of traffic. It's in any case important to approach the frightening stimulus slowly, and also to practice the next approach only when the dog no longer demonstrates any fear behavior when he's presented with a weaker stimulus.

It's critical that you remain close to your dog whenever you approach a frightening stimulus during the exercise. This is the only way in which you'll be able to tell when his fear subsides. He should also experience the weakening of his fear, i.e. his relaxation, when he's near to you. He'll then perceive closeness to you as something positive and so will seek you out in future when he's afraid of unfamiliar stimuli or otherwise feels uncertain.

18.5 Flooding

The psychologist Thomas Stampfl developed this form of therapy in 1967. Flooding is an exposure therapy like habituation, but it differs from habituation in that exposure to the frightening stimulus takes place in a substantial and rapid manner. Flooding has to be performed in 'real life' in dogs (in vivo flooding), although it can also be performed in the imagination in humans (imaginal flooding).

Flooding exposes a dog to the stimulus that causes him the most fear. He then needs to survive this exposure until his fear level decreases. The procedure is therefore primarily about overloading the dog's responses. There will initially be a significant surge in his fear responses, but this will be followed by a spontaneous reduction of his fear. The dog learns that the frightening situation has no negative effects on him.

As flooding places an incredible strain on your dog, it's very important to assess whether he's able to process the frightening stimulus by himself. He should have built up a strong relationship of trust with you before flooding is used to combat his fears. If he isn't able to process the overstimulation or if the exercise is carried out incorrectly, his mental state could worsen and he may develop phobias.

The length of the exercise is dependent on the dog. In some cases, it may last for up to several hours.

You can introduce your dog to the frightening stimulus in a step-by-step manner during the exercise, but the steps need to be passed through much faster than in systematic desensitization. You shouldn't wait for the stimulus to stop triggering fear behavior; the dog should be exposed to the next stimulus as soon as his fear has passed its peak. He shouldn't demonstrate any further fear behavior once the exercise is over. Repeating the exercise will subsequently accelerate the stimulus processing and allow you to see whether your previous attempt was successful and lasting. Your dog should require less and less time to consider the stimulus as insignificant with each future repetition.

18.6   Fear of vacuum cleaners

A dog will always consider a vacuum cleaner to be frightening if he isn't already accustomed to it. I'd like to use the example of the vacuum cleaner to explain the differences between the two types of exposure therapy that are described above.

18.7   Practical example: Habituation

Place your vacuum cleaner in a room, turn it on, and watch how far your dog distances himself from the situation. Go up to him and then approach the vacuum cleaner together, continuing until he demonstrates slight signs of fear. Stay close to him and calmly lay your arm around him. You'll now be able to check how his breathing rate changes and when he becomes calm. Offer him some tasty food if he processes this first approach and eventually relaxes. If he takes the food, you can assume that he's overcome his fear in this stage of the approach process. You can use food to counter-condition the negative, frightening situation into a positive situation – or you can help him to surmount his fear by requiring him to approach the vacuum cleaner in order to obtain the food. You dog will be motivated to overcome his fear more quickly of his own accord, and he'll also experience food as something positive. He'll then at some point stop seeing the frightening stimulus as something negative.

Now lead him gradually toward the noise source. Reward him eagerly if he looks at you or moves to the vacuum cleaner by himself. Avoid making any vocalizations or hectic movements. Behave in a calm and balanced manner, and force yourself to move in slow motion if necessary. If your dog responds too sensitively to an approach, remain patient and don't be afraid to take a step or two back.

18.8   Practical example: Flooding

Bring your dog to his bed area and attach him to a collar and a short leash. Now go right up to his place, place the vacuum cleaner behind you, and squat down so that you're between the vacuum cleaner and your dog. Hold on tightly to your dog's collar and turn on the machine. You'll now need to stop him running away from the noise. He should learn that he's safe in his place and that the vacuum cleaner doesn't present him with any threat. Wait with the machine until he stops trying to escape, and then begin to vacuum his bed area's floor. Continue to hold him tightly so that he can't get away. You can also ask your partner to operate the machine while you stay with your dog. Be careful not to get too close to him if you want him to see his bed area as a safe place in future. If you do get too close, he'll associate closeness to you with a feeling of security. This isn't a bad thing, but it isn't particularly useful within the home. Your dog should feel safe when you're not at home, and he also shouldn't jump into your arms in every situation just because he feels safe with you.

Once he no longer tries to escape, let him go and continue to vacuum in his immediate vicinity. Everything should be done slowly and without any hectic movements. When he's mastered this situation, stand up and carry on vacuuming around him. Behave as you normally would while vacuuming. If he processes this situation well, continue to repeat the exercise over the coming days until vacuuming becomes something familiar for him. Wait a day before starting your repetitions if possible, as your dog will then have the intervening night to process his experiences and impressions.

18.9 Street noise

If your dog is afraid of passing cars or bustling streets, slowly approach a busy street with him. Stay close to him and look out for his frame of mind. If you recognize fear from his behavioral changes, move back from the street until he only shows slight signs of fear. Continue to remain close to him. Consider crouching down and placing your arm around him as well, as doing this will stop him from unexpectedly escaping and possibly even running into the street. If you place your hand on his chest from this position, you'll also be able to feel his heartbeat and so will know when he finally relaxes.

Secure your dog in an escape-proof harness to further reduce the risk of accidental escape. A panicking dog won't have much difficulty in freeing himself from a collar or conventional harness.

Now remain where you are and watch your dog's fear diminish. You can only successfully combat his fear if you stay in your current situation until his fear has clearly reduced. Only then can you continue to approach the fear trigger or end the exercise for the day. Repeat the process until your dog no longer demonstrates any fear response when he's directly confronted with the fear trigger.

By staying near to your dog, you ensure that he connects the emotional state of relaxation with closeness to you. You can also touch him or place your arm around him. Only stroke him when his fear has significantly diminished, however, and avoid all forms of vocalization throughout the exercise.

18.10 Separation anxiety

It's rare for a dog to experience separation anxiety when he has to stay alone. The issue will usually only exist if a dog has found himself in a threatening situation while he's been alone in the past. Separation anxiety will see a dog withdraw – usually to a corner or a specific other location – and whine, tremble, drool or pant heavily.

A dog isn't suffering from separation anxiety if he runs through your home, destroys objects, barks loudly, or yelps or whines while hectically wandering around. Such behavior usually results from one of two reasons.

On the one hand, a dog may become stressed because a social partner's absence causes him to lose both a bond and the direction that this bond provides. Such stress will usually be expressed as whimpering or whining. The dog will calm down once he's reoriented himself, and this process will normally require fewer than 20 minutes.

On the other hand, panic may similarly be induced when a dog loses control. He no longer has any influence over the social partner who's left the house, and this powerlessness can prompt an enormous stress response.

A dog will suffer from stress in both situations if he has to remain alone. The stress will often manifest itself as displacement behaviors, e.g. barking, howling or destroying objects. These behaviors will normally subside if they successfully relieve the stress. If the stress remains, however, there's a danger that these behaviors will become routine. They'll then be shown compulsively and will no longer be sufficient for relieving his stress.

A dog won't suffer from a loss of direction or control if his owner has control over the territory and the dog knows where he's safe (see Page 95, 'Taking responsibility').

Even if your dog does become fearful when he has to stay alone, consistent blanket training should alleviate this fear (see Page 97, "At home"). He'll then have somewhere that's safe from dangers to which he can retreat. He'll initially experience his fear here just as he does elsewhere. If his fear subsides and relaxation sets in, however, this emotional experience will always be focused on a single place. This place should be his bed area. If the dog repeatedly gains this experience in the same place, he'll later withdraw here of his own accord whenever he feels threatened or uncertain.

18.11   Shyness toward humans

Fearful dogs will also usually behave in a cautious manner toward unfamiliar humans.

Shyness toward humans can have numerous causes. Some dogs will have developed a learned caution toward humans as a result of having had very sporadic or even no contact with humans during their developmental phases. These dogs will only tend to avoid humans because they're unfamiliar.

An alternative cause is instinctive shyness toward humans, such as is seen in wild animals. Dogs that have learned to live without humans over multiple generations will generally show instinctive shyness that will only subside very slowly – and will probably never entirely disappear. This characteristic is normally reinforced via a process of natural selection.

If you adopt a dog that's shy toward humans, you should start by helping him to overcome his uncertainty toward you.

To establish a bond with a shy dog, use all of the previously described interaction options and also remain close to him during rest periods when he's relaxed. Take him with you while you're reading the newspaper or lying on the couch, for instance. He may be tense on the first few occasions, but he'll soon learn to relax in your vicinity. You should rest together in these situations until your dog really relaxes and realizes that you don't pose him any threat. Don't touch him at all in the beginning. You should only stroke him when he lies next to you and is genuinely relaxed. If he finds it difficult to relax while he's close to you, start by staying further away from him. Gradually decrease the distance on each attempt until you can finally lie next to one another without issue. Always choose a starting distance at which he doesn't attempt to escape and is eventually able to relax.

You should rest together at night as well – providing your dog is happy to do so and you don't have a problem with this. The closer and longer you're in contact with one another, the more strongly he'll associate closeness to you with positive experiences and relaxation. He'll also learn that you don't present any form of danger. Avoid all vocalizations and simply enjoy closeness in all of its forms.

The effect of lying together is often underestimated when it comes to building up a relationship with a dog. Lying together is a demonstration of affection among dogs that similarly encourages their bonds to other social partners. Your dog should therefore also have the opportunity of lying together with you in future.

Once your dog stays within your reach, offer him food as motivation for overcoming his uncertainty.

Motivate him with especially tasty food so that he reduces his distance away from you of his own accord. Most dogs prefer moist, strongly smelling foods to those that are very dry. Start by placing the pieces of food at ever-decreasing distances from yourself. He'll then need to make himself approach you if he wants to take the food. You can later place the pieces in your open hand and then bring this hand closer to yourself on each attempt. Give him enough time to smell your hand or arm before he takes the food.

Spread the food all around yourself at the end of the exercise. Place it over your body and hide it in your pockets, under your legs or in the folds of your clothes. Your dog will search for the food on you and rummage in your clothes if he's sufficiently motivated. He'll then connect closeness to you and your smell with the experience of food, and you'll consequently reduce his final hesitation about approaching you. This exercise obviously requires him not to demonstrate any aggression toward you or to see you as a rival for food.

18.12 Fear of other dogs

Keep your dog away from other dogs for a while so that he's not exposed to this fear trigger and can instead rebuild his self-confidence and inner sense of security. Introduce him to an unfamiliar dog once this period has passed. Stand between the two dogs, and then start moving around the other dog in a wide circle so that your dog doesn't demonstrate any signs of fear. Gradually decrease the distance between the animals, but only so long as your dog remains unafraid. You'll now be converting his negative association toward other dogs into a positive association. Reward him for establishing eye contact with you, as he'll then learn to take direction from you during critical situations. Also reward him if you see that he notices the other dog but doesn't become afraid, as doing this will further reinforce his positive association toward other dogs. Give him the time that he needs to learn that you can control the situation and that other dogs don't always present him with a threat. Remain calm and assured in your actions throughout, and favor slower movements over hectic movements. The more often you practice meeting other dogs, the faster your dog will consolidate what he's learned.

Always stand close to your dog and in between him and the danger, as these actions will help you to win his trust. Follow him if he moves away. Stay near to him and remain attentive, as he otherwise won't ever be able to trust you. You can't protect him if you're several meters away, and your dog knows this. He'll think that you're shirking the responsibility and leaving the work up to him.

18.13 Uncommon stimuli

Certain fears can't be relieved with desensitization and counter-conditioning because their triggering stimuli appear too infrequently for habituation to occur. Examples of such conditions include fear of fireworks and fear of thunderstorms. A dog will find it useful if he can decide where to stay in these situations. Create areas with few stimuli that offer your dog protection and allow him to rest.

18.14 Touch and overcoming fear

It's often said that you should never stroke your dog when he's afraid. You'll then reward his fear and so strengthen it. This naturally isn't the case, as fear can't be rewarded. Fear can only be initiated or strengthened by a fear trigger. If you always stroke your dog when he's afraid, he may associate your touch with his emotional state and therefore avoid your touches in future or become afraid of them in expectation of a fear trigger. If you stroke him while his fear's subsiding or when he's relaxed, however, he'll actually associate your touches with a positive experience.

18.15 Success in practice

I've obtained the best results with fear therapies by only stopping the exercises once a dog shows no more fear. He should also have taken the food so that I've been able to associate the situation with a positive experience. The time that a dog requires to become habituated to a fear trigger is subject to great variation. Most dogs won't need longer than between 10 and 20 minutes per approach, but it can sometimes take several hours before accustomization to a fear stimulus takes place. When you repeat the exercises in future, you'll see that your dog now overcomes his fear much faster and so is able to approach his fear's source.

The older a dog is, the longer he'll require for overcoming his fears. You should remain patient and give him all the time that he needs. If you end a situation before he's habituated and while the symptoms of his fear are still present, he may demonstrate more fear when you subsequently repeat the exercise.

18.16 Using your voice during fear therapy

Many of the methods used in human fear therapy can't be successfully used on dogs. Some of these methods can even worsen a dog's condition. Examples of non-transferable methods include suggestion and the use of relaxation techniques. The voice is also an essential component within human therapy, but using it with dogs can strengthen their insecurities and fears.

A dog interprets our voices in accordance with what voices mean in his world. As such, he can't interpret our vocalizations in a positive manner unless he first learns what they mean among humans. In his world, vocalizations serve as warning signals or as signs of stress and frustration. A dog won't use his voice if he feels comfortable. He'll only make a sound when something isn't right. If we talk incessantly to our dogs as a means of calming them down, they must hear that we're totally stressed or that we want to tell them that something's wrong. They already know that something's wrong, as they otherwise wouldn't have become afraid. It doesn't help them to combat their fears if they think that we're stressed by the same situation. Even if you believe that your voice has a calming effect, it's easiest to avoid all forms of vocalization until your dog really knows what human voices mean.

19 Mistakes in handling problem behavior

19.1 Avoiding problem situations

Dog owners often take the path of least resistance when they're confronted with problem situations. Such situations are then regularly avoided so that everyday life is simpler. You can see owners wandering through parks late at night or very early in the mornings so that they can avoid all confrontation with other dogs.

These owners are certainly avoiding stress for their dogs, but they're also not solving their problems. If you constantly look for ways of avoiding problems, it's possible to end up with a significant, long-term reduction in quality of life for both yourself and your dog.

Use the opportunity that's presented by a conflict situation and show your dog that you're able to solve the associated problem.

If he becomes aggressive toward other dogs, seek out confrontation and show him that you can control these situations. If he's afraid of street noise, search for it and then help him to reduce his fear.

19.2 Distraction and problem situations

If your dog becomes aggressive toward passers-by and dogs at the garden fence, don't correct this issue by distracting him with games. As in similar situations, the cause of his problem behavior will then remain unaffected. It may subside while he's distracted, but he won't learn that you can take over his tasks. And what will happen if you don't distract him in good time in future? Correct: He'll bark at passers-by at the fence once more.

If a dog has problems with other dogs, you'll often see his owner distracting him during encounters with other dogs. He may do this by simply throwing a ball in the opposite direction to another dog. His dog will then leave the problem situation as a result of his chase drive. If his dog confronts another dog, however, he'll be able to throw the ball as much as he likes without gaining his dog's interest. Quite the opposite will occur, in fact: His dog's chase drive will now be triggered, in turn increasing his aggression level and so making the ball a piece of prey that needs to be competed for.

19.3 Ignoring undesirable behavior

A dog considers all actions to be allowed if they haven't been forbidden. If you ignore undesirable behavior, your dog won't necessarily adjust what he's doing. Why should he? He doesn't feel hurt, disappointed or provoked by your disregard. He won't change behavior that he currently sees as worthwhile just because you ignore it.

If he's aggressive toward other dogs, he won't change this aggression because you ignore his behavior. You can ignore his loud barks at the doorbell as much as you like, but doing so won't result in a change in his behavior.

Issues such as fear or uncertainty may resolve with time, but this will occur as a result of habituation and not your disregard. If your dog can't become accustomed to a fear trigger, his fear will actually worsen if you ignore this issue.

If your dog begs at the dinner table, his behavior will quickly change if you ignore him. This won't be because you're not giving him any attention, but rather because his behavior hasn't been successful and his begging hasn't led to a reward. Psychology refers to this type of behavior disappearance as 'extinction'.

Extinction

Extinction describes the erasure of learned behavior through a lack of reinforcement. A stimulus that isn't reinforced loses its ability to trigger a response. If the situation at the dinner table previously acted as a stimulus that triggered begging, the learned begging behavior can be erased if acknowledgment (the dog receiving food from the table) is removed.

Your dog's goal is always need satisfaction. Attention alone doesn't satisfy any of his needs. If you give him attention, it's normally one of your subsequent actions that actually satisfies his need. You may give him food or spend time with him, for instance. He'll then develop a sense of expectation whenever he receives attention.

If we humans receive too little attention, this has a direct impact on our wellbeing. A dog doesn't have this need in the same form. He doesn't need pure attention to the same extent as us humans, and he certainly doesn't need it from humans. If a dog learns that our actions have no effect on him, he'll be able to relax quicker and more effectively than if we constantly and expectantly stare at him. If he's affected by all of our actions or is continuously spoken to, he'll be constantly tense because he's trying to work out what we want from him. He won't be able to relax, and simply because we want to be attentive toward him.

Remain alert and watch your dog, but refrain from constantly talking to him, taking him all around your home with you, and allowing him to share in every small matter.

Instead create routines so that he can recognize whether or not he's affected by a situation. If you want to occupy him with search games, for instance, you might lay out a small rug on which to play with him. He'll then learn that a search game starts whenever the rug is unfurled. There are no games going on when the rug isn't present, however, so he'll then be able to relax.

19.4   Castration and problem behavior

The decision to castrate a dog will often be made in the hope that doing so will have a positive effect on his behavior. Other people fear that the surgery will have more negative consequences. The belief that males become fat, lazy, weak of character or vicious once their testicles have been removed remains widespread, for instance.

Castration will basically only reduce or eliminate those problems that arise from directly testosterone-dependent behaviors. Such problems among sexually mature males include straying, restlessness, constant whining, refusal of food and increased irritability – all of which develop with the sex drive when one of the neighborhood's bitches is in heat.

Castration won't necessarily make male dogs calmer. Castrated males tend to put on weight as a result of their altered metabolic states, and after they've put on a certain level of excess weight, they of course also develop corresponding energy-saving behaviors. This problem is nevertheless easy to avoid with proper feeding.

The lowering of a dog's testosterone level will have no effect on his temperament, his urge to move, or his vocalization behavior. Undesirable behaviors that result from territoriality can similarly not be eliminated via medical intervention. Castrated dogs will continue to monitor and mark their territories and demonstrate aggressive behavior when it comes to defending their property.

Castration is an invasive procedure and so is always associated with risks. As a result, this surgery shouldn't be carried out in the absence of medical necessity.

19.5 Punishing problem behavior

Punishment is a common and often-subconsciously used method of changing problem behavior. Before we talk about punishment, we should clarify what it means.

By 'punishment' we refer to a penalty for an undesirable behavior. A punishment is always a negative interaction, although our dogs won't see all negative interactions as punishments.

This matter is best explained using the example of a reward. If you offer your dog a piece of food for a desirable behavior but he refuses your offer, food isn't currently a reward for him. If you then move away from him because you don't want to focus on him at that point, he won't necessarily see your moving away as a punishment. He just has one fewer potential action in this situation; other potential actions remain open to him.

The point at which a negative interaction becomes a punishment is dependent on how strongly you act against one of your dog's needs. Interactions are assessed differently by all dogs and depend on both the situation and each dog's individual motivation.

A negative interaction only becomes a punishment if it's sufficient to influence a demonstrated behavior in a sustained manner.

A threat is often equated with a punishment, but it actually has a different function within a social community. A threat gives notification of a penalty, but it isn't itself yet perceived as a punishment.

A dog's decision-making freedom isn't limited by a threat. All he knows is that a punishment will follow if he chooses an undesirable behavior. If he's confronted with multiple potential actions, he'll opt for the one that offers the most pleasant consequences. A threat assists him in avoiding a punishment and also gives him the opportunity of preventing a penalty.

Mistakes in handling problem behavior

It's within the nature of all creatures to punish wrongdoing. No human would bring up his child and completely forego penalties. We can similarly see that wolf pack members are punished for wrongdoing, although only on irregular basis. The affected wolves are either threatened or bitten.

So does it make sense to punish your dog for wrongdoing? Yes: If you notice wrongdoing, you can punish your dog for it. Wrongdoing doesn't mean undesirable behavior from a human perspective, however, but rather incorrect behavior from a canine perspective.

It may be undesirable for a dog to bark, but this isn't incorrect canine behavior. A dog makes a sound when he wants to draw the pack's attention to something, e.g. danger. You can't punish a dog for barking, as he's really acting in the correct manner.

If a dog barks at passers-by from a fence, he's protecting his territory because his owner has consciously or subconsciously given him this task. Punishing the dog wouldn't just be wrong in this instance: It could also make him unpredictable as a result of avoidance behavior or displacement actions.

Senselessly punishing your dog can similarly lead to him developing aggressive defense behaviors. His original behavior was correct from his perspective, so he won't understand what he's being punished for.

If a usually housebroken dog relieves himself in the house because he's suffering from diarrhea, you'll see that he recognizes his behavior as being incorrect. It would nevertheless be wrong to punish him in this circumstance. We don't know which punishment would be appropriate for him to understand his error, not to mention when or how strongly to apply it.
If you use punishments to stop behavior that you interpret as incorrect, you place your dog's trust in you at risk. If he doesn't understand why you're punishing him, he'll avoid closeness to you in future. He'll no longer be able to assess when and whether you're about to punish him. You'll essentially make yourself unpredictable for him.

Mistakes in handling problem behavior

As such, avoid using punishments in training whenever possible. There's a considerable danger that you'll lose your pleasure in your dog as a result of destroying your relationship of trust with him on a long-term basis.

Animals in the wild learn almost exclusively through punishment. In a wolf pack, for example, wrongdoing may be punished with a bite that causes the subject animal pain. This animal will then refrain from such wrongdoing in future.

Puppies also learn their bite inhibitions through punishment. This form of conditioning is equally normal among other carnivores. The animals usually require only a single painful learning experience to permanently refrain from an action or recognize a boundary.

Why, then, do we not use punishment when training our dogs? On the one hand we're not usually able to correctly punish canine wrongdoing, while on the other hand we have different demands from other dogs in our co-existence with them.

In a pack, every animal fulfills his role and so is a part of the community's wider survival strategy. All of the animals rely both on one another and the entire pack's functioning as a hunting weapon. Subordination and compliance with rules are prerequisites for this arrangement.

We humans don't need our dogs for survival. From our perspective, a dog is simply another social partner. He's a family member and a companion in our lives. He should gladly associate with us and feel comfortable alongside us. We want him to search out closeness to us and allow our children to stroke him. He shouldn't become aggressive toward our family members or us. If our dogs are to develop such trust, they first need to learn that we don't pose them any threat.

If we punish a dog, he won't understand our reasons and so will distance himself from us out of pure self-protection. We'll become too much of a threat for him if we try to solve our training weaknesses and impatience with physical violence.

We'll often subconsciously punish our dogs. A punishment can arise from holding back a reward, our dog being frightened, or him feeling threatened as a result of our body language. We should therefore aim to consciously avoid the use of punishment when we train our dogs.

19.6 Training or coercion?

Coercion is unavoidable in the coexistence between humans and dogs. We coerce our dogs simply by keeping them in captivity and making them dependent on us for food. You can similarly refer to our demanding of behaviors with commands as coercion. A dog is coerced by everything that doesn't correspond to his will.

Coercion is necessary for containing a dog's freedoms, taking him on the leash, and specifying certain paths during walks. We can't do without coercion if we want to enable our dogs to live among us.

The observance of rules requires the respecting of boundaries. A boundary is a limit on a dog's freedom of action, so boundaries are equally a form of coercion. There are multiple types of coercion, however, and all are perceived differently in accordance with their respective natures.

You can coerce a dog by exposing him to either direct or indirect coercion.

Direct coercion only permits a single action. Indirect coercion allows a dog to choose between multiple potential actions.

A dog only has one choice when his leash is jerked: He has to choose the path that you've specified with the jerk. No other paths remain open to him. If you contain him with your body language, however, you only prevent him from choosing one of multiple possibilities. You restrict his freedom in the precise place that this freedom ends, both now and in the future. You don't do anything more or anything less. He can continue to do anything that he wants to behind this boundary: He can escape, run around, sit, lie down, or whatever else makes sense for him. Everything is allowed providing he adheres to the rules and only moves within his free area.

19.7 Training aids

Many dog owners highly regard training aids such as spray collars or head halter. These tools are not panaceas for training or behavioral problems, however. When you use such tools, you never solve the issues that really cause problem behaviors.

The only tool that you need in dog training is motivation. A leash and possibly a muzzle may also be used for the safety of third parties. All other tools are unnecessary and can harm your dog more than they assist him in his learning.

If you're thinking about using a head halter, for instance, first consider why your dog isn't attentive, why he doesn't look at you of his own accord, and why he doesn't seek out your help in conflict situations. If he trusts you, he'll ask for your help, regularly establish eye contact with you, and take direction from you during conflicts.

He may eventually look at you if you force his attention by pulling on a head halter – but not because he wants to, but rather because he doesn't want you to tug on the training tool.

A head halter as a training aid. You don't need this kind of training aid, and neither does your dog.

Some groups of trainers still use strong coercion for what they call 'securing' commands. Their aim is to make a dog follow a command almost 100% of the time.

But who needs this? It begs the question as to who wants a dog that works like a machine. Certainly not me!

Who needs drill on the dog-training field? Definitely not the dog. No dog will ever perform a conditioned command with absolute reliability in every situation. There's also no need today for our pets to demonstrate unconditional obedience. A dog is a living being and not a machine. He has his own interests and needs, he'll make mistakes, and some of his days will be better than others. A dog is fallible, just like us humans. And that's a good thing.

20 Contradictions in dog training

You can only expect your dog to demonstrate behavior that he understands. He'll act in a certain way if doing so makes sense and is appropriate from his perspective. As a result, many different activities and sports that we offer to our dogs actually contradict what we want to convey with our training.

You can't expect your dog to walk on a leash, for instance, if you've handed over your territory to him. The fact that he has property compels him to monitor his territory, and this also involves a protection element. He needs to monitor the territory ahead of anyone else so that he can recognize dangers in good time. If other dogs approach, he'll be the first to check whether they pose a threat. He'll therefore want to walk up to other dogs and so will pull on his leash.

Don't expect your dog to walk on a leash if you've trained him in protection work. In protection work, you expect your dog to protect you from dangers. He needs to independently detect and ward off threats, so he has to make every decision by himself. He'll also need to walk ahead of you so that he can carry out the tasks that you've given to him.

Don't expect your dog to allow visitors onto your property if he's been tasked with protecting this area. He can't determine which people you do and don't want on the property. He sees all non-pack members as threats, and he'll bark to announce such threats. Don't think that he's guarding your property: He's long since claimed the property for himself. This may mean that he at some point also defends the area against you.

If you occupy your dog with ball games, don't expect him to ignore hares or other live prey. You're training your dog to hunt, and if he learns that he can satisfy his drive by himself, he'll also want to hunt doves, deer and rabbits. You'll lose control over his hunting behavior.

Don't expect your dog to walk on a leash if you train him in human tracking. This activity requires him to independently look for people and make decisions. He can't take direction from you or become distracted by other people. He should follow a trail entirely by himself until he finds the missing person. Such a dog will struggle to distinguish between work and leisure, so he'll also usually have difficulty in walking on a leash.

21 Behavior explained

21.1 Enthusiasm for walks

A dog only needs to barely note an imminent walk before entering into a state of excitement that we interpret as enthusiasm. We can only determine whether he's really enthusiastic in this situation if we consider the causes of his behavior.

If you trigger your dog's hunting drive during every walk by playing ball games, for instance, he'll learn over time that when you put on your shoes, you're both about to go hunting. He'll eventually develop expectation that leads to stress long before a ball game actually takes place. Adrenaline is released into his body to prepare him for the upcoming hunt. Adrenaline has a vasoconstrictive, blood pressure-increasing and heartbeat-accelerating effect within his circulation. It expands his bronchial tubes, dilates his pupils and promotes the flow of oxygen through his body. He enters a long-lasting, high-drive state as soon as he sees signs that a walk is imminent. He'll instinctually attempt to relieve this stress via movement or displacement actions. We humans often interpret this agitation as enthusiasm, but it's really just his anticipation for the hunt.

Your behavior and routines allow him to quickly recognize when need satisfaction is probable. His body adjusts at an early stage, reacting with various states of agitation long before the actual event begins. We see him as being full of anticipation, but this situation is often really associated with considerable stress.

The state of agitation that's built up during prey or tugging games will also tend to remain for a long time after a game has ended. This is because adrenaline is only removed from a dog's body on a gradual basis. Many dogs are therefore still very restless once a walk is over. It's common for people to think that their dogs aren't worn out at this point, but in reality there's just adrenaline in their bloodstreams.

There are equally some dogs that become uncertain when they notice that a walk is imminent. We often interpret these signs of uncertainty as enthusiasm, but what should an uncertain or fearful dog be enthusiastic about? Many of these dogs consider their bed areas within their homes to be much safer than the outside world. Urban environments can be very frightening for dogs: Traffic noise, crowds of people, machinery noise, exhaust fumes, street crossings, subway tunnels, elevators, shopping noise, cigarette smoke, aircraft noise, escalators etc. don't belong in a dog's natural surroundings. Many dogs are therefore uncertain or afraid of things that we humans consider to be entirely normal.

There are also dogs that only live in cities and so are shaped by the stimuli of urban life. These dogs will frequently demonstrate uncertainty or fear when they're in a forest, field or unfamiliar environment. Dogs are shaped by what they learn and experience, and this shaping is often the cause of behavioral issues.

21.2 My dog licks me

Your dog may lick your hand or arm if he's relaxed and you're stroking him. The hormone oxytocin will be released if he perceives your touch in a positive manner. He'll then be in a state in which he feels affection. It's unlikely that this feeling is comparable with the human feeling of affection, although licking a social partner is certainly the result of a positive emotional state. Dogs groom one another via licking and so also show affection in this manner. Licking as an expression of affection isn't a declaration of everlasting love: It's simply your dog showing you what he's feeling in that moment. Licking on the face will often have different causes (see Page 276, "Licking the corners of other dogs' mouths").

21.3   My dogs mounts me

Dogs demonstrate mounting or mock mating for the most diverse of reasons. If the behavior is directed toward other dogs, it can have a sexual motivation. There's also an assumption that it's a dominance gesture when it's not used for actual mating. In my opinion, however, this behavior isn't an attempt at winning dominance.

Dogs usually demonstrate this behavior among one another long after the situational hierarchy has been clarified. Dogs that mount have usually recognized other dogs' dominance. They never act in this manner during rank challenges or initial confrontations with entirely unfamiliar dogs.

You can only normally see mounting behavior among dogs that already know one another. It's therefore likely that the behavior is encouraged or influenced by the relationship between the dogs. It can often be seen during play, for example. It should be noted that mounted dogs don't see their positions as being questioned. They'd otherwise demand the other dogs' submission once the mounting was over.

I see mounting behavior as more likely to be a momentary demonstration of affection or an expression of an inner feeling of happiness toward another social partner. This is why the dog that does the mounting can be seen to be in an increased state of excitement. This excitement is caused by the release of the hormone oxytocin, which was in turn triggered by a positively experienced emotion. The hormone has a sexually stimulating effect and encourages behavior patterns that are associated with sexual activity.

Mounting is often seen as rude behavior and so can provoke a defensive response.

When the mounting occurs, however, the two dogs' interests may collide. This collision will often lead to a defensive reaction from the dog that's being mounted. One of the dogs wants to run around, but the other wants to act out his arousal. The mounting doesn't lead to any serious consequences, but it may annoy the mounted dog.

Mounting is especially evident in dogs that have already submitted to others. These are usually dogs that are uncertain, afraid and withdrawn. They don't normally want to dominate situations, and they generally demonstrate a strong willingness to submit. If a dog wanted to dominate another dog and demand his subordination in a serious confrontation, the idea of mounting would never enter his thoughts.

I believe that a dog similarly isn't showing a dominance gesture if he mounts a human. There isn't any reason for a dog to dominate an unfamiliar human. If he sees a visitor as a rival for his territory, he's far more likely to become aggressive, growl and bark.

Unfamiliar humans will usually cause a dog to feel uncertain. He'll see a visitor as an unfamiliar predator who's invading his territory. This situation is normally associated with stress: The dog can't anticipate the stranger's intentions, but it remains up to him to monitor and guard his territory. He'll usually be hopelessly overwhelmed by this task, so he may actually use mounting to relieve his stress.

We humans can't show a dog any reassurance signals that he'll understand. Stressful situations therefore last much longer between dogs and humans than between only dogs. Mounting subsequently becomes a displacement action that helps a dog to reduce his stress hormones. If he's learned that mounting has a calming effect, he won't look for alternative coping strategies. He'll instead try to use mounting for stress relief whenever he encounters stressful situations.

If you look at the natures of dogs that show mounting behavior, they'll often tend to be uncertain or afraid. These dogs will instinctively try to reassure rather than dominate. It's therefore very unlikely that mounting should serve to establish dominance.

It's also common to see dogs that mount humans' arms. They'll often show this behavior during a period of relaxation, and in combination with licking the human's arm or hand. The hormone oxytocin is released whenever a dog experiences a positive emotion. Oxytocin is also referred to as the 'cuddle hormone' or the 'love hormone', and it has a sexually stimulating effect that may lead a dog to demonstrate mounting behavior.

Dogs may similarly mount pillows, stuffed animals and other objects. They'll often use these objects as replacement bitches for the purpose of masturbation.

If you want to prevent stress-related mounting, reduce your dog's responsibilities and create routines that give him security and from which he can take direction.

21.4   My dog laughs

The actions that we interpret as laughter in a dog are usually signals that he's using as submissive gestures. He'll let his ears fall to the side and will pull back the corners of his mouth so that all of his teeth are visible.

Many people want to see laughter in their dogs, but you need to consider the entire situation in which such behavior is shown and not just the expression itself.

We laugh because we recognize jokes and irony. A dog can't recognize these matters. You similarly can't make a dog laugh by teasing him or pulling faces.

When a dog meets another dog, the gestures that we interpret as laughter actually show submission. But why does he show these gestures to humans? Dogs instinctively show submissive signals. They're born with this capability and don't need to learn how to do it.

We humans also instinctively use body language and understand it when we see it in other humans. If we're told off, for instance, we look to the floor and lower our heads. If we're happy, this emotion is immediately evident to other people through our expressions. We don't show these gestures consciously, but rather subconsciously like our dogs.

If a dog feels threatened by a human or is uncertain around us, he'll instinctively show us signals of reassurance and submission.

A dog will also pull back the corners of his mouth and 'laugh' when it's very hot. This action allows him to gain maximum airflow through his respiratory passages and so regulate his body temperature. I'm inclined to doubt that he finds this situation funny.

21.5 My dog is jealous

Jealousy is a painful emotion that's felt toward a loved one. It consists of affection for the other person and also a deep dislike of a rival.

This feeling is entirely foreign to dogs. They're unable to feel sympathy, dislike, hate or envy. If your dog behaves in a jealous manner, he may really be showing protective behavior against someone who's close by.

When we acquired our foster dog Dunja, I suggested that only my wife should initially work at establishing a bond with her. I withdrew entirely from the training and only interacted with Dunja when necessary.

After a week, we observed the following situation. My wife was sitting on the couch and reading the newspaper. I sat down next to her, moved up to her and gave her a hug. When Dunja saw this, she jumped up between us and growled at me. She wasn't jealous: She just wanted to protect the social partner with whom she was associated. My wife pushed her away forcefully and so demonstrated that she already had the situation under control.

We often also see jealousy in barking or defensive behavior. These actions may actually be expressions of uncertainty that result from a dog not recognizing a situation, e.g. two people hugging or kissing. It's not usually a good sign in the wild if two predators fall onto one another and bite one another's faces. A dog will interpret what he sees in accordance with his own understanding. If he doesn't understand a situation, he'll respond with uncertainty and in a reassuring manner.

A dog may equally demonstrate uncertainty if you stroke another dog and he has to watch. He may begin to whimper, whine or even bark. This also isn't jealousy. It's not normal among dogs for everyone to interact with everyone else. Interaction will normally only take place upwards in a hierarchy or within the same hierarchy level. If you engage with a social partner that's below your rank, your dog won't understand what you're doing and so will respond with uncertainty. We often interpret this uncertainty as jealousy.

21.6 The wagging of the tail

When a dog wags his tail, most people see this as an expression of joy. If you consider the whole situation in which this behavior is displayed, however, it soon becomes clear that this isn't the case. A dog can't experience joy in the human sense. Canine joy can only be experienced through security.

But what is joy? A happy moment? Euphoria? Expectation of a positive event?

From a dog's perspective, joy is the satisfaction of a need. He'll most likely experience the feelings that we humans label as joy in an entirely different manner. Positive emotions can also be triggered in a dog by completely different experiences. We might be happy when we receive a gift from a loved one, someone compliments us, or we go on vacation. A dog will see the same situations entirely differently. Gifts don't have the same symbolic character for him as they do for us humans. He can't strictly speaking interpret any symbolism in gestures or their representative actions. He also can't do anything with a compliment, and he isn't able to share in our joy about a vacation to the same degree. If a dog experiences joy, it's because he sees something as positive from his own perspective and not from ours. Even then it remains unlikely that his joy will be comparable with our human emotion of joy. Human joy is normally an expression of interpersonal happiness. We experience such feelings because we've developed a need for them over the course of our evolution. A dog has never developed this need in the same form, so he'll consequently feel joy in a manner that we can never imagine.

The wagging of the tail that we interpret as joy will in most situations really mean that a dog is uncertain. Uncertainty isn't something negative in principle. The dog knows that something's happened, but he doesn't know what. There isn't any routine from which he can recognize what will happen next in the current situation – or whether this situation will have an effect on him. It's not clear to him whether what's happened will have a positive, negative or even no effect on him. The unclear nature of the situation will generally cause stress.

Watch your dog when you throw him his favorite toy, for instance. You'll notice that he isn't wagging his tail during this moment of total bliss. If you take his prey away from him and then look at him, however, you'll see that it doesn't take long for the wagging to start. It will then often be accompanied by the pulling back of the corners of his mouth. He isn't pleased that you now

Behavior explained

have his prey. Your dog can't assess the situation and isn't sure how you'll behave. Will you give him back his prey? Will you claim it for yourself? He'll express this internal conflict by wagging his tail. As soon as he's given back his prey, the wagging will once again cease.

Your dog may wag his tail in 'joy' when you return home after a long day at work. But is he actually showing joy in this moment?
We dog owners are far too keen to anthropomorphize our dogs' behaviors, so we generally see what we desire in their actions. You naturally want your dog to be pleased when you return. Who doesn't want that? You want to be missed and loved. But these are all things that our domestic predators can't provide.

How does your dog experience this situation? Being alone is a fundamentally foreign and frightening situation for him. Pack animals are almost never alone in the wild. They're never forced to separate themselves from their packs. It's an individual pack member's decision whether to follow the pack. His life will often be in danger if he's forcibly separated from his group. He'll have been separated either during a confrontation with a hostile pack or because an injury means that he can't keep up with his pack. A pack animal won't ever choose to stay behind. Doing so will on the one hand cost him his security and direction, and on the other hand will prevent him from helping his family if they need his assistance.
If you see your family as a replacement pack for your dog, leaving him alone will cause him to go through the same experiences that he would if he were separated from his pack in the wild. If a family member leaves the house, the pack is no longer complete. If you've given him control over the pack and the territory, he'll become unsettled whenever a family member leaves or comes back to your home.
He'll lose control over the pack if he's left alone in the house. He won't be able to fulfill his tasks within the community or appreciate why the other pack members have left. Will they return, or might they expose themselves to danger?

Your dog believes there to be far more dangers lurking outside than humans recognize. If you leave home, he considers you to have left his area of influence and so exposed yourself to significant danger.

He has to adjust to the new situation in your absence and take on new tasks. He therefore becomes uncertain, not joyful, when you return. The entire situation has now changed once more, but he doesn't know in what way or how your return will affect him.

Are you in an amicable or a hostile mood? Is his status in danger? Do yesterday's rules still apply?

The answers to these questions are vitally significant to your dog and essential for his survival. The whole situation is stressful for him. You can observe such stress every day in innumerable homes when dog owners return from work. These owners never consider whether their dogs are actually demonstrating joy. Many dogs are even unable to hold their bladders as a result of this considerable burden of stress, and they end up urinating on the floor when their owners reappear. If we assessed the symptoms in an objective manner, we'd soon see how stressful this situation is for dogs. In reality, pure selfishness often means that we don't want to know what our dogs actually feel.

You can also see this 'reunion joy' among wolves in the wild. It's not uncommon for individual animals to sometimes hunt smaller animals by themselves. This form of hunting is called 'solitary hunting'.

The animal that decides to break away and hunt has a specific motivation for leaving the pack. There always needs to be a very important reason for a wolf to hunt alone. He'll ultimately be abandoning his task of protecting the community. The motivation that drives him is hunger.

The wolf will return from hunting after a few hours, or perhaps even a few days. As soon as he finds the other pack members, he'll be met by a welcome delegation far in advance of the other animals. These animals will greet him by wagging their tails and licking their lips. The group will generally be quite excited, although this excitement will promptly subside after a short period.

This greeting ceremony has nothing to do with 'reunion joy'. It's actually a precautionary measure for the pack's protection. The animals that welcome back the wolf show him their amicable intentions by licking their lips. They

Behavior explained

also expect a sign of peace from him in return. It's not self-evident that the returning wolf will be amicable. He was already starving when he left the pack, so if he hasn't caught any prey during his absence, he may now become a rival to his own group. He might even kill his own mother to obtain food. It's therefore important to check his intentions far in advance of the rest of the pack. If he's peaceful and shows this state via signals, he'll go back to the other animals. All of the wolves will stop wagging their tails as soon as reassurance and submission gestures have been exchanged. Until the situation has been clarified, however, the uncertainty about the returning wolf's intentions will cause all of their tails to wag. This tail wagging occurs instinctively and subconsciously, much like most of our dogs' body language signals.

21.7 Strangers and visitors

If you've left your territory to your dog, he'll also bear responsibility for this area's protection. It'll normally take some time before he develops aggression toward strangers, and this delay is indicative of how much weaker a dog's natural protective drive is versus that of a wolf.

A wolf would immediately kill unfamiliar invaders of his territory. A dog may allow our visitors to live, but the rudiments of his monitoring and protective behaviors and the undesirable behaviors that result from these actions can all be traced back to the typical behavior patterns of his ancestor.

Your dog may fundamentally tolerate unfamiliar people, but he'll still strive to fulfill his monitoring tasks. He'll behave in the same manner toward these people as he would toward predators from other packs. Visitors always present a dog with the potential of danger for himself and his pack.

Your dog won't initially be able to assess the situation when a visitor enters his territory. The visitor's intentions will at this point remain unclear. The dog may have met the visitor in the past and the visitor may have always been amicable, but this won't necessarily continue to hold true. Your dog won't make this assumption, in any case.

He's not able to predict future events based on prior actions. If he doesn't meet visitors with aggression, he'll instead wag his tail and perhaps bark as a means of demonstrating his inner conflict.

Your dog will usually have expectations about social partners that he knows and anticipates. If he's previously had numerous positive experiences with such a partner, he'll also have established a positive set of expectations about this partner. These expectations will potentiate your dog's stress. He now won't just face the decision as to whether this social partner is amicable or hostile – he'll also consider whether they'll satisfy his positive expectations. Dogs therefore respond differently to different people and wag their tails to varying degrees. They at some point associate expectations with all of their social contacts, and these expectations go on to influence their subsequent states of excitement.

Dogs with weak control compulsions may not demonstrate any unusual behavior.
Your dog will prefer to watch visitors from afar if he learns that you control situations. Control means stress, as a dog must be prepared to defend his territory in the case of doubt. Control has nothing to do with joy – at least not for a dog.

21.8 Canine greetings

The greeting ritual that occurs between two or more humans serves to confirm the people's statuses and show acceptance of each another as communication partners. Our Stone Age ancestors used communicative signals just like our dogs – to recognize each other's intentions.
We consider it standard conduct and good manners to welcome other people and offer to shake hands. It's been a long while since these actions concerned sending peace proposals to one another. But what happens if another person doesn't reciprocate your welcome or pointedly refuses to shake your hand? Such people still won't generally be our best friends. Greeting rituals have developed to express the relationship between the involved parties. All of our greeting forms require smiling at the other person if you're pleased about the meeting, for example. Over time, we've developed many other greeting forms to similarly show our counterparts whether we're happy about a meeting, and then just how happy we are. We end up embracing one another and accepting all of the relevant social conventions. These rituals assist mutual recognition and appreciation and have ultimately become an element of our interpersonal communication.

Behavior explained

As we don't know any better, we show our dogs that we're happy to see them in the same manner. A dog can't understand such greeting rituals, however. He doesn't have any need for human recognition or hugs. A greeting fulfills a different purpose among dogs, and they don't take any pleasure in reunions. Why should a dog enjoy a reunion with a rival if he can't even assume that this rival has amicable intentions?

Rituals during canine meetings are used to secure status. When everyone's status has been recognized and it's clear that everything remains as before, the 'greeting ritual' will end and the dogs will tolerate one another.

We behave as if we we're meeting a beloved human when we greet our dogs. All they want to know is whether they and their statuses are secure and if the rules that they previously knew remain valid.

We can see a dog's uncertainty and inner conflict about how a meeting will affect him through the wagging of his tail. A more dog-friendly greeting would reassure him that everything is still the same and that your mood hasn't changed since your last meeting.

We're unfortunately unable to offer our dogs reassurance signals that they can understand and that relieve their uncertainties. A dog nevertheless expects these signals in every meeting with another social partner. It doesn't matter whether he's meeting a dog or a human: He needs these signals so that he can take direction from them. They provide him with information about his counterpart's mood. As we can't provide him with these gestures, he'll remain uncertain about our attitude toward him for a long period. His uncertainty will only subside once he's seen that everything remains the same and that we're behaving toward him in our usual manner. The time that he requires to feel secure in these situations will depend on his self-confidence and your relationship toward him. Older dogs will generally have sufficient experience to recognize earlier on when everything's okay with their humans. These dogs can interpret many behavior patterns and recognize when you're in good or bad moods.

You can create simple routines from which your dog can take direction if you want to relive him of his tension and stress. He'll then be quick to lose his uncertainty in unclear situations and will be able to use the familiar routines to recognize that everything's okay. If a routine is always the same, your dog will know that everything else will remain constant as well.

What do we do instead? We embrace, stroke and hug our dogs as if there were no tomorrow. Their uncertainty is then only strengthened – which we interpret as an increase of their joy in the reunion. A dog will often endure mortal fear in these situations, and the considerable stress may cause him to lose control of his bladder, whine or bark. The stronger your 'assaults' on him, the more reassurance signals he'll show to you. Listen to your dog: He wants to tell you something.

"Please be amicable – I don't want to provoke you. I have peaceful intentions, so please show me that you have the same."

Create a routine for meeting your dog to show him that everything's okay and that yesterday's rules remain valid.

You could take him to his bed area and give him a piece of food from your hand, for example. Behave calmly and avoid all vocalizations as you do this. He's already learned that he's safe in his place. For meetings that take place outside of your home, you might make him lie down and then reward him. He'll very quickly be able to take direction from these or other routines. You'll then avoid unnecessary stress for both your dog and yourself.

When I discussed this topic with a friend, she didn't initially want to believe me when I told her that her dog was very stressed whenever she met him. She nevertheless eventually allowed me to talk her into practicing a routine for a few days. Her dog would be able to take direction from this pattern and recognize that everything was the same as it was yesterday. The routine was intended to help reduce Peppo's stress level.

Peppo was a small Dachshund that often came to visit me during the day. Whenever his owner came to pick him up in the evenings, he'd go completely berserk. He'd cry and bark until he eventually calmed down after quite a while. It wasn't uncommon for him to also have an accident; he couldn't control his bladder as a result of his considerable stress.

I asked Peppo's owner to now wait by her car, open its rear door, and then place Peppo on the backseat without making any comment. She should next close the door, and this would be the end of our routine. We practiced this sequence consistently over the next few days. Peppo's owner found it visibly difficult to place him onto the backseat without saying a word. After just four days, however, his stress had completely subsided and he was taking direction from the routine. On the fifth day I asked her to leave the car door closed while I brought Peppo to her. I took him over as usual, and he sat directly in front of the closed door and waited. He was totally relaxed. He noticed after a while that the door wasn't going to open, and a short while later he began to wag his tail, cry and bark. His owner now opened the door, and he jumped onto the backseat and immediately relaxed.

You can see from this example how simple it is to provide your dog with a routine from which he can take direction.

Peppo's owner was of course somewhat disillusioned to realize that her dog was showing stress rather than pleasure at seeing her. The relationship between Peppo and his owner didn't change after we introduced the routine, however. They're still soul mates, but Peppo's owner now pays attention to when he gives her genuine affection, and not just what we humans misinterpret as canine pleasure. A dog shows his affection in other ways, and these don't include wagging his tail.

If you want to establish reunion routines, it's important to maintain them consistently so that your dog accepts them as guides. You'll soon see that his uncertainty disappears and he's much more relaxed in reunion situations in future.

21.9   My dog jumps up at people

A dog jumping up at people is usually seen as rude behavior that needs to be prohibited in all circumstances. No dog behaves rudely, however. They'll always behave in a manner that they see as correct. We therefore shouldn't prohibit jumping up, but should rather first find out why dogs act in this manner.

Reassurance is the most common reason for a dog to jump up at people (see Page 276, "Licking the corners of other dogs' mouths"). He'll be uncertain of our intentions and so will demonstrate his own amicable intentions with reassuring behavior.

If he sees a human as a threat, however, he may jump up with aggressive intentions.

In both of these situations, the dog feels responsible for his own security and is reacting to the situation. He isn't doing anything wrong; he's behaving in a typical canine manner. If we don't want to tolerate this behavior, we need to provide him with security so that he has no reason to become aggressive or want to independently clarify uncertain situations (see Page 95, "Taking responsibility").

Some dogs will also jump up at people for another reason. Many dog owners have bags full of treats for their dogs. If a dog knows that food comes from his owner's bag, he may jump up or climb his owner's leg so as to claim this food. A dog that's used to doing this to his owner may do the same to other people when they place their hands into their bags, for instance. The dog will assume that there's also food here that can be claimed.

21.10 Enthusiasm for other dogs

The idea that a dog can be enthusiastic about other dogs is a purely human interpretation. Dogs most likely see these situations in a very different manner. Are you pleased to meet entirely unfamiliar other people? Certainly not. We enjoy meetings with people whom we know and like. If we meet someone that we know but absolutely can't stand, our pleasure is contained within strict limits.

Unfamiliar dogs are basically enemies and rivals for resources. We humans find it difficult to understand this fact because we haven't existed in direct competition with other humans for thousands of years. Competitive behavior

Behavior explained

within our species has virtually disappeared over the course of our evolution. It's no longer necessary for us to compete for resources, and we fundamentally tolerate and accept one another as a result. It's only because of this situation that civilization is possible. All of this is unimaginable for a dog.

Dogs don't trust other dogs that they don't know. Two dogs that haven't met in a long while similarly won't automatically trust one another when they next meet. This lack of trust is why dogs should learn to take direction from humans in conflict situations. Your dog will be quicker to tolerate other dogs if they don't pose any threat to his security or resources.

A dog isn't necessarily happy about a meeting if he 'gladly' runs up to other dogs – even if he's wagging his tail. He'll remain uncertain for as long as these other dogs' intentions remain unclear. The situation will make him tense, and this tension will only be relieved when clarity about the others dogs' intentions has been established. He'll therefore strive to clarify such situations early on. If he also has control over the pack, he needs to recognize dangers and threats before these risks are able to jeopardize the pack's safety. He'll often dash toward other dogs so that he can subsequently establish their intentions in a calm manner.

A considerable information exchange will normally have taken place long before we notice the signals that dogs send to each other during meetings. A dog will become uncertain if he can't interpret another dog's signals – perhaps because that dog is too far away or because there remains doubt about his intentions. Situations cause stress if it's not clear whether they'll lead to war or peace. A dog will look for clues as to other dogs' intentions in such situations, and he'll also express his uncertainty by wagging his tail, becoming restless or even barking. Such situations will generally relax quickly if submission or reassurance signals are shown.

Younger dogs will generally show greater uncertainty toward older dogs that don't reveal their intentions. The older dog may stand calmly without even batting an eyelid while the younger dog barks and jumps around in anticipation of information. Such behavior will usually have little to do with an invitation to play.

Behavior explained

A dog is equally in an uncertain, conflicted situation when he 'invites another dog to play' by lying down on his front legs, wagging his tail and baring his teeth in a submissive manner. This gesture can be easily explained by reference to the hunting behavior of wolves.

The image shows how a pack of wolves hunts a bison. You can often see the 'invitation' gesture as soon as a wolf enters a head-to-head situation with his prey. One matter ultimately becomes clear: The wolf doesn't want to play. He also isn't looking forward to the tasty bison leg that he might later eat. He only chooses his posture for a single reason: He can now react to all of his counterpart's actions, including escaping sideways if necessary. He's completely alert and prepared for however the bison might respond. He'll wag his tail as well, although still definitely not out of joy.

Dogs demonstrate exactly the same behavior pattern with one another. If a situation is unclear or a counterpart's reaction is unpredictable, your dog will adopt a posture that allows him to respond to all occurrences and avoid danger. He'll also adopt this posture during play – either as a provocation or as a reaction to a provocation. He may similarly display this behavior toward

Behavior explained

humans. If you move toward your dog while he's in this position, he'll respond by swerving away in an instant.

When a dog shows submission during a confrontation with another dog, he knows that this sign of deference or reassurance is simply a peace offer. The other dog can either accept or decline his proposal. Conflict will remain until both dogs have accepted the other's offer of peace.

Don't rely on dogs not harming one another simply because one of the dogs shows signs of submission.

The notion that dogs will 'work it out among themselves' is correct. When they resolve conflicts in their own way, however, you won't have any influence over the altercation's course or result. Your dog's character may alter if he's seriously hurt when a situation escalates. You should therefore closely observe how the two dogs communicate. It won't normally take long to see whether they've agreed to peace or whether a real dispute is imminent. Dogs might know one another from prior meetings, but this doesn't necessarily mean that they'll always tolerate one other. They'll always check each other's intentions at the start of every encounter. They'll also try to establish whether the rules and freedoms of their last meeting still remain valid. It's difficult to predict whether war or peace will follow, as we don't know what intentions the other dog harbors or what experiences he's gained during the intervening period.

The wolf is prepared for the attack of the bison.

21.11 Making eye contact and baring teeth

Direct eye contact between dogs doesn't necessarily constitute a declaration of war. Multiple clues are always necessary for interpreting behavior. It's nevertheless undisputed that dogs can reassure one another by looking away. This instinctive gesture is how they show their lack of interest in a confrontation. We humans similarly avoid direct eye contact with people who threaten us or might present us with danger. A dog isn't likely to interpret a human making or avoiding eye contact as he would if these actions came from another dog – although staring an already-irritated dog in the eyes will demonstrably increase his aggression.

We express our emotions more through facial gestures than body posture, so dogs quickly learn to recognize our moods from our faces. Attentive dogs will often independently seek out eye contact with us.

Dogs can distinguish human faces. This isn't a ubiquitous skill in the animal kingdom, and it's as a result of this skill that dogs often look at our eyes.[12] A dog knows that you're not a dog and that you therefore send out different signals from other dogs. We don't use our bodies to communicate in the same ways as dogs. He'll nevertheless learn to interpret your body language over time. He won't interpret aggression when you show your teeth while laughing, for example. Loud laughing can cause a dog to feel uncertain because he won't know why you're making this noise or what it means. When he learns that you're in a good mood when you laugh, however, he'll no longer consider you 'baring your teeth' to mean danger.

21.12 Avoidance behavior and displacement actions

All dog owners should know by now that desirable behaviors can't be encouraged with remote trainers, electric collars, choke chains or prong collars. These training aids use pain to teach a dog to avoid certain behaviors such as barking or growling. The triggers for these behaviors will nevertheless continue to lurk within him. When he's exposed to these triggers, he'll still

---

[12] Mongillo P: Animal Behaviour, Oct. 2010.

Behavior explained

react as he did in the past, e.g. with aggression. As he can no longer express this aggression with barking or growling, he may now instead opt to bite.

All behavior patterns that are suppressed with heavy-handed coercion can lead your dog to demonstrate unpredictable alternative behaviors or displacement actions. These new behaviors will generally develop over a long period and will erupt when he's exposed to strong drive triggers.

The term 'displacement action' refers to certain unexpected behaviors that don't appear to bear any direct relation to another behavioral sequence. Example behaviors include yawning, scratching, barking and mounting. Displacement actions help a dog to relieve stress in threatening situations. They also serve as replacement behaviors for reactions that he's planned but hasn't carried out.

If displacement actions aren't sufficient for relieving a dog's stress, he'll demonstrate his forcibly suppressed original behavior in a new, stronger form.

As an example, a leash-aggressive dog's behavior may develop in the following stages:

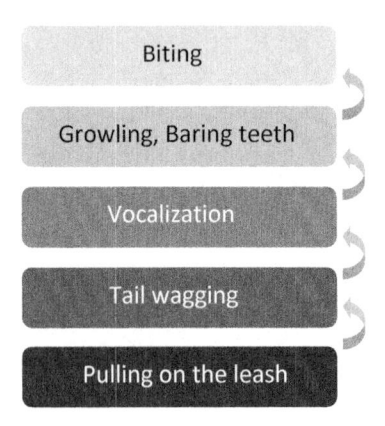

- Biting
- Growling, Baring teeth
- Vocalization
- Tail wagging
- Pulling on the leash

Example:
Your dog didn't have it easy even while he was a puppy. He's quite reserved and fearful by nature. His previous experiences with other dogs haven't been especially positive. He mostly has to submit to unfamiliar dogs, and they'll often demand this submission with violence. He's therefore learned to become aggressive toward other dogs at an early point.

He can't escape from danger while he's on the leash, so he's always very tense during confrontations with other dogs. He now barks at all unfamiliar dogs. You don't tolerate this barking and so punish him for it. He'll stop barking after he's endured this torture on a few occasions.

As he no longer barks, you now search out contact with other dog owners on a more frequent basis. You assume that he's overcome his problem with other dogs. When another dog approaches, however, you see from his bared teeth and growling that he sees this other dog as a threat. You punish him for his aggression once more. He'll subsequently avoid baring his teeth and growling in future.
You meet another unfamiliar dog during a walk some time later. Your dog has long since recognized the threat. As you approach this unfamiliar dog, you already notice that your dog has become very unsettled. The other dog suddenly runs energetically toward you.
If your dog remembers not to bark or growl in this situation but hasn't learned an alternative behavior, he may end up biting without warning.

He has a choice between accepting your punishments and suppressing his aggression. You haven't taken away his reason for becoming aggressive, so he'll continue to demonstrate this behavior – although he will suppress his aggression up to a certain point. He'll release this aggression if a threat becomes too strong, however. He may even raise his aggression to the next level in the case of doubt.

21.13 My dog suddenly stands still

Puppies and young dogs may suddenly refuse to continue during walks. One possible cause for this issue is that the dog is already exhausted. Strangely enough, however, he may abruptly restart if you change your direction.

Think about how a wolf behaves and the rules that apply in his world to unfamiliar territories. It's easily conceivable that another dog's scent marking might cause your dog not to enter his territory. He's respecting the other dog's territorial boundaries and is aware of the danger that lurks within an enemy's area.

A young dog won't yet usually see any reason to follow you. He considers walks that only go in a single direction to be extremely uninteresting. Everything's more exciting than simply moving in one direction. He'll show you this desire by suddenly not wanting to continue and so instead standing still. Encourage him with food and show him that following you makes sense. Don't lure him with the food, but rather reward him for walking with you. If he remains in his standing position, go in the direction that he suggests and stay very close to him. Distance yourself from him somewhat a short while later, and reward him if he then follows you. Move in a big circle so that you can continue on your original path, and encourage him to stay with you throughout by using food.

You'll often notice behavioral changes in your dog when you enter unfamiliar territories. He'll suddenly become very attentive, will look around for other dogs, will respond to you less well, or will become jumpy and fearful. His marking behavior will also normally change in enemy areas.

Such behavior will usually stop if you move through these areas more frequently and your dog learns that he's not really in any danger.

Fearful or uncertain dogs will often stand still when you encounter forks in paths. They'll want to decide which paths to follow and which paths they'd rather avoid.

These dogs will be reluctant to move through unfamiliar terrain. They'll always see unfamiliar paths as posing more threats, so they'll instead prefer paths that they know and paths that seem safe.

21.14 Why does my dog paw at the ground after defecating?

There are various theories and opinions about why dogs paw at the ground.

The action is supposedly part of a dog's marking behavior, for instance. It helps him to distribute the scents that he's just deposited with his feces. These scents let other dogs know who's in control of that territory.

Pawing is also said to act as a visual marker, and the odors that a dog's paws leave on the ground during the action are similarly attributed to marking behavior.

These assumptions about marking behavior certainly don't apply to all dogs. You can see pawing in dogs that don't otherwise demonstrate any marking behavior, are quite fearful by nature, and travel far away from paths before relieving themselves.

It's also possible that pawing is intended to cover up what a dog leaves behind so that no attention is drawn to the associated odor. The action may not be well enough targeted to completely cover the feces in most instances, but it may alter the scent's concentration in the air and so eliminate clear signs about how long ago the odor was left. Dogs that are concerned about not standing out or provoking anyone could therefore cover their tracks and so reduce the risk of a confrontation with a rival.

21.15 Why do dogs roll around?

Some researchers believe that dogs roll around in muck, feces or grass as a behavioral relic from when they used to catch prey. Other animals won't be able to sniff out a dog if he's masked his scent.

Rolling around will often simply be associated with a dog's sense of wellbeing. He may also be demonstrating marking behavior if he only brushes his neck on the ground. This action will cover him with a prey item's scent and similarly cover this prey item with his scent. He can then show other dogs that he controls this prey item. His pack will equally be able to find the prey item later on by following the scent trail that he'll subsequently leave through the territory.

21.16 Why do dogs bury food?

A dog may bury his food if he's being over-fed. You should reduce such a dog's food ration so that he recovers a natural food drive. Dogs will often also demonstrate this behavior directly at their bowls – or they may paw at the floor next to where their food is placed.

21.17 Aggression while on the leash

A dog's range of movement is very limited by the length of his leash. He can't escape from danger, so he's forced to develop alternative strategies for dealing with threats. His limited movement also means that he can't communicate at all well with other dogs. Misunderstandings will therefore often arise between dogs, and these can soon escalate. It's common for a dog to demonstrate considerably more on-leash aggression if he's walking far ahead of his owner. He's now alone and knows that there's no one to resolve conflicts on his behalf. As escape isn't an option, his only way of handling danger is usually attack. Once he's developed this problem-solving strategy, he won't independently give it up going forward.

21.18   My dog's tricking me

No matter what your dog does, his actions won't ever be intended to trick or annoy you. What you're really seeing in his behavior are the consequences of his training. Your dog has learned that particular routines equate to the prospect of need satisfaction. Certain actions that you've repeated have led him to take direction from these routines. He's now picked up on regularities from your everyday life and is using his observations to his advantage. He'll only ever do what you've consciously or subconsciously taught him.

21.19   It's not a question of size!

You may have wondered why a larger, more powerful dog will sometimes submit to a much smaller dog in a confrontation. We can barely understand this behavior, but it's a result of dogs not having any self-perception. They can't compare their body sizes with other dogs. They don't know how big they are or how much physical superiority they possess. It's therefore unimportant how big or small another dog might be. All that's important to a dog's self-assertiveness is his body language.

When dogs confront one another, the superior animal is the one who can control resources and also express this ability through his body language. Such body language makes him appear more self-confident than the other dog, and similarly makes it clear that he's in command of the situation. The superior dog isn't always the largest or strongest. It's really intelligence and experience that are decisive when it comes to establishing a predator's superiority in conflict situations. Dogs that want to gain mastery over others with aggressive behavior aren't usually dominant. Genuine dominance doesn't require aggression.

A dog's self-awareness is determined via how others behave toward him. He may be a Great Dane, but he'll still seem small and inferior if he's always had to submit to others in the past. In contrast, a Pinscher that's always managed to dominate other dogs is likely to appear large and superior.

21.20   Calming signals

Wolves have developed behavior patterns over the course of their evolution that allow them to resolve conflicts between one another, relieve tensions in their pack, and thereby ensure social harmony within their group. Physical altercations can therefore be avoided. This is particularly important for retaining the capability to hunt. Dogs show reassurance signals when they're uncertain, afraid, concerned or in response to another dog's gesture. The aim here is to relieve stress or tension and also prevent a conflict from escalating. The ability to dissipate conflicts with reassurance signals is genetically determined and so not learned. All dogs are born with the ability to show these signals. Dogs see them as offers of peace. There's no fundamental obligation for another dog to accept such an offer, however – and especially not if that dog comes from a different pack.

Licking above the nose
Dogs demonstrate this behavior on a very frequent basis. It's intended to show their counterparts that they don't want to provoke them. They also show this signal to humans.

If you stroke your dog on the stomach, for instance, and he responds by rolling over and licking above his nose, you can see that he wants to reassure you. This is a sign that he isn't enjoying being touched. He's uncertain about what effect your behavior will have on him, and he therefore wants to avoid provoking you.

Licking the corners of other dogs' mouths
Wolves tend to live together in small packs, with the parent animals providing food for their offspring. Once the parents have found food, they transport it back to their young by eating more than necessary and then regurgitating it when they return. The cubs lick at the corners of their parents' mouths to stimulate this regurgitation.

All dogs now understand licking at the corners of the mouth to be a reassurance gesture – although it can equally be a means of begging among adult dogs. Most dogs will also lick humans' faces and the corners of their mouths. Your dog isn't happy if he licks the corners of your mouth while he's excited. He instead wants to reassure you and so is trying to make you aware of his peaceful intentions.

He often won't be able to assess your behavior in exciting situations. He therefore uses this means of reassurance to forestall any hostility that you may present.

We humans are normally much larger than our dogs, so they'll often jump up at us to lick the corners of our mouths. Your dog isn't behaving in a joyful or rude manner if he jumps up at you or your visitors while he's excited: He simply wants to offer reassurance.

Lifting a paw, Pawing at you, Nudging you with his nose

A dog 'paws at you' if he nudges you with his paw. In older dogs, this gesture is a hangover from how they stimulated the flow of milk as puppies. Pawing is often shown when a dog begs, invites you to do something, or wants to reassure you. Nose nudging similarly has its origins in how a puppy prepares his mother's teats to give milk.

Laughing

A 'laughing' dog will often let his ears fall to the side and pull back the corners of his mouth. You'll be able to see all of his teeth with this gesture. Your dog is actually signaling to other dogs that he's not looking for a confrontation (see Page 255, "My dog laughs"). He'll simultaneously avert his eyes from his counterpart and thereby reinforce his submission.

Rolling onto his back

Dogs use this gesture to submit to other dogs. They adopt this entirely helpless position to demonstrate that they won't put up any resistance and that they're completely surrendering to their counterpart. The action will often be their final signal before a situation escalates. If the other dog doesn't accept the peace offer, it may not be long before serious injuries are inflicted. As a dog's breast and stomach area are very vulnerable to bite wounds, such an attack can easily have life-threatening consequences.

21.21 My dog is inquisitive

Humans have a particularly strong desire for new information. This is partly because we can enter new situations without fear; we're the masters of solving problems. It's also because new information can contribute to our social status. People are welcome in our society if they can entertain others with news. A dog doesn't have this need for social recognition. He's much happier when everything carries on as normal, and new or unfamiliar things cause him more uncertainty than pleasure. He'll only tend to behave in an inquisitive manner if he's collecting information that concerns his own status or security. He won't sniff at other dogs' marking places or 'curiously' explore unfamiliar terrain because he's genuinely inquisitive – but rather because he wants to ensure that his safety isn't at risk.

21.22 False pregnancy

A bitch may develop a false pregnancy a few weeks after she's been on heat. Her mammary glands will enlarge and she'll begin to produce milk.

Wolves have their cubs in spring when the meadows are green and food is abundant. It makes sense from a biological perspective to bring offspring into the world at this time of year. The cubs have a much greater chance of survival due to the availability of food. It'll usually be the alpha bitch in a pack that breeds, but the other bitches will develop false pregnancies so that they can produce milk and act as replacement mothers. They can subsequently nurse the cubs if anything happens to the leading animal. In sociobiology, this phenomenon is referred to as a 'Helpers at the nest' system.

False pregnancies secure the life of the litter and so serve the survival of the species. Our domestic dogs have retained this entirely natural process.

22 What's meant by 'species appropriate'?

Every dog owner at some point considers whether he's handling his dog in a manner that's appropriate to his species. But what does it mean to handle an animal in a species-appropriate manner? And is doing so what's best for this animal?

All that's ultimately important is ensuring that a dog can lead a happy and fulfilling life. We therefore have to ask whether our current understanding of species-appropriate animal ownership is an automatic path to happiness for our dogs.

In Ethology, we consider the behavior of wild dogs and wolves and then use this information to determine what is and isn't species appropriate. Our current understanding of species-appropriate animal ownership directs us to try and replicate our pets' natural habitats in the best possible manner within our civilized, unnatural surroundings. It makes absolute sense for a zoo or wildlife reserve to simulate an animal's natural habitat in this way. But this form of animal ownership doesn't work when a different species is supposed to be integrated into a family as a social partner. We want to co-exist with our dogs and share living spaces with them.

For this to succeed, we have to open our worlds to our dogs and allow them to become parts of them. We have to give them the same level of protection that we afford to vulnerable humans. They should receive help just like all others in the world who need help. And just as our dogs should participate in our lives, they should also know that we have a fixed place in their lives.

If we don't allow a dog to become a part of our life, he'll carry on living in his own world. Problems will then arise in our co-existence with him. Humans and dogs can live in parallel without problems, but they can't live together in this manner. As soon as two living spaces coincide, certain standards and rules need to exist that are understood and accepted by all of the parties involved.

A dog sees the world through the eyes of a predator whose existence depends on acquiring food and holding out against rivals. We haven't had to lose sleep over these issues for a very long time. Who among us has to fight for his food, stand up to rivals or constantly guard against threats? These are everyday concerns in a dog's world. This situation can quickly lead to problems when dogs live alongside us.

A dog will often have a completely different take on things that we find fun or see in a positive light. From a dog's point of view, for instance, the huge parcel of land in front of our house isn't a playground: It's a huge amount of work. This area is first and foremost a part of his territory, so it needs to be guarded and also defended in the case of doubt. His compulsion to take on these tasks comes from his lupine heritage, and it's a necessary behavior for his survival in the wild. Such behavior exists in all dogs and is important for securing critical resources, although it's less pronounced in some dogs than in others. A dog can only really relax and live a worry-free life once all of his important tasks have either been completed or taken over by someone else.

Our human perception of species-appropriate animal ownership often causes the exact opposite of what we want to achieve with our mostly well-intentioned laws and regulations.

Even if a dog acts as he would in the wild when among other dogs, we still need to ask ourselves whether he's happy to behave in this way.

The best example of species-appropriate animal ownership comes from the only mammal that's able to live a self-determined life: Man.

We humans decide how to shape our environments and create our own habitats. Only we have these capabilities. If we had to live in a species-appropriate manner, we'd live in the forests and consume nature's fruits – just as we did for the past four million years. We've instead cut down more than 90% of the original forests in Europe so that we can realize our own ideas of suitable living.

These forests were once our natural habitat, but we've chosen to destroy them in favor of living in concrete, stone, steel and glass. When this is the case, why do we presume to decide what's suitable and unsuitable for another type of living being? An animal may live in a naturally grown habitat or demonstrate a certain behavior when in the wild, but this doesn't imply that he likes or chooses this state of affairs. In their natural surroundings, most creatures have no option but to act as they do.

When animals live alongside humans, lots of their behavior patterns cease to make sense. Many of our dogs unfortunately don't know this, so we need to show it to them.

But why are we such bad dog owners when we only want the best for our four-legged friends? It's because we project our human needs and emotions onto our dogs and so end up ignoring their real requirements (see Page 62, "Empathy").

If we see a dog with a limp, for example, we empathize with him because we think that we can understand his suffering. We image how we'd feel and what pain we'd experience in the same situation.

We act in the same manner when a dog's in a kennel or wearing a leash. We fall back on our own experiences and infer how the dog must feel. We subconsciously expect his experience to match our imagined versions – and we thereby project our emotions onto him.
Dogs will actually experience most situations and emotions in a completely different way from us. We treat them in accordance with our human emotions, but we're not aware of what our resulting actions mean to them.

It's common to see dog owners using retractable leashes. They're convinced that they're doing their dogs a favor with these tools, as they wouldn't want to be on a fixed leash if the relationships were to be reversed.

The owners are really just transferring their emotions onto their dogs in this situation. A dog isn't human, so he'll interpret situations in an entirely different manner from us. He doesn't walk ahead on a leash because he wants to, but rather because he has to.

We humans can fill our freedom with activities that give us pleasure. We can enjoy our spare time and realize our aspirations. These needs don't exist in a dog's world. His life predominantly consists of work that secures his existence. Freedom has a completely different meaning for him than it does for us. His freedom is the basis for his existence – just like going to work every day is the basis for our existence. The more freedom he has, the more duties he has to perform. A dog that has a large territory needs to monitor, guard and defend this area. He'll instinctively take on these tasks because his life depends on them in the wild. He needs to pull on his leash to complete his tasks, and we sometimes use retractable leashes to make our lives easier as a result. Our dogs then have the freedom to walk far further ahead. We end up giving them the task of monitoring everything, so they now have more work for the same salary. If I were treated this way in a job, I'd quit.

The responsibility that we give to our dogs when we use retractable leashes causes them considerable stress. We want to do something good for them, but we ultimately only add to their problems.

You often hear dog owners say that their male dogs only have problems with other male dogs. This is another situation in which we project our subjective feelings onto a dog's emotional world. No dog only has problems with other dogs of a certain sex. This is a purely subjective perception that's perhaps given weight by our own prejudice. Another dog's sex is never the cause of aggression.

Some dogs are given bed areas near to windows so that they can watch the world go by when they're not outside. A dog doesn't need to watch others, however. He also doesn't have any appreciation of aesthetics, art, symmetry or nature's beauty. Even Homo sapiens only developed this ability some 35,000 years ago. The Neanderthals weren't able to develop an appreciation of art or painting, for instance. So why do we give dogs bed areas near to windows? Because we'd rather sit by a window than anywhere else in a house.

Our care for our dogs actually produces a negative result yet again. If unfamiliar dogs or other uninvited guests walk past a dog's window, he'll want to defend his territory and so will bark. He'll have to remain constantly alert and watching for rivals that might be prowling around in his area. An attempt to do something good for a dog will have actually left him with more stress than he had before.

Many owners also claim to know that their dogs don't like having other dogs sniff around their hindquarters. Human feelings are transferred onto the dogs once more. We wouldn't like our counterparts to sniff around our rears on every meeting, and we unconsciously assign our notions of this situation onto our dogs. We don't sniff at other humans' rears and we've never done this, either.

Dogs find out a lot about other dogs from their scents.

This action is nevertheless part of how a dog communicates. It's important for preserving the social order, as it allows him to recognize his position within the community and also obtain information about his counterpart. There therefore aren't any dogs that don't like having their hindquarters sniffed. If your dog responds aggressively when another dog approaches, this is generally because he sees almost all other dogs as presenting a serious threat. He'll respond with defensive behavior whenever another dog crosses into his personal space.

When we rescue a dog, we liberate him from a kennel and give him a new home. This home will sometimes have a huge plot of land where he can really let off steam. He should have a good life with us, after all. He'll nevertheless see this land privilege from a very different perspective. We humans consider land to have a recreational value, so the more land we have, the better. Dogs associate a large territory with significant work, and the larger the territory, the greater the workload. Look at a dog that spends all day protecting his area by standing at a fence and barking at passers-by – and then reconsider whether access to an open space really makes a dog happy.

We often think that a dog is excited and wants to play if he wags his tail when he sees an unfamiliar dog. We therefore let him off his leash. But why should a dog be excited about an unfamiliar rival? He can't tell whether this other dog has peaceful intentions toward him.

If you can evaluate your dog's behavior in an objective manner, you'll also be able to recognize his needs correctly and treat him in the right way. You probably won't let him off his leash so readily in future once you realize that confrontations with other dogs will always cause him stress and come with risks.

A dog sees our world through different eyes. He assesses situations from a predator's perspective. He'll only object to being attached to a leash if it prevents him from running ahead while he's constantly forced into doing so.

A kennel can also be the most wonderful place on Earth for a dog. It doesn't matter that we think this place seems horrible: He'll consider a kennel to be paradise if all of his needs are satisfied here.

It's up to us to design our dogs' living quarters. We have opportunities that aren't open to other creatures because of the resources that we control. We're masters over our own survival-critical resources, and we also control these resources for our dogs. We can therefore satisfy all of their needs. We should nevertheless avoid the desire to satisfy needs that they don't really have.

A good dog owner should consciously think like a dog – and not subconsciously treat his dog like a human.

23 Keeping a dog occupied

There's always something to do, at least for a dog. To survive in the wild, both dogs and wolves are almost continually occupied with sourcing food, rearing their offspring or ensuring their own safety. Dogs are workaholics. They don't ever clock off and they don't recognize any fixed working hours or spare time. Even when they're doing nothing they're fulfilling a need to do nothing, and this in turn also serves a purpose. Rest allows a predator to recharge and relax so that they're ready to hunt once again.

The activities that occupy a dog are first and foremost aimed at ensuring his existence. Like humans, dogs work to guarantee their livelihoods.

Our domestic dogs have also had jobs during their evolution. They were no longer required to secure their own existences, so we humans gave them tasks. We didn't need to think about keeping our dogs occupied: They had to search for tracks, guard the farm, hunt game, catch mice, or help the shepherd to tend his sheep.

We've increasingly kept dogs as pets over the last century. They no longer have any special functions, and they now fulfill the roles of social partners more than employees. Most families who adopt a dog today also have these requirements. In consequence, however, people often forget that these animals continue to demonstrate behaviors that are important to their survival in the wild. They don't have to act in these ways any more, but they do so nonetheless. As an example, a dog won't go for a walk: He'll go to work. He can't recognize that he doesn't have to work in our human world and that supermarkets provide an alternative to hunting. He's equally unaware that doors and gates protect him from danger.

We humans can take work away from our dogs and allow them to enjoy lives of leisure. They'll then have the freedom to do whatever gives them pleasure.

A dog's freedom still needs to be filled in a meaningful manner. This occupation should ideally consist of activities that he enjoys.

Keeping a dog occupied

We've now arrived at an important question: How can you keep your dog occupied?

In answering this question, you first need to clarify what you want to achieve by keeping your dog occupied. Should he enjoy what he's doing, or do you simply want to tire him out?

It doesn't matter what activity you choose if your sole objective is to tire him out. Everything is suitable providing it challenges him in mental and physical terms. Options include human tracking, trail finding and dog sports.

You need to pay closer attention to your choices if you want him to enjoy what he's doing. Once you've worked out what he likes, you can select activities that will make a good contribution to your human-dog relationship. You'll be able to use these activities to interact with him in a positive manner – and you'll then actively satisfy his needs as a result. Just be careful not to choose activities that you enjoy but that aren't well suited to him.

I'm not a dog, so I naturally don't know what dogs enjoy. We need to answer this point by establishing what we humans enjoy and why this is the case. We can then transfer this knowledge to our dogs.

Does physical exertion make us happy?

If we had to live in accordance with our species like we demand from our dogs, we'd have to hunt for our meat or roam in forests for hours to collect fruits. We're physically able to walk long distances in an extremely resource-efficient manner. By walking upright, we expend about a fifth of the energy that's used by chimpanzees. It was chiefly this efficient form of movement that made us into the successful hunters that we remain today. We've become the only species on Earth that can control its own resources. Even major incidents such as the extinction of big game in Australia some 50,000 years ago can be traced back to Homo sapiens' incredible hunting success. Big game vanished from the area at the same time as Homo sapiens arrived. The only kind of big game that survived the Pleistocene period in Australia was the kangaroo.

But what made us into such good hunters given that we're not actually predators?

Some of our ancestors developed a reduced amount of body hair. Sweating onto their bare skin allowed them to regulate their body temperatures better than most predators.

We consequently became extremely good distance runners. We could chase our prey for between 40 and 50 km until they were exhausted. The prey animals were normally much faster than us, but they couldn't continue for such long periods.

Our bodies are able to walk between 40 and 50 km every day (more than 150 km at peak points). It's therefore appropriate to our species to walk long distances. We've done little else for the past four million years. But what do we do now? The average human currently walks no more than an average of a kilometer each day![13]

We do everything in our power to ensure that we don't have to exercise any more than is absolutely necessary. We build cars, escalators and elevators, and we design our workplaces to be ergonomic.

If we enjoyed walking 40 km every day, we could do so; no one's stopping us. And yet we don't. Walking was only a means to an end for our ancestors. Their survival depended on it, as it was only by walking that they could exploit new food sources. We only endured the associated strain so that we could survive.

A wolf or a dog equally doesn't hunt because he enjoys hunting, but rather because hunting ensures his survival.

It's similarly not in his nature to be nocturnal. He'd immediately shift to day shifts if these hours offered him better prospects of success. A wolf isn't happier during the nights than the days simply because we think of him as being nocturnal.

---

[13] According to the German Health Ministry, the average German citizen walks around 2,000 steps each day – amounting to an average daily distance of 1.4 km.

Keeping a dog occupied

Hunting causes stress and uses up a lot of energy. You can't assume that this stress or physical exertion makes a dog happier. A dog will run alongside you as you cycle 20 km every day, but I doubt that he'll enjoy this activity.

Would you like having to run a marathon before breakfast every day just because someone said that doing so was appropriate for your species? I certainly wouldn't.

The situation is exactly the same for a vast number of other domestic pets. These animals are happy even though they don't exercise to the same extent that they would in the wild. Many cats solely live inside houses, for example. They've never seen the open sky, and yet they don't appear to be unhappy. Rabbits, hamsters and birds often live similar existences, but they're also not necessarily unhappy. Dog owners are the only pet owners to measure their animals' happiness levels by how much they exercise.

I don't want to imply that exercise is bad for our dogs. Quite the opposite, in fact: From a physiological perspective, exercise is vital for maintaining fitness. Considerable exercise is nevertheless far from able to maintain fitness by itself.

When it comes to maintaining your dog's physical fitness, what's really important is the type and intensity of strain to which his musculoskeletal system is exposed. I know many elderly dogs that are no longer able to raise their hind legs, so they now drag their claws along the floor when they walk. Their restricted movement is often accompanied by a hardening of their spines. The issue wasn't caused by a lack of exercise, but rather by a lack of variation in exercise. If a dog only ever walks on surfaced paths and at a moderate pace, the muscle groups that are responsible for raising his legs will reduce in size. Other muscles will shorten or harden as a result of their lack of stretching. The dogs' health problems will have ultimately been caused by their bodies' self-adjustment in accordance with the resource-saving principle of minimization.

A dog's subjective feeling of wellbeing isn't so dependent on how much he exercises or whether he's fully worn out each day. His muscles will deteriorate if he exercises less and build up if he exercises more – exactly in line with the economical principle of the natural world.

Every organism is designed to remain alive with the least possible energy usage. If something isn't required for survival, it'll degenerate so as to avoid wasting resources. This concept applies to muscles and bones as well as to mental capacity.

When we humans run today, we do so because we enjoy this activity. There's no need for us to run, and we determine how far and how intensively we travel. Dogs and wolves can't make these decisions.

We exercise because we want to and not because we have to. Even when we do exercise, it's often not the actual exercise that gives us pleasure. It's common for other matters to be far more decisive in whether or not we enjoy what we do.

When we play tennis, for example, we certainly exercise and make demands of our bodies. But we only have fun if we also win. You won't find any tennis players who enjoy their games but always lose. The actual exertion is of secondary importance to gauging your own strength and beating your opponent.

One of my friends similarly told me that he enjoys cycling. He actually rides more than 10,000 km each year. But he doesn't really like cycling. Why? If he really enjoyed the activity, he'd also love cycling uphill or riding an old ladies' bicycle that has half-deflated tires. What type of bicycle does he use? A 9 kg racing bicycle with rock-hard 20 mm tires. And why? Because he doesn't like cycling as much as he likes exerting as little effort as possible. Crazy, right?

Only a very small percentage of the human population takes part in sport. Even fewer people actively pursue competitive sports. More people would be involved in these activities if effort and physical exertion alone made us happy. Competition is only fun if you have the prospect of winning against others, and very few people have this prospect.

The same situation applies to non-competitive exercise: Any enjoyment that we derive will usually come from factors that aren't related to the associated physical strain. We'll take little or no pleasure from the activities without these factors. Aerobics and dance classes are largely popular due to the opportunities that they provide for communicating and interacting with others. Most people will have less fun dancing alone at home than they will if they dance in a group. Watching sport in front of a television is equally not the same as exercising with other people. The better you know these other people and the more positive your relationships with them, the more fun you'll have in exercising alongside them.

Mental occupation also isn't enjoyable because it requires intellectual exertion. If you solve crosswords, for example, you'll experience success when you work out the correct words. If you never find the right solutions, you'll never enjoy crosswords, mahjong, sudoku puzzles or memory games.

When groups of friends come together every week to play cards, they don't just do so for the mental effort of the games. I know people who meet for this purpose on a weekly basis but always lose. They enjoy the social contact, the interaction with the others, and not least the satisfaction of their human need for recognition when they eventually manage to catch a good hand.

There are also fun activities that don't require competition against someone else or even another person's involvement. I'm thinking here of many sports that are enjoyable because they make you overcome your fears, cross boundaries or successfully learn new things. Lots of these sports also cause you to uncover completely new emotions, which in turn induce states of excitement that make you want to do the sports again. Examples of such sports include paragliding, base-jumping, snowboarding, surfing and skating. These activities often start by causing inner states of stress that later subside and are instead perceived as feelings of pleasure; you'll have achieved something that was previously impossible. Once again, we only participate in these activities to a certain extent because we're successful at them. Our nervous systems reward us with endorphins for what we've done and how we've overcome our states of stress.

Our urges to satisfy our individual needs also drive us to do certain things that aren't always enjoyable. We've developed a need to be acknowledged and respected as individuals by those around us. We show our personality – and so who we are – in everything that we do. This is the only way that we can find like-minded people and social connections. We don't just buy any items of clothing; we search each item out. The same applies with furnishings, cars, vacations and leisure activities. Much of what we do isn't founded in pure joy, but is rather a means of highlighting our individuality and so satisfying an entirely human need for recognition of our uniqueness. It's the satisfaction of this need that makes us happy and also justifies the purchase of extremely expensive cars or totally overpriced vacations.

It's therefore not physical or mental exertion that makes us happy, as other matters will usually play a much more important role. Physical or mental activities are often just a means to an end. It's much more common for success or need satisfaction to give us pleasure. Specific sources include the care that we give to interpersonal relationships, the states of excitement that we gain from experiences, and the recognition that we're awarded by our social environments.

It's not sufficient to simply expose a dog to physical or mental strain if we want him to enjoy an activity. All creatures will become stressed and unable to derive much pleasure from an activity if it exposes them to burdens that aren't worth their while to bear.

Sheepdogs act as an example here once again. As has already been mentioned, these dogs are forbidden from grabbing the animals that they herd. They develop a strong desire to seize their prey as they hunt, but they're never able to satisfy this urge. It must be frustrating to never obtain need satisfaction in this manner. It's only the dogs' inner drive for success and the simultaneous prospect of success that prevents them from losing their motivation for herding.

A wolf also doesn't hurt because he enjoys physical exertion, but rather because hunting secures his survival. Hunting causes him stress and requires considerable energy. A wolf's success rate when hunting is around 6%, so he'll

Keeping a dog occupied

fail on 94 of every 100 approaches that he makes. If you apply Freud's drive theory to this situation, he can only achieve drive satisfaction if he's successfully able to grab prey. Frustration will therefore dominate 94% of his hunting efforts, giving him in turn absolutely no sense of pleasure.

It's similarly no guarantee that a dog enjoys a behavior simply because he decides to act in this manner. It may be 'in his nature' to hunt, but this doesn't necessarily mean that he enjoys hunting. A wolf may run up to 200 km a day, but he won't do so out of choice.

I'd like to present a conversation that I overhead between a mother and her daughter as an example of this issue.

I came across the pair in a bookshop. The mother wanted to buy her daughter a book and so do something good for her. The daughter seemed less interested in the idea. They discussed which book to buy for a short while before the daughter said that she didn't really want one at all. Her mother responded: "But you enjoyed reading so much while you were with your grandparents during vacation. Why don't you want a book now?" The daughter answered: "I don't like reading at all. Grandma and grandpa don't have a TV, so what else was I supposed to do?"

As you can see, even things that seem obvious can present different pictures on closer examination. Just like the little girl, dogs and wolves in the wild have few options about how to behave. It's all about survival. Wolves don't have plentiful food supplies, so they can't afford to give up hunting. If you want to treat your dog well, you need to question any behaviors that seem to be 'parts of his nature'.

Does a dog enjoy taking part in sport?

Of course not! A dog would never independently choose to complete an agility course, crawl through a tunnel, dash over a seesaw or run laps of a racetrack.

I was visiting a friend at a dog-training ground one afternoon. An agility group was just starting to assemble their equipment. While the people were building up the course, their dogs were running around the ground. When the assembly was complete, the owners went back to the clubhouse for a coffee and left the dogs to their own devices. I stood at the training ground fence and watched how the dogs behaved. Once the group had calmed down and all of the dogs had established that the others were amicable, they all lay down to relax and do nothing. None of the dogs decided to complete the course. There were almost 20 dogs in the group, but not one went over the seesaw, crawled through the tunnel or ran through the slalom course.

A dog needs to be given the prospect of success before he'll undertake these actions. We use food or prey (toys) for this purpose. He won't do anything without these motivators.

We might go jogging or complete an obstacle course, but we'll do so for completely different reasons from a dog. We may enjoy these activities or be motivated by other factors, whereas a dog will do them because they're worth his while. He'd be equally excited about his reward if he didn't have to struggle so hard for it.

If a dog were to voluntarily participate in and derive pleasure from the activities, we wouldn't need treats or toys to make him try his best. You don't need any incentive to do something that you enjoy.

We similarly need to consider whether dogs actually enjoy chasing substitute prey items such as balls or sticks.

Chasing an object satisfies everything that a dog basically needs to experience pleasure. His hunting drive will be triggered when you throw the item, and he'll then chase after it and attempt to grab it. He'll at some point be successful, so you can assume that he enjoys the activity as a result. For a more accurate view, however, you need to know what's going on in his head during the chase.

Why does a dog really run after a ball? And why don't all dogs do this? A dog needs a clear desire to claim an object if he's going to give chase – or at least a pronounced hunting drive. He won't be interested if has little or no need for his own property and similarly no hunting ambition.

Keeping a dog occupied

He needs to want to claim the ball if he's going to run after it. He'll try to seize your property by reaching it before you can do the same. You release the ball from your possession by throwing it, and he'll subsequently try to take it ahead of you and therefore win it for himself. He won't normally bring it back to you once he's taken it. It's now his, after all. It's even likely that he'll run around in front of you with the ball so as to show off his trophy. He'll only return it if he's learned that doing so is worth his while – either because you reward him or because you throw the ball again so that he can satisfy his hunting drive once more.

A dog will usually be quick to lose interest in his captured prey if you wave another ball in front of him. His attention will rapidly be drawn to the new item. It's therefore a competitive situation between you and your dog that first drives him to chase after a ball. He wants your ball and not the ball that he already has.

If you consider this situation in the context of your human-dog relationship, such competition isn't especially conducive to interacting with your dog in a positive manner.

If you want your dog to see you as a leading figure, you need to be able to provide him with security. He consequently needs to trust that you're sufficiently superior to ward off threats in conflict situations. He'll perceive you as a weaker social partner if he always ends up taking charge in such situations. No one – and certainly no dog – would entrust their safety to someone weaker than or inferior to themselves.

Imagine that several other people are threatening you. Who would you place your trust in? A boxing champion or a weak young boy? This is exactly the choice that your dog has to make when he's faced with impending conflicts. He won't trust you to ensure his safety if he sees you as a weak young boy. He'll actually feel responsible for your safety instead.

The same situation occurs with tugging games. A dog may approach his owner with a stick or other toy in his mouth and propose a competition over the object. Most owners will take up the offer. They'll tug at (compete for) the object and ultimately allow their dog to win. The dog won't want to give up the toy after his victory, so he'll run away with his prey if his owner subsequently goes up to him.

Why does the dog propose a tugging game in the first instance? Does he enjoy the activity? Yes, and because it offers him the prospect of success. If you emerge as the winner whenever you play in future, he'll eventually lose interest in the competition and will stop asking you to play.

It's solely the prospect of success that motivates him to initiate the duel. The problem here is that his resulting image of you isn't desirable if you want to bear responsibility for his security. No dog will challenge another dog in the wild if he knows that this other dog will always emerge as the superior. Your dog will consequently only challenge you if he sees you as a potentially weaker party. It's only in this situation that he'll have a relatively good chance of winning the competition.

We humans don't act any differently. No one enjoys losing, so we'd never initiate a competition with someone if we only had minimal prospects of success. Boredom wouldn't make me want to fight a boxing champion, for instance. I wouldn't enjoy this activity because there simply isn't any chance that I'll win.

Your dog will assess his prospects of victory or defeat against you even if the activity in question isn't a serious competition.

If you play a small, friendly tennis game with a friend, for example, both parties will still want to know who'd win in a real match. You'll both enjoy the game, but you'll also learn to assess your opponent in the correct manner.

A dog can read situations equally well. Just like with your tennis match, pack animals pick up on the likely victors of serious competitions by playing with one another. These competitions are therefore extremely rare in pack environments.

You'd soon lose interest in a tennis match if your friend intentionally allowed you to win. Any potential success would have become worthless.

Keeping a dog occupied

When raising a child, it's advised to let him win from time to time – although naturally so that he doesn't notice what you're doing. If a child has low self-confidence and so finds learning difficult, this action allows him to see that working to solve a problem can be worthwhile. The positive experience has a rewarding effect and motivates him to learn independently in future. Dogs don't need this kind of learning motivation. Food is a much better motivator for encouraging a dog to learn his own problem-solving strategies and so boost his self-confidence.

One or two competitive games won't challenge a stable, trusting relationship with a dog, of course. I nevertheless think that you should know what you're doing when you consider how to keep a dog occupied.

Another problem that arises from occupying a dog with hunting games is the lasting state of excitement from which he'll suffer. Hunting causes a dog stress. When he hunts, adrenaline rushes into his bloodstream to prepare him for a confrontation with prey. His digestion also comes to a standstill and he enters into a highly driven state of mind. The longer a ball game continues and the more excessively the dog hunts, the more likely it becomes that he'll end up addicted to these physical consequences. Adrenaline functions as a naturally produced drug. The more often adrenaline is found in the body, the more frequently a dog will search out excitement during periods of calm. He'll ultimately become dependent on this state and will at some point become unable to relax and enjoy rest.

We humans can see this effect in so-called 'adrenaline junkies'. They can't wind down after their adventures, so they become easily frustrated during calm periods and are constantly on the lookout for new ways of raising their adrenaline levels. They're also frequent sufferers of depression, and they often appear restless and uneasy in their surroundings.

Similar effects can be seen in dogs that are constantly occupied with hunting. There's a small difference between dogs and humans here, however. A dog is a predator. We lose control over his hunting behavior if he learns that he can satisfy his drive with anything that moves. In the case of doubt, he'll hunt everything that moves. This may be a cyclist or a playing child. A moving shadow will often be sufficient to trigger such a dog.

You can prevent this problem from arising by never occupying your dog with hunting if he already has a very pronounced hunting drive.

No dog needs to hunt – but if you need to occupy your dog with ball games, an option is to limit these games to a certain area. This place will act as a discriminatory stimulus if it's only ever here that your dog is allowed to hunt. His drive and excitability will then be limited to where the drive is both triggered and satisfied.

But how can you keep your dog meaningfully occupied?

Going for a walk? A walk is just as exciting for a dog as reading a Dostoyevsky novel would be for a six-year old child. A dog will follow you, but only because he doesn't question the meaningfulness of your action.

If you're responsible for the outer territory when you go for a walk, your dog won't be particularly interested in investigating any scent markings, chasing prey, or fighting with other dogs. He doesn't have any tasks, and he'll only follow you because it's in his nature to follow whoever makes the decisions in his pack. Dogs aren't able to question why we do things, to think about the meaningfulness of our actions, or to anticipate our potential plans. Not even primates are capable of such intellectual achievements.

You can nevertheless give a simple walk meaning or highlights. By using your hand to integrate food, you satisfy one of your dog's needs and similarly promote the establishment of a positive relationship with him.

Keeping a dog occupied

You can also meaningfully occupy your dog with a food search. Go to a field where he's safe and won't encounter any rivals. Throw a handful of food into the air so that he has to look around the field for it. You'll now be in the center of the action, and he'll only be able to find food in your near vicinity. You can equally sit down in the field and place the food on and around yourself. Hide it in the creases of your clothes, beneath your legs, under your armpits or between your knees. Your dog will then search you for the food and will positively associate the experience of food with proximity to you.

As with chasing a ball, a food search satisfies all of the conditions that are required for a dog to enjoy this kind of activity. His need to search will be awakened by the food's smell. His pleasure will be ensured by the success that he experiences when he finds the food. If he weren't successful, his motivation for the search would gradually decrease. Trainers of tracking dogs encounter this problem during both training and real jobs. They need to praise their dogs even when success can't be realized; the dogs have to remain motivated even when what they're looking for can't be found. Dogs don't derive pleasure from nose work, but rather from success. Without success, they won't remain interested in the search.

All food searches will unfortunately end negatively at some point. Everything will smell of food and the dog's motivation for the search will remain, but there won't be any more food to find because he will have eaten it all. What's negative for him, however, gives you another chance for positive interaction. He'll look at you quizzically once he's determined that there's no more food. If you reward this gaze with a final piece of food from your hand, you'll end the game in a positive manner and will then be able to continue with your walk.

The fetching of objects also satisfies all of the conditions that a dog requires to have fun. Practice this activity by making him fetch hidden objects, and reward him with food when he returns a found object to you. He'll be mentally challenged, will enjoy himself, and will also associate the positive experience with you.

Another option is agility, which similarly meets all of the criteria that are required for a dog to feel enjoyment. When his efforts are over, he'll have been successful in what he's done.

Agility requires swiftness and maneuverability. You can develop your dog's motor and co-ordination skills with a variety of different exercises. You don't need a fully equipped dog-training field for this purpose, either. Walk with him over rough terrain, for instance, and encourage him to jump over, crawl along or balance on logs. These experiences will make him more confident in his movements and will ultimately teach him how to move in a more certain manner in many different environments. A varied exercise regime is especially important for young dogs so that they can develop their motor abilities.

The physical exertion that's required to complete the course may be of less importance to the dog than the prospect of reward. The associated diversity of movement and variation from routine are nevertheless good for the maintenance of his motor and physical fitness. It's important for a dog to be successful in what he does. Success is guaranteed by the reward that you give him once he completes the course. This reward also allows a form of positive interaction that's vital for building up your relationship.

A dog doesn't satisfy any of his own needs when he works at his maximum performance level. The only need that this effort satisfies is his handler's need for recognition. Winning a competition certainly doesn't satisfy any canine need. Taking over responsibility from your dog means being able to determine when you're boosting his health and equally when you're overexerting him and so putting his health at risk.

We can also take further guidance from humans if we want to explore new ways of occupying our dogs.

We can enjoy activities that don't in any way match our species, for example. We can race cars, go surfing, or slide down snow-covered slopes with boards on our feet. We have to learn how to do all of these activities before we can derive pleasure from them – but once we've picked up an activity, we can make our own decisions about whether to repeat it in future. If we want to go skiing, we don't need any incentive to make this happen. We'll enjoy the activity for itself.

A dog can equally take pleasure from learned behaviors. There are some dogs that enjoy riding on skateboards, playing the piano, or gliding over water on surfboards. They need to learn how to do these activities, but once they've acquired the necessary skills, they can independently decide whether to do the activities again in the future. All that we end up providing are offers. We can assume that a dog enjoys an activity if he takes us up on an offer. When we give a dog a new way of keeping himself occupied, we also provide him with a way of satisfying a need that he'd never have known without us.

A dog can't enjoy activities that satisfy our human needs for recognition, self-realization or individualism, however.

Dogs are similarly unable to appreciate art and aesthetics or to understand humor and irony. They also don't require these abilities for their happiness. We humans have developed certain needs over the course of our evolution that are entirely unfamiliar to our dogs. We can nevertheless satisfy those needs that our dogs do know.

Regardless of the activity, you should always ensure that need satisfaction doesn't become routine for your dog. A need will lose its value if it's satisfied on a regular basis. If your dog can satisfy his needs by himself at any time, his desire to satisfy these needs will reduce. In practice, this means that we need to make the decisions about when our dogs receive need satisfaction. We should only intermittently present them with offers of things to do. They'll then continue to derive pleasure from the activities over the long-term – and their experiences of need satisfaction will also remain perceived as rewards.

Be creative when it comes to keeping your dog occupied and presenting him with a variety of interaction options. Don't force yourself into constantly tiring him out, either. You won't enjoy doing this and your dog doesn't need it.

Take pleasure in what you do and allow your dog to share in these activities. He'll end up having fun as well.

Do dogs really play?

A dog isn't always playing when we assume him to be doing so. If you throw a ball for your dog and he chases after it, he won't necessarily see this situation as a game. Scientists have examined the concentration of the stress hormone cortisol in dogs' blood and found out that such chasing games may cause them stress.[14] A dog is primarily compelled to run after prey by an instinctive drive; running after prey promises him drive satisfaction. When we play chasing games, we use this instinctive drive to keep him occupied. His protective and defensive drives are also primary drives like his chase and prey drives. We'll never understand how a dog feels when one of his drives is satisfied, although I doubt that he enjoys defending his territory or life even though he's driven to act in this manner.

When does a dog play?

Play is an action that serves no purpose other than the realization of pleasure.

A dog will only act out of pure enjoyment if all of his other needs have been satisfied, none of his survival-critical drives are taking priority, he isn't afraid, and he's made an independent decision to behave in this way. He'll therefore only play if he doesn't need food and he's also safe. No one can be challenging his resources or threatening his security. If all of these conditions are met, we can then assume that he's either playing or deriving pleasure from a non-result-oriented behavior.

Young wolves have been seen to slide down snow-covered slopes on their hindquarters before re-ascending the slopes and repeating their actions. This clearly isn't a result-oriented behavior; the cubs are just having fun. They can only enjoy this experience, however, because their parents are satisfying all of their survival-critical needs and they don't bear any responsibilities themselves. They're able to afford to have fun.

---

[14] Dr. Gansloßer U., Strodtbeck S.: The Dog, Jun. 2011.

Puppies don't yet have to provide for themselves or worry about their safety. They have time to discover the world in a playful manner and experience pleasure. When considered from a purely biological perspective, the puppies' actions certainly help them to develop coordinative and motor skills and to learn social behavior. These actions nevertheless do nothing to satisfy their survival-critical needs.

In contrast, adult dogs only play on very rare occasions. They'll only play if they know one another well and there's no territory to watch, mark or defend. Play behavior is equally dependent on neither dog presenting any risk to the other's resources.

Adult dogs use non-serious clashes to check their relative strengths. The information that they gain is used to determine whether the same rules now apply as did during the last meeting, and also which dog is allowed to claim which resources. Wolves use similar confrontations to playfully check and assert their ranking orders. If one of the wolves questions the established order, such a confrontation can quickly escalate into a serious ranking conflict.

If a game involves competition over prey, it may not take long for a serious confrontation to develop.

Supposed games among adult dogs normally have purposes and specific rules. The dogs will make various gestures to one another so as to make clear their intentions. They'll only usually tolerate and engage in the 'game' if it's clear that their counterpart doesn't present any danger and isn't asserting any claim to their resources. The short conflicts that occur between dogs are nevertheless not games in the human sense. They're normally associated with stress for the dogs involved because it's never clear how the confrontations will develop. Dogs are also aware that different rules could apply today in relation to another dog from those that applied yesterday. All meetings between unfamiliar dogs therefore contain a danger of escalation. Even dogs that meet everyday on walks will see one another as coming from different packs.

Humans don't play together very often either, although it may well seem otherwise. You may play tennis with a colleague who's equal to you in the workplace, for example. The match might not be formally competitive in any way, but it'll still be about asserting position, reputation or ranking over one another. You certainly don't want to lose against the weakest member of your department. You similarly won't play against your boss in the same was that you'll play against a good friend. As you can see, play usually has a purpose – and it's often used to assert rankings by humans as well as by dogs.

We humans can only enjoy games during our spare time. We can only relax and have fun once we've completed the jobs that we consider to have existential significance. Your dog is the same: He'll only be able to have fun if he's completed his survival-critical tasks or never had these tasks in the first instance.

There's often a fine line between playfulness and seriousness among dogs. You should therefore never leave playing dogs unattended, and you should also be aware of the potential risks that are associated with canine games. Watch whether both dogs are friendly toward one another and whether they continue to maintain their peace agreement as their game goes on.

You can assume that unfamiliar dogs will never play during a first meeting and that there's a constant danger that this meeting will escalate. Play will also only ever take place between two dogs. It's similarly important to note that

Keeping a dog occupied

one dog can be playing while the other isn't. If one of the dogs is occupied with tasks that prohibit him from demonstrating play behavior, another dog's game can quickly turn into a serious affair.

You can recognize a typical game from features such as role-play. One dog will give chase, and then the other dog will chase back. One dog will submit to the other, and then the roles will reverse. One-sided behavior, constant submission or continuous submission demands don't constitute play. Even if role-reversal seems evident, the situation may still be a one-sided confrontation that needs to be taken seriously. Dogs will often demonstrate their superiority by allowing another dog to give chase before they suddenly become the chasers themselves. Once again, this isn't a game.

Play behavior can only occur in a completely relaxed atmosphere and between dogs that have peaceful intentions toward one another.

Active subordination does not mean peace in any case.

Play always requires a relaxed environment. Typical features of play include the frequent repetition of behavior and the free combination of actions without recognizable aims or final actions. Dogs leave out the final actions when they demonstrate fighting or prey behavior in play; with prey behavior, the final action would be the killing of the prey. Exaggerated movements are another characteristic of game elements.

Remember that submission and reassurance signals that occur in playful situations are only peace offers (see Page 276, "Calming signals"). A dog with hostile intentions doesn't have to accept these offers. Don't underestimate the danger that supposed play can present to your dog. Unfamiliar dogs won't play together in most instances.

24 Final remarks

All that remains is for me to wish you much success in dog training and considerable fun with your four-legged friend.

This book should help you to find your own solutions for dealing with your dog. The Alpha Project isn't a training method: It's a core philosophy.

You'll encounter many obstacles on your path to successful dog training. It'll never be easy to implement a species-appropriate training approach in practical terms. The approach isn't especially demanding in itself, but you'll end up facing many hurdles along your way that you can't even imagine at present. You'll meet considerable resistance once you've learned how to act in your dog's best interests, and this resistance will make you question your thoughts on countless occasions. You'll eventually need to decide between liking your surroundings and wanting to be there for your four-legged friend. You'll have to address the issues associated with dog training in a more intensive manner so that you can form your own unalterable opinions.

You'll end up understanding a dog's nature, although most other dog owners in your area won't share this knowledge. Be prepared to endure half-truths and maybe even critical remarks about the decisions that you make for your dog. The other owners will unsettle you, and you'll often query your attitude to dog training questions as a result.

Dealing with social surroundings is only one of the difficulties that you'll have to overcome when you implement your dog training. Another problem is – and will remain – empathy. You'll constantly and subconsciously allow yourself to rely on human decisions and evaluations. After a few months, you'll have fully returned to assessing possible canine behaviors against human standards. You won't even notice what you're doing. At the same time, you'll also avoid other people's empathetic evaluations and will learn to assess their points of view in entirely objective terms. It's difficult to renounce the human way of thinking, and doing so requires much bravery and motivation. It's nevertheless worthwhile to recognize how much positivity you can get back from a dog by acting in such a manner. He'll ultimately be grateful if we can see him for what he is: A dog.

Final remarks

This book may help you to see your dog's world through different eyes. You'll then be better able to understand him and communicate with him – although without talking to him.

Your genuine love for your dog is evident in your wanting to understand his nature and your preparedness to learn about this topic. Share what you know with others and always be ready to challenge existing knowledge.

> **Truth isn't that which we know.**
> **We only think that we know what truth really is.**

The search for the WHY helps you to keep your mind free and ready to absorb new things.

Now it's your turn: Help your dog to be a dog among us humans.

Yours, Daik Lalyon

Printed in Great Britain
by Amazon